A PARENT'S SURVIVAL

GUIDE TO THE

INTERNET

CLARK L. AND KATHRYN H. KIDD

Bookcraft
Salt Lake City, Utah

For Jeff and Beth Trestrail,
living proof that silicon-based friendships can be
as tangible as those based in carbon

Library of Congress Catalog Card Number 99-72622
ISBN 1-57008-641-9

First Printing, 1999

Printed in the United States of America

CONTENTS

INTRODUCTION

Back in the Digital Dark Ages (early 1970s), the authors of this book were both attending college. One sad fact of life for college students was that just about every course required the dreaded term paper. This involved research at the library, taking pages of notes, shuffling those notes together into some attempt at organization, writing the paper in longhand, and then (if you wanted a professional look) typing the paper.

This last step was the worst part. You either had to bribe a friend (usually with pizza) who was not keyboard-impaired to do this task, or you had to suffer through it yourself. If you chose the latter course, this would mean several nights of frustration, sore fingers, and general misery. Even then, the results were usually less than professional, with oceans of "white-out" fluid decorating each page, and lines that sometimes went off the right side of the page because (unlike Pavlov's dog) you forgot to push the button when the bell rang. No wonder many students would wait until the last minute and then pull an all-nighter to get the paper in by the deadline.

After the paper was completed, you would invariably find that you had put a section in the wrong order or had forgotten to include something important. The part you left out would almost always be on page two of a ten-page paper. You then faced the choice of wasting more nights to retype the thing or submitting the paper and hoping your less-than-perfect effort would at least secure you a passing grade. Then you had to hope the professor didn't lose your term paper and then accuse you of never having written it—a nightmare that once happened to Kathy.

Even though Clark was a computer science major in college, he didn't have an advantage when it came to getting his term papers written. In those days computers weren't designed to benefit the average person, at least not directly. They were owned by governments, large corporations, and universities, and they were kept in locked rooms with raised floors and lots of air-conditioning. They were used for printing payroll checks and keeping track of credit card balances and student grades—not for something as mundane as helping a student write a paper.

Looking back on those times makes us wonder how we ever survived without a personal computer and the friendly glow of its monitor. Today, computers are as essential to our lives as flush toilets. In fact, given the choice of giving up the computer or giving up indoor plumbing, most professional writers would sadly bid farewell to the porcelain throne.

Today we can visit a museum and gasp in astonishment over the crude tools that were used for surgery and dental work. "You mean, they would actually use that to drill into your teeth, and with no anesthetic?" But children of parents our age would be equally astonished if they saw a manual typewriter in a museum. "You mean, you actually used that to write a term paper? Where is the screen, and where does the printer attach?"

Today's college student lives in a different world from that of his parents' generation. He may still crack a book or two, but a lot of his research is probably done on the Internet. If he uses an encyclopedia or other reference work, he doesn't have to sort through huge, alphabetized volumes. Indeed, he can find sources from all over the world, and he doesn't have to turn a single page to do it.

Once research material has been found, our student will highlight the sections that are useful, and click a few keys to transfer them into a word processing program. There, all kinds of magic can be performed. The author can move the sections around, insert new paragraphs, or include photographs and line drawings. Naturally he'll want to generate a table of contents, an index, and footnotes. He'll also create a header and footer that will appear at the top and bottom of each page.

Not sure how to spell a word? Don't worry about it. The word processor will underline words that it doesn't recognize. If our student can't figure out the correct spelling, the word processing program will give him suggestions, let him pick the one he wants, and then automatically change that word throughout the entire document.

When the paper is complete, our student will print it out on his laser printer, producing a result that is as professional looking as something you would get from a typesetter. But then he remembers that important paragraph he forgot to include on page two. Not a big deal. He can pull up the document, add the text, and print it out again. Five minutes later, the paper's ready to submit.

If a college student is less than honest, he could even visit several Internet companies and use his credit card to buy one of thousands of completed term papers purchased from other students. This has become so commonplace that many educators are beginning to question the value of term papers as tools for measuring learning. At first computers allowed students to produce better work, but then the situation "evolved" until those same computers can be used to allow students to avoid any work at all.

In light of the potential for cheating, there are some educators who wish computers had never been invented. You, too, may wish you and your family lived in a time when computers weren't a potential temptation to your children. Although you may not agree that computers have made life better, you must concede they have made life different. For better or worse, computers will affect just about every aspect of your children's lives. Whether they want to or not, your children will live in a world where computers are as commonplace as automobiles, telephones, and microwave ovens.

The important thing to remember is that computers are neither good nor evil. They are machines, and like all machines they can be used for evil purposes as well as for good ones. Automobiles are weapons that maim and kill when they're operated by drunk drivers. Cameras can be used to create priceless treasures, or they can be used to generate pornography. Musical instruments can produce symphonies, or they can produce "music" that tempts children to go out and commit acts of crime. Television can bring stories of adultery and incest into your home, but it can also expand your world with religious programming or that of science and learning.

Would you throw away the automobile because some people use it improperly, or banish all music from your home because unscrupulous musicians advocate the killing of policemen? No—if you're like most Americans, you own a car and a television and a stereo or two, but you make rules that govern how those tools can be used by your family members. Computers fall into the same category. Yes, they can be misused. But if you'll go back to our example of the student writing his term paper, having a personal computer can free that student to concentrate on the important things that he is attending college to learn—research, organization, summarization, and critical thinking. You don't want to deprive your children of those opportunities without at least studying the issue first. That is why we wrote this book—to allow you to make that informed decision, and to supervise your children's computer experience.

THE OSTRICH APPROACH

We recently had the following conversation with a friend. He lives quite a distance from us, but we need to send him things occasionally. So we wondered if we could contact him through the Internet:

Clark:	"You have a personal computer, don't you?"
Friend:	"Sure do."
Clark:	"Do you have an e-mail address?"
Friend:	"Heavens no! I would never expose my children to that stuff!"

All we were asking was whether it was possible to contact a friend of ours electronically. What he heard was a different thing altogether. In his mind we'd questioned his fitness as a parent. As far as he was concerned, no decent father would ever allow such an evil tool as the Internet into his hallowed home.

This is what we call the ostrich approach to the Internet. *If I don't know what's out there, I won't have to worry about it. If I don't tell them about it, they will never find it. If I don't let it into the house, my children won't know it exists. If I pretend there is not a problem, there won't be one.*

There is certainly no one who is entitled to tell you how to raise your children. Every child is different, and every parent has to learn through trial and error what methods will work for each individual child. Perhaps in some situations the "no thanks, not for me" approach is the best one to take. But the key is for you to make an informed decision, and you can't make an informed decision until you know what the Internet has to offer and where its pitfalls lie. Many parents don't know enough about the Internet to make such a decision. They base their opinions on what they read, or see on television, or hear through their friends. At best, those kinds of reports are at least unbalanced, and at worst they are purposely misleading. It is only the sensational stories that make the news. "Child Kidnapped by Internet Pen Pal" is a news story. "Granny Uses E-Mail to Communicate with Twelve Grandchildren" is not.

By the time your first child enters kindergarten, you should be well aware that he'll learn certain things even if he is not exposed to those things at home. Children are separate entities from you, and they learn about the world by communicating with others—just as you did. They'll learn to read and write in elementary school. They'll also come home with bad words and dirty jokes and folklore that may or may not be correct.

If you're old enough to have children, the chances are fairly good that you were raised in a home where parents just didn't talk about sex. Perhaps your parents were just too ashamed to broach such a sensitive subject. Maybe they thought you weren't old enough to learn about sex until you reached a marriageable age—say, age sixty. Perhaps they assumed your school would take on the responsibility of teaching you about human procreation. Or maybe they handed you a textbook and presumed you would read it, never checking up afterwards to learn that you were too embarrassed to do so.

If your parents didn't teach you about sex—for whatever reason—it's apparent you eventually learned about sex anyway. If you hadn't, you wouldn't have children, and you wouldn't be reading this book! If you're like most children whose parents didn't explain the birds and the bees, you probably learned about procreation from sharing speculation with your friends. They most likely didn't get all the facts right, but eventually you picked up the basics. By the time you were ready to start a family, you had learned what you needed to know; you just did it in a way that was far less wholesome than it might have been if your parents had mustered the courage to tell you the facts of life.

Although modern parents seem to be more open when discussing sex with their children than parents were when we were growing up, that openness has not extended to the computer. Most parents are perfectly contented to trust that their children will learn about computers through osmosis, or at school, or on the street. And they're right. Just as you learned about sex even if your parents didn't teach you, your children will learn about computers even if you don't teach them. More than likely, they will learn at school. This is not necessarily a good thing. In this politically correct age, do you think the schools will emphasize the same values that you would if you were the one doing the teaching?

Let's put a best-case spin on this. Let's assume your children have excellent teachers who are only concerned about making sure their students are computer literate. Unfortunately, those teachers are still dealing with potentially explosive material. The knowledge your children will get from their computer classes can be used to find perverted and even evil things on the computer if they are inclined in that direction, or even if they are only curious.

If your children's schools do not teach computer classes, your children will more than likely learn about computers in their friends' basements. This is even worse than having them learn about computers in school. Yes, many of their friends can probably give your children a real education, but are they teaching what you want your children to learn? You can bet that many of the parents of your children's friends have very different standards from yours.

One of Clark's coworkers regularly lets her son visit Internet areas containing pictures of naked women. Her philosophy? "There is nothing dirty about the human body, and I would rather have my son do such things openly than behind my back." This woman is basically a decent person, but not all decent people have values that would conform to the values you're setting for your own family.

Even if your children don't have any Internet-connected friends, there is always a public library, most of which have Internet connections. Many libraries block access to the really repulsive material, but most libraries certainly grant access to a whole variety of material that you would find inappropriate for the members of your family. And even the libraries that used to block access to pornography are being challenged in the courts—and losing. Apparently, the right of adults to view pornography in the public library is more important than a child's right to be shielded from it.

It's not surprising that parents who hear the horror stories about the Internet often react by denying their children the use of computers. But if that's your attitude, you're just shutting your eyes to the inevitable. Your children are part and parcel of the computer age. They wouldn't know how to live in a world that didn't have computers. The very toys they played with in their cribs contained computer chips. They use a computer chip every time they change television channels with the remote control, or pop up a bag of microwave popcorn.

No matter what occupation your children eventually choose, they will have to understand computers and be able to use them. Even your local garage mechanic has to be computer-literate to diagnose the family car. Don't handicap your children by trying to hide them from a technology that also has much good to offer. Instead, teach them to use these tools properly—just as you'd teach a child how to use an iron or an electric drill.

The best alternative is for you to have an understanding of the technology and its dangers, have honest and open discussions with family members, and then agree on rules that all can accept. We cannot set the rules for your family, but we can give suggestions and help you understand the other pieces of the puzzle, so that you can set reasonable rules and make wise decisions.

GOALS OF THIS BOOK

The ultimate goal of this book is to teach you to be a better parent, to build stronger relationships between family members, and to increase the feelings of harmony that exist in your home. Granted, that is a pretty big goal for a book about the Internet. But we believe management of the Internet can best be approached through understanding, intelligent discussions, reasonable rules, a certain amount of trust, and suitable punishment when it is warranted—in other words, by using the same techniques that successful parents already use to manage most aspects of family life.

We hope that by the time you have turned the last page in this book, you will have learned four things:

1. You will understand the technology—and the dangers. You will have a basic understanding of how computers connect to the Internet, the things they can do once they are connected, and the potential areas that may cause trouble. It is a sad fact that most children have already passed their parents in terms of the tricks they can perform on the family computer. We recently read a joke where a father asked his son what he was doing down in the basement. The son said he was adding some Java and hot links to his web site. Reporting back to the mother, the father said he didn't know what his son was doing in the basement, but it involved coffee and sausage.

Depending on your degree of computer expertise, you may not get the joke. (Don't worry, you'll be able to do so by the end of the first chapter or two.) If you *do* get the joke, the punchline may make you wince instead of laugh. It's hard to have a meaningful discussion when your child is talking in another language. Is it surprising that children get annoyed when you make attempts to set rules for the computer based on your limited understanding? That's like setting rules for the family auto when the parents don't routinely drive it, even though they may have taken it for a test drive and read some good articles about driving.

We do not have enough time or pages to convert you into an Internet expert. You will not be ready to go out and get a job as a web designer or network administrator after you finish reading this book. But we should have given you enough information that you can at least understand some of the things that your kids are saying. Perhaps when they realize you're not totally hopeless, they will even take the time to explain some of those things you still won't understand.

We also hope to give you enough knowledge that you won't be afraid to sit down at the computer and try a few things. Sadly, many adults who own computers are still at the "cautious" stage. They don't even want to touch that thing, because it might bite them. Or they know how to do a few things, but don't want to try anything different because they might break something. Children don't have this fear, and they adapt rather quickly. Just like learning to play the piano, you must learn a few things and then practice. Then learn a few more things and practice. Soon your fear will go away, and you might find yourself actually enjoying it.

We will also show you the things that your family will want to avoid while they are exploring the Internet. Don't let anyone tell you otherwise—there are some dangerous places out there. But they can be managed and avoided once you have the understanding of where the real threats exist. We will try to make you aware of all the potential problem areas, and give you suggestions for staying out of trouble.

2. You will be able to have good discussions and make fair rules. Once you have an understanding of the technology and the dangers, you should be in a good position to start having intelligent discussions with family members. That still does not mean you will be on their level in terms of understanding. In fact, your children may even try to thwart your efforts by throwing out some technical buzzwords they know you won't understand. Your son may say, "Well Dad, this dumb computer won't let me into chat rooms anyway, because the crummy down-level BIOS does not interface correctly with the stupid TCP/IP packet handler, and you don't give me enough allowance to afford a better graphics card." If anyone tries this trick on you, don't fall for it!

Don't be intimidated by attempts to steer you away from meaningful discussions because you don't know as much as your children do. This book should give you enough of a technical foundation that you will be teachable. If your kids say something that you don't understand, ask them to explain it. They may complain, and roll their eyes a bit, but eventually they will understand that you really are serious about this, and then the communication will start. Of course, there is always the possibility that after reading this book, you will know more than they do. That would be an even better situation, and it's entirely possible. We don't subscribe to the common myth that parents today will never be comfortable with computers because it's something you have to learn at an early age. Hundreds of thousands of grandparents and great-grandparents are learning how to use computers, and are just as fearless about learning new things as a young child. You can do it, too.

Once your children have decided that Mom and Dad can learn new tricks, you should be able to make some reasonable rules, and explain the need for those rules. Obviously, the rules will vary greatly depending on the age of your children, their capacity for getting into trouble, and their disposition towards mischief. And of course, children being children, they will insist that any rule you make is much too strict. But keep the lines of communication open, continue the ongoing discussions, and adjust the rules as necessary as you observe their behavior.

3. You will be able to make sure the rules are being followed. Even after you have set reasonable rules, this does not end the process. Your household computer guidelines should be flexible. There should be a cycle of ongoing evaluation, discussion, and adjustment of the rules based on behavior and maturity. But an important part of that cycle is making sure existing family rules are being followed. This can be done in several different ways:

- In some cases, the technology will enforce the rules for you. We will show you how to set the options on your computer so that it won't allow certain things to occur.
- Enforcement of certain rules is beyond the capability of the technology, so a certain amount of trust is necessary. As with any rule, you should explain why it is needed, explain what is expected, and explain exactly what is prohibited.
- Whether rules are enforced by the technology or through trust, a certain amount of monitoring may be necessary to make sure the rules are being followed. We will show you ways to detect violations of rules, not only through the monitoring of the behavior of your children, but also by using certain features of your computer that keep track of what it has been doing.

Let's talk for a minute about that last one. No parent wants his child to accuse him of "spying" or of not trusting him. Hurt feelings on the part of the child can be minimized by making sure your children understand from the first that you have the right to monitor the adherence to the rules you are setting. You don't need to make a big production of any monitoring that is done. Saying, "Well, it's time to get on the computer and see if Julie has been a good girl this week," will probably not get you a nomination for Parent of the Year. But the computer is a family tool, and you certainly have the right to use it, and to see what others have been doing with it. We will talk more about this in Chapter 2.

4. You will have an appreciation for the Internet. Based on what you have read so far, we hope you don't have the impression that the Internet is a terrible place, and the only reason for buying this book is to defend your family from it. There is a whole world of information and tools out there that can save you time, money, and frustration. The Internet has become a valuable tool in our family, and we use it for everything from finding hotel rooms to ordering books. We have come to rely on it, much as we rely on the telephone or the electric lights.

This book should give you the knowledge that will allow you to use this hidden giant in your family. You will certainly not use it in the same way as your children, but you will be able to find things that are just as valuable, informative, and entertaining. We will explore more of the positive aspects of the Internet in Chapters 1 and 7.

CHAPTER ORGANIZATION

Chapters 0 and 1 will give you the background you need to understand computers and the Internet, including the process of getting yourself connected. If you already feel knowledgeable about these topics, you may want to skim these chapters or skip them altogether.

Then in Chapter 2 we'll take a break from the technology to expose the dangers of the Internet. We also propose methods for creating and presenting the usage restrictions and access rules that will apply to all family members. Finally, we will give some general guidelines and suggestions for what should be included in those rules.

In Chapters 3-6, we'll explore each of the four most common functions that are used during an Internet session. For each of these we will explore:

- The nature of the function, common features, and how to go about using it.
- Dangers that are introduced by the function if it is used incorrectly.
- Suggestions of rules or techniques that will minimize the dangers.

To conclude on a positive note, in Chapter 7 we will show you some friendly and useful places the family can visit while navigating through the Internet neighborhood. This is by no means an extensive list, but represents some of our favorites. Yet it probably represents less than one tenth of a percent of the family-friendly places that exist. We will also touch briefly on the topic of building your own Internet resources, so that you may publish family or business information for all the world to see.

At the end of each chapter, we will include answers to common questions that may have come up while you were reading the chapter. This makes for a different way to include new material, and also serves as a place to cover issues that don't fit well into the previous sections of the chapter. These questions and answers are always fun to write, and we hope they will be fun and informative for you as well.

SOME ASSUMPTIONS

One thing you will find when working with personal computers is that no two computers have exactly the same "configuration." By this, we mean the combination of parts and programs that come together to make the computer. Different parts of the computer are made by different manufacturers, and can be bought in different sizes, and with different options. Similarly, no two computers are the same in terms of the programs that are installed on them. Even if they were the same when they left the factory, you have probably installed new programs or changed the options to tailor the computer to your family. This is not a bad situation, because it makes the old family computer a much more valuable tool as it can be customized to your needs—much as you might customize the family car by installing a better radio or one of those dogs with the bobbing head in the back window. But the idea that your computer is different from everyone else's does cause problems when you're reading a book like this. Perhaps the illustrations in the book will not exactly match what you see when you look at your computer. Or maybe you are running a different version of some programs that makes them behave just a little differently from what we describe here. This certainly does not mean the end of the world, but it may mean that you will have to do a little experimentation, or do some reading in the manuals that came with your computer or its programs.

It would not be practical to try and account for all of these variations in this book. Doing so would double the size (and cost) of the book, and require you to have the biceps of a weight lifter. A more practical approach is for us to assume that your computer runs with certain of the most common configurations (there's that word again). We will assume that your family computer is "IBM-compatible," and that you are running one of the versions of the popular Windows operating system from Microsoft. If you are confused already, don't be. This configuration probably applies to well over ninety percent of the personal computers being used in homes today. And the ten percent who are brave enough to use the less-popular computers and programs are also usually the ones who are so determined to learn things on their own that they would never "cheat" and buy a book like this anyway. Also, as we discuss Internet tools and commercial Internet services, we will only concentrate on the more common ones.

Nevertheless, don't despair if the examples we show here don't apply exactly to your computer. We can still accomplish our goals, and you can learn what you need to learn. The basic functions of the Internet and the rules you set to govern it will be the same no matter how your computer is put together. As we said earlier, we just may force you to do a little bit of homework outside the covers of this book.

A JOINT EFFORT

Since we have been married, this is the sixth book we have written together as coauthors. We tend to think that our writing styles complement each other, and we hope that you will agree.

Clark has a background in computers, and tends to immediately jump into a level of detail that is far beyond what is required. Although he could talk endlessly about number systems and Internet protocols, his explanations would be about as fascinating to most readers as the label on the bottom of a mattress, and would go light-years beyond the level of understanding needed to accomplish the goals of this book.

That is where Kathy comes in. As a professional writer, she can translate Clark's ramblings into something most people can understand, and can eliminate or simplify the technical details that aren't essential to gaining a practical understanding. She also knows her way around computers enough that she can talk to the experienced user while remembering what it's like to be a beginner. Her writing style tends to use a lot of humor and personal examples. She could even write a description of how to overhaul a carburetor that would be understandable to the average reader.

We hope this joint effort on our part will produce a book that will teach you, while being fun to read at the same time. You may have bought this book out of duty, much as you would go to the dentist to get a root canal. You are determined to educate yourself about something of vital importance to your family, even if it means reading a technical manual about something you fear may be overly complex and dull. We can't make any promises, as this is a complex subject, but we hope that when you close the back cover you will say: "Wow, that wasn't as bad as I thought! May I use the family computer for an hour or two?"

Chapter 0—Remedial Computer Basics

• • • • •

RIGHT NOW YOU PROBABLY HAVE ONE QUESTION you want us to answer before you go any farther: "Why did you clowns start the book with Chapter 0, instead of Chapter 1?" The answer is easy. We did it for you. Our reasoning is that many of you know enough about computers already that you'll want to skip this chapter, but you may not be able to justify skipping a chapter if it has a real chapter number. Some mathematicians believe that 0 represents nothing. If you want to skip this chapter without having to feel guilty about it, the 0 allows you to do so and then be able to truthfully say you read the whole book.

In fact, we didn't even want to write this chapter, but we were convinced that it was necessary. You see, a certain percentage of the people who buy this book have never wrestled with a computer. If you're one of those people, you don't know the difference between memory and disk space, and you have no earthly idea what to do with a mouse. Without this chapter to give you some background into computers, you'll only set the book aside in frustration. Then you'll tell all your friends this book is only suitable for wrapping fish or starting campfires, and we won't sell a million copies and build our dream beach house in Hawaii. So this chapter is for you folks— the potentially frustrated, fish-wrapping, fire-starting homewreckers.

Before we can give you advice that will help you make the Internet a positive experience for your kids, we have to assume you have a certain base level of knowledge. We have to assume that we can use such words as RAM, mouse, and Windows without you thinking of sheep, rodents, and glass cleaner. The most obvious alternative is to assume that you know nothing, and then to stop every paragraph or two and explain everything. If we take that approach, the reader who already has a working knowledge of computers will resent being treated like an idiot, and he'll quit reading before he ever learns anything useful. So we think this chapter represents a good compromise. Experienced users can skip or skim, while beginning users can read the chapter and reach that level of basic knowledge needed before we can proceed with intelligent discussions of the subjects covered in later chapters.

It is our experience that most married couples possess different levels of computer knowledge. Quite often, the husband bought the computer, he and the kids use it, and Mom pretty much ignores it as just another one of Dad's toys. But more and more often, it will be the wife who bought the computer for her work or hobbies, and it is Dad who doesn't know much about it. We hope this chapter will level the playing field in these kinds of situations. As with any aspect of family life, kids are more apt to follow the rules if both Mom and Dad are involved in making them.

COMPUTER SCIENCE 101

If you are tempted to skip this chapter, please take this little quiz first. It is very simple, and should take less than a minute. Look through the list of the ten words and phrases below. You should have heard them before, and should know what we are talking about if we use them in a sentence later in this book. Ready . . . Go!

RAM	(not a sheep)
megabytes	(nothing to do with table manners)
Pentium	(not a car or a camera)
modem	(not a prescription drug)
double-click	(nothing to do with the telephone)
GUI	(pronounced "gooey")
cut and paste	(nothing to do with a scrapbook or coupons)
ICON	(not a piece of religious art)
menu bar	(nothing to do with food)
radio button	(not the ones you find in the car)

Now, use the results from this little quiz to determine how you should proceed. If none of these words rang a bell, you should read every word of this chapter, and then probably start over and read it again. If you regularly use most of these words on a daily basis, you should go immediately to Chapter 1. If only some of the words were familiar, you should browse through the rest of this chapter, reading those topics that sound interesting or unfamiliar.

See you at Chapter 1. With a little bit of luck, we will all arrive with enough of a background to jump right in and learn about the mysterious and fascinating Internet.

HARDWARE

You will often hear the terms "hardware" and "software" thrown about when discussing computers. Hardware refers to the physical parts that make up the computer, while software refers to the programs (or applications) that run on the computer. Most cars these days come with either a tape player or a CD player. Consider that the player itself is the hardware, while the songs that you play on it are the software. They are two different things, but they both have to be there before you can hum along while you motor down Route 66. Similarly, your hardware and software work together to allow you to accomplish your computer tasks. Like the old song says about love and marriage, you can't have one without the other.

In this section we talk about the hardware, or the actual cables, boxes, and physical things that you unpack when you come home from the computer store. We assume that you probably have a desktop system, meaning several different boxes that are cabled together and take up most of your desk. If you have a laptop system, everything is squeezed together into one little box that you can take with you as you travel. This discussion still applies to laptop computers, but just remember that everything is in one package.

System Unit

If your computer were an old gangster movie, then the system unit would be the brains of the operation. It does all the thinking, planning, and decision making. All the other gang members just send information back and forth between the boss and the outside world.

The system unit is what does the actual computing, or thinking, on your computer. All of the other pieces of hardware are really Input/Output (I/O) devices. Their job is to get information from you to the system unit, and to get the results of the system unit's work back to you. An example of an input device is your keyboard, while an example of an output device is your printer. Some devices, such as disk drives, can be used for both input and output.

The system unit is a rectangular box that sits on the desktop, often underneath the monitor. It usually has lots of cables coming out of the back, because all the other devices are connected to it. Some system units are known as "towers," because they are designed to sit on their sides and tower into the air, much the way your VCR would look if you stood it on its side.

If you take the cover off the system unit, you will find a whole collection of wires, boxes, and circuit boards. Although we won't get into the physical details of how these parts work together, we will cover some of the logical functions they perform.

Stopping for a Byte First

We need to detour for just a minute and talk about computer memory. This is something that confuses a lot of people, even a lot of veteran PC users. If you can understand computer memory, everything else you read in this chapter will make more sense.

Your kitchen probably has all kinds of drawers and cabinets for storing kitchen items. The hard-to-access spaces are reserved for utensils you seldom use, but the things you use every day are kept within easy reach for your convenience. Your computer needs a similar way to store pieces of information that it is using. This storage is referred to as memory.

For example, let's say you fire up your word processor program and start writing a letter to your Aunt Undine. As you type your letter, the words appear on the computer screen, but they are also stored in the memory of the computer. When you print out the letter on your computer printer, the program will read your letter from the text that is stored in the computer memory, rather than the text you see on the screen.

Perhaps your letter to Aunt Undine is so brilliant that you'd like to use pieces of it in a letter you'll write to Cousin Horace tomorrow. In that case, you'll use yet another option that reads the information stored in the computer memory and writes it to a file on your disk drive. This is called "saving" your text.

The concept of saving illustrates an important attribute of computer memory—whether it is temporary or permanent. The memory within the system unit is temporary, because it is only active when the computer is on. If you are typing away on the last paragraph of the novel of the century when a power outage turns off your computer, you'll never get that million-dollar contract unless you've saved your masterpiece to a disk file before the power outage. A disk file is permanent memory in that it stays in your computer after the machine is turned off.

Here's a rule of the computer biz that you should tattoo on your forehead: *Save early, and save often.* Don't just assume the power is going to stay on long enough for you to save your masterpiece when you've finished writing it. In fact, one of the little ironies of life is that the more important the document is, the more likely it is that some million-to-one freak accident is going to erase it unless you've saved it on your hard drive. If something's important, save it—and then save it again.

Although your computer memory may hold your last will and testament, or that Great American Novel, or the love letters that have been exchanged between you and your dearly beloved, your computer doesn't have the same sentimental attachment to your documents as you do. In fact, as far as your computer is concerned, computer memory is nothing but a series of switches that can be turned either on or off.

Imagine having a whole wall full of light switches that you can flip up (for on) or down (for off). In computer memory, each of these switches is called a "bit." As a convention for displaying the status of bits, the computer uses a value of "1" to represent "on," and a value of "0" to represent "off." For example, if you had three bits in memory, and only the middle one was on, the computer would show this on your screen as 010. This just makes it easier to visualize than saying "Off-On-Off."

Let's be realistic. Unless you're trying to light the Astrodome, there's not a lot of use for a machine that only has an on-off switch. A computer must be capable of doing far more than just turning switches on and off. Even if all you ever plan to do with a computer is write that occasional letter to Aunt Undine, you'll need to have some way of displaying (and saving) the alphabet, in both small letters (lowercase) and capitals (uppercase). You'll also need the numbers zero through nine, plus all the punctuation marks. But that isn't all. You'll also need all of the different combinations of keys you can press on the computer keyboard, plus some special "control" instructions, such as a command you could send to the printer to have it skip to the top of the next page. If you add those up, you will find that just one simple letter to your aging aunt will require your computer to represent at least a hundred different values in memory—perhaps even more. This is not an easy task to require of a machine that only knows the values of "on" and "off."

Somehow, those on-off bits have to be manipulated so they can represent all the concepts they need to represent. This is done by bunching them together, so that a group of bits can represent a particular letter or symbol. If we had four bits, each with a possible setting of on or off, we would have sixteen possible on-off combinations. We need a lot more than that. Five bits would give us 32 combinations, six would give us 64, and seven would boost the number to 128. Just to be safe, most computer systems use eight bits of memory to represent a single value, which gives us the possibility of 256 different combinations. Each group of eight bits that work together to store a different value is known as a "byte."

Once the concept of bytes made it possible to assign 256 different values to a single piece of information, computer designers had to define what combination of bits would represent each value that needed to be defined. Just as the people who developed your VCR came up with different formats (Beta and VHS) that were not compatible with one another, computer developers came up with different ways to represent the same value on a computer. But for our purposes, it is sufficient to say that most home computers are designed to use a standard called ASCII (American Standard Code for Information Exchange). Although what you've already read probably represents more than you'll ever need to know about ASCII, here are a few of the keys from your keyboard, together with the combination of bits used to represent each character in memory using the ASCII standard:

A	0100 0001
B	0100 0010
a	0110 0001
b	0110 0010
2	0011 0010
3	0011 0011
$	0010 0100
%	0010 0101

The computer keeps track of memory by assigning each byte of memory a unique memory address, much as each house on your street has a unique street address. The address of the first byte of memory is 0, followed by 1, 2, 3, etc. If your computer had 1000 bytes of memory, it could be addressed with the addresses 0 through 999.

If this is all clear as mud to you, don't worry about it. You really just need to understand the terms bit and byte, because you'll run into them quite often when reading instructions and other computer literature. In summary, a bit is the smallest unit of memory in the computer, and it can only be set on or off, represented as 1 or 0. Because there is not a lot that can be done with a two-position switch, bits are clustered together in groups of eight to form bytes, which are the basic storage unit of the computer. A byte is often referred to as a "character" of memory, because each one can represent any of the characters you can type on your keyboard.

Now that you understand a little about memory, let's get back to the system unit.

Processor Chip

We said earlier that the system unit was the brain of your computer. We lied. Actually it is the processor chip living in the system unit that provides the brain power. This chip makes all the calculations and does the decision making. Other parts of the computer simply move data around as directed by the processor chip, which in turn runs under the control of a program.

Unlike human intelligence, the processor chip has a limited number of instructions that it can understand and perform. These are known as the "instruction set." The chip cannot really learn and it cannot really think, in a human sense. It's not a thinking machine as much as it is a pocket calculator.

When you use a pocket calculator, you can press buttons that cause it to perform the basic math functions, such as addition, subtraction, multiplication, and division. You can also do things such as clear memory, and save results in memory to be used in future calculations. As you use the calculator, you are actually "programming" it by giving it a series of instructions to follow in a specific order. That's what a computer does. The computer's processor chip is simply the big brother of the chip in your calculator, and it can do a lot more tricks.

The instruction set of each processor chip can be divided into several general categories of instructions. We're going to list them for you, but before we do, we want you to know that this information is something you will never need in this lifetime, other than to satisfy your curiosity. If all you want to do is to learn how to run a computer, skip the following list:

❑ **Math**

Instructions are provided inside the chip to perform the basic mathematical functions of addition, subtraction, multiplication, and division. All other math functions can be built from these basic functions.

❑ **Data Movement**

Instructions are provided inside the chip to move the contents of computer memory from one location to another. Also, because all math operations are performed in special memory areas called "registers," instructions are provided to move the contents of regular memory into a register, and then back out again. As we said in the previous section, each byte of memory has a unique number, or address, and this address is used in the instruction to specify which bytes to move.

❑ **Comparison and Branching**

Comparison instructions are the ones that allow the chip to appear human. They allow the contents of registers or memory locations to be compared. Based on the results of the comparison, branch instructions allow you to branch, or jump to, different parts of the program. Let's say you are writing a program to calculate the number of months until a car loan is paid off. Your program will calculate the monthly interest due, add it to the total due, and then subtract the monthly payment. At this point you will need to compare the total due, to see if it is less than zero. If so, the loan is paid off, so you will need to print some final information on the computer screen (such as the total number of months to pay off the loan), and then stop the program. If it is not less than zero, your program will have to return to the section of code where you do the calculation. This section of the program is called a "loop," because you loop through the same part of the program until a certain condition is satisfied.

❑ **Device Control**

This final group of instructions allows the chip to communicate with the devices that are attached to it. The program may wish to obtain information from the keyboard, or send some information to the printer, or read data from a disk drive. The device control instructions are used for all of these functions.

As noted above, the instruction set is nothing but a set of basic tricks that the processor chip can perform. To actually perform any useful work on a computer requires a "program"—a series of instructions executed in a certain order to perform a specific function. Programmers design, write, and test their programs, and then save them as files on a disk drive. Then the consumer buys the program and installs it by copying it to a disk drive.

Every time you run a program, it is copied from the disk drive into computer memory, and then the processor chip starts following the list of instructions it was given—much as someone who is sent to the store with a shopping list will pick up the items specified on the list. So all programs, no matter what their function, are built from the same basic building blocks—the instruction set of the processor chip. This is why the art of programming is fascinating to many people. Everyone starts with the same materials, and yet the things you construct are limited only by your imagination. You can write programs that allow you to play a game, write a letter, balance your checkbook, keep track of recipes, monitor your investments, connect to the Internet, or do a thousand other things.

Although the processor chip can only perform a few dozen instructions, it performs them very accurately and quickly. One measure of processor speed is called MIPS, or Millions of Instructions executed Per Second. Scientists have developed some experimental chips that exceed 1000 MIPS, which is a billion instructions in one second. Granted, the chip in your computer is probably not that fast, but it is fast enough to do most of the things you request without breaking into a sweat. The speed of home computer processor chips is measured in megahertz, usually abbreviated as MHz. The larger the MHz number, the faster the chip.

The reason you have a computer sitting on your desk today is because of the advances that have been made in the manufacturing of microprocessor chips. In the 1970s, computers were so expensive that they were only purchased by large organizations, such as corporations, universities, and the military. These large computer machines, which were called "mainframes," filled entire rooms, consumed significant amounts of electricity, and had to be cooled by running cold water through them.

But researchers weren't satisfied with these behemoth computers. As soon as they saw the potential of large mainframes, they started to work to make computers smaller and more efficient. New materials and processes were developed that could produce chips that were faster, smaller, more energy efficient, and less prone to generate heat. Eventually, chips were produced that were efficient enough that it was practical to produce a "personal computer" (PC) that could be kept in the average home, and which was affordable to the average citizen. But researchers still aren't satisfied. As long as PCs have been available, they have continued to get faster, smaller, and cheaper each year. Most of the processor chips that run PCs are made by Intel Corporation. Because these PCs also usually run Windows software (more about that later in this chapter), these machines are often called "Wintel" machines (a combination of Windows and Intel). Since the PC emerged, Intel has designed a succession of processor chips, each of which has been faster, cheaper, and smaller than the previous model. Shown in the table below is a summary of Intel chips used in the PC:

Year	Chip	Speed	Comment
1981	8088	4-12 MHz	PC, XT Class Machines
1984	80286	8-20 MHz	AT Class Machines
1986	80386	16-40 MHz	386 Class of Machines
1989	80486	25-100 MHz	486 Class of Machines
1993	Pentium	60-200 MHz	Pentium Class Machines
1995	Pentium Pro	180-200 MHz	Faster Pentium
1997	Pentium MMX	166-200 MHz	Video Enhancements
1997	Pentium II	233-300 MHz	Combined Pro & MMX

When buying a new (or used) computer, it is important to know which processor chip is used, because you should be charged far less for a machine that uses an older chip. Notice also that processor speeds vary, even among machines that use the same chip. Using the table above, you can see that a 200 MHz Pentium is more than three times faster than a bottom-of-the-line Pentium that runs at 60 MHz.

Processor chips have become so small and cheap that they're almost throwaway items. Not only do high-end products such as televisions, microwave ovens, VCRs, and automobiles have processor chips, but chips can even be found in cheap toys. Equipping an appliance with a processor chip allows it to behave much more intelligently, with less human intervention and less chance of error. As processor chips continue to get faster and cheaper, expect this trend to continue.

RAM

RAM is another acronym. Computer people love acronyms, and this one stands for "Random Access Memory." That is just a fancy name for the memory that lives inside the system unit. RAM is the temporary memory we mentioned earlier, which only remembers its contents while the computer is turned on. If you have a power failure (whether caused by a storm, a kid, or a dog), whatever was stored in RAM is gone.

The processor chip uses RAM as a resource to accomplish work. You might want to think of RAM as a chalkboard where information can be stored for temporary use, because that's almost what it is—minus the chalk. When you start a program, the program will use RAM for temporary work areas, such as to hold the characters that are read in from a keyboard or displayed on the screen. Turning off the computer erases the data from that computerized "chalkboard."

Remember that each byte of computer memory can be accessed by its unique address, which starts with address 0 and goes upward sequentially. Because the processor chip can access any memory location by its address, this is known as random access, and is the reason for the RAM acronym for internal computer memory.

When reporting on the size of memory, several terms are typically used. A kilobyte (KB) is "approximately 1000" bytes. A megabyte (MB) represents "approximately a million" bytes, and gigabyte (GB) represents "approximately a billion" bytes. Early PCs usually contained no more than about 64 KB of RAM. But faster processor chips and more complex computer programs have constantly pushed against this limit, and have caused PC users to have to purchase more RAM to run the latest versions of new programs. Also, complex software such as Windows allows multiple programs to run at the same time, which also requires more memory. As a result of this growth in demand for RAM, it is not uncommon for new PCs to arrive with at least 8 MB of RAM, and often 32 MB or more.

If you have an older computer, you may find that the computer "crashes" or "freezes up" when you're trying to run complex programs, or when you're trying to run several programs at a time. You can fix this problem by purchasing additional RAM for an existing computer. If you don't have your RAM installed where you purchased it (always a good option for novices!), you'll have to open the computer and plug the memory chips into the "motherboard," which is the main circuit board in the system unit that contains the processor chip and other goodies.

Buying new RAM is not the problem it once was, because RAM, like processor chips, has benefited from rapid technological advances. RAM memory has become cheaper and smaller over the years. Because of this, any new PC you buy should come with adequate RAM to run most of the programs you will want to run.

The designers of the original PC used an architecture that limited the amount of RAM to a maximum of 640 KB, thinking that no program would ever use such an incredible amount of memory. Obviously, they were wrong. To overcome this limitation, the software was changed to allow the use of additional memory over that 640 KB limit. The details of how this was done are unimportant, but the RAM addresses over 640 KB are referred to as "extended memory," or "expanded memory." Don't be confused by these terms; you won't need to know about them when you're using your computer.

Hard Drive

A hard drive is a type of disk drive that is installed inside the system unit. It can be thought of as another type of memory, but this is permanent memory that remembers its value when the computer power is off. If RAM can be described as a chalkboard, a hard drive is one of those white boards where markers are used to store information on a semi-permanent basis. The information can be erased from a hard drive, just as it can from a white board—it just takes a little more effort to do so.

Information is stored on the hard drive using magnetic technology, much as music is recorded on a cassette tape. But information recorded on the hard disk is still in digital format, meaning it is stored in the same series of ones and zeroes that are used in RAM to represent the data. The hard drive itself is made up of one or more "platters" that are three to four inches in diameter. These platters rotate while the computer is turned on, much like a music CD. A read/write head travels across the surface of the drive, and is used to write new information, or to read the information that is already stored there.

Information is stored on the hard drive as a series of "files," each of which represents a logical collection of data. If you use a word processor, for example, each letter or paper you write will probably be stored as a separate file on the hard drive. Programs you buy and install on your hard drive are also composed of one or more files. You keep track of each file by giving it a name. When using Wintel computers, file names are usually composed of a one- to eight-character name, followed by an optional one- to three-character extension. The name and the extension are connected using a period. Examples of common file names are:

LETTER1.DOC
AUTOEXEC.BAT
PAYROLL.XLS
MYGAME.EXE

Although the three-letter extension is often optional, it is suggested you always supply one. That is because the extension is used to identify the kind of file that has been saved. For example, the last file name shown above has an extension of "EXE," which means it is a file that can be executed. This is a fancy way of saying that this file is a program. It is a series of instructions that can be run on your computer to achieve a desired result. Because the file name is "MYGAME," it is a pretty good bet that this program runs some kind of game on the computer. The first file name shown above has an extension of "DOC," which usually means that this is a document. Because the file name is "LETTER1," this is probably a letter that was written using a word processing program. Some programs are written to force you to save files produced by that program with a given extension, but other programs allow users to name their own files in any way that makes sense to the user. Theoretically, you could save a word processing document with an extension such as "EXE," even though that extension usually indicates an executable program. But if you don't come up with some sort of identification system, you'll only be frustrated when you come across those files in six months and try to remember what they contain. The appendix contains a listing of the most common file extensions you will come across.

Current versions of the Windows software (to be discussed later) remove this limitation on the length of file names, and allow you to name a file, "My Favorite Potato Salad Recipe, Miracle Whip Version" if that's what you want to name it. But keep in mind this is a trick that Windows performs for you. The file is still stored on the hard drive using the 8.3 limitation, so that the computer thinks of your potato salad recipe as being MYFAVO~1.DOC. When you access the file, Windows uses another file known as a registry to convert the actual file name to the long file name that you used when you created the file.

Because a typical hard drive contains thousands of files, some type of organizational method must be used to keep track of them. This organization is achieved through the ability to create things known as subdirectories. Assume you buy yourself a file drawer to keep track of important papers. At the beginning, you just have a few papers, so you just throw them in the drawer. Later, as the volume of papers increase, you realize that a better system has to be found. You buy yourself some manila file folders and label them with categories, such as "Paid Bills," "Bills to Be Paid," "Insurance Documents," and "Letters." Then you go through all the papers in the drawer, place them in the proper file folders, and place the folders in the drawer. A subdirectory is the hard drive's equivalent to the manila file folder. You can create a subdirectory called "LETTERS," and place all your word processing letters in it. Subdirectories can be created in other subdirectories, so within "LETTERS," you could create two more subdirectories called "BUSINESS" and "PERSONAL." The starting directory on your hard drive is known as the root directory. It will probably contain a few files, but most of it will consist of subdirectories for products you have installed or personal files that you have created. As you explore each subdirectory, again you will probably find files and/or subdirectories leading to other logical collections of data. There are many software tools supplied with your computer that allow you to display the contents of your hard drive. The file structure of the hard drive is often called a "directory tree," because you start with a given "branch" (subdirectory) of the tree, and that branch may be connected to other "branches" (other subdirectories) or to "leaves" (files).

Probably the worst disaster that can happen to your computer is to have the hard drive "crash." A crash is a failure in the drive or in the software that causes you to lose all the data stored on the drive. Although crashes are not that frequent, they happen often enough that you should plan for the worst. Keep the disks and documentation for all the software you install on your computer, in case you have to install it again on a new hard drive. For important files you create on the computer, the best defense is to make a second copy on a different drive, such as a floppy drive. There is also software known as backup software that allows you to copy (or backup) all the data on your hard drive. Although backup software has a lot of powerful options (such as the ability to copy just those files changed since the last backup), backup is still not easy due to the large size of most hard drives. The best solution is to use backup software in conjunction with other special hardware devices designed specifically for making backup copies. These devices are discussed later in this chapter. Every time you create something on your computer, ask yourself the question, "What would happen if this file were lost?" If loss of the file would cause serious disruption in your business or personal life, you need to think seriously about getting a reliable backup system.

It is possible to have multiple hard drives installed in your computer. Consider this an option if you run out of space. It is usually easier to install a second drive than to replace your existing drive with a larger drive, and have to copy all your files to the new drive. Also, there is software that allows you to "partition" your hard drive into multiple "logical" drives. This makes it appear that you have multiple drives installed, although all of the data really reside on the one drive. This often makes it easier to manage your data.

Like other areas of computer hardware, there have been great advances in the area of hard drive technology. Each new generation of hard drive becomes faster, smaller, and cheaper. Early PCs would often come with hard drives that would store 10-40 MB of data. If you go buy a new PC at the store today, it is not uncommon to find a hard drive with a capacity of 12 GB (that's approximately twelve billion bytes!). As with RAM, as hard drives have increased in capacity, new software has come along to take advantage of that capacity. Word processors that used to consume 2MB of your hard drive now consume 30 MB. Why? Because the producers of those products know you have larger drives, so they supply more material that may be useful. Many word processors now come with an extensive library of sample documents, self-study lessons, and artwork that may be included in your documents.

Floppy Drives

Similar to a hard drive, a floppy drive allows you to read or write data on a small removable disk. Early versions of floppy drives used disks that were 5 1/4 inches across. The actual magnetic disk was enclosed in a flexible plastic container that was thin enough to be easily bent, especially if you didn't care about damaging the data on your disk! This is probably the origin of the term "floppy disks."

Later drives used smaller disks, 3 1/2 inches across, that were enclosed in a thicker plastic housing that did not lend itself to bending. Although some older computers have both size drives (5 1/4 inches and 3 1/2 inches), most new computers sold today accomodate only the smaller, sturdier disks, which have become the industry standard. Each of these disks will hold 1.44 MB, or just under a million and a half bytes of data. This is not a lot of data compared to the capacity of a hard drive, but a floppy can hold a good-sized novel on it, and sometimes a backup for that novel as well.

Why would you use a floppy drive? There are three primary reasons:

❑ **Transfer of Data**

Floppies are a convenient way to transfer data between computers. Mom or Dad may start a report on the computer at work, and then take it home to finish it on the home computer. Or the kids may do research on the computer at school, then bring the research home to turn into a report.

❑ **Software Installation**

Often when you buy software it comes on a series of floppy disks. When you install the program on your own computer, the files that comprise the program are copied from the floppy disks onto your hard drive.

❑ **Data Backup**

As previously explained, making a second copy of an important file on a floppy drive is a good safety precaution. This will ensure the information is not lost due to a hard drive crash, or some other disaster. If the file is really important, keep the copy in a location away from your computer, such as at work or school. That will protect you from disasters such as fire or theft, which could affect the computer and any floppies stored nearby.

The technology of a floppy drive is identical to that of a hard drive. For example, you can create subdirectories on a floppy drive, although they are not as common, due to the small capacity of the disks.

One nice feature of a floppy disk is the ability to write-protect the data. Each disk has a small rectangular hole near one edge, and a plastic tab that can be moved to cover the hole or expose it. When the hole is covered, you can both read the disk and write data on it, just like a hard drive. If you open the tab so that you can see through the hole, the disk is "write-protected." This means that you can read any of the files on the disk, but you cannot alter it by writing new data. This is a nice feature to have, especially when using floppy disks to keep copies of important files.

CD-ROM Drive

Most new computers sold these days come equipped with a CD-ROM drive that reads compact discs (CDs). You are probably already familiar with CDs, because they have become the most common medium for the distribution of recorded music, and you probably have at least one music CD player in your home already.

Because you are probably already familiar with a music CD, let's look at that technology for a moment. Music to be placed on a CD is recorded with a special kind of digital recorder. This converts the sounds into digital data, or a series of ones and zeros, much the way that data are stored on computer disks. When the digital data representing the music are transferred to the CD, a laser is used to cut pits into the surface of the disk. Each pit represents a "one" in the data, while a gap with no pit is used to represent a "zero." These rows of pits and gaps are so small that a human hair would cover fifty of them. Playing the CD on a music player is a similar process. A laser scans the surface and converts the pits and gaps back into digital data, which are converted back into music. Music on CDs has several advantages over previous technologies, such as vinyl records or cassette tapes. A music CD should be able to be played thousands of times, because reading the surface does not cause damage as it does with records or tape. As long as the CD is protected from damage, it should play back without error. Also, making multiple copies does not result in a loss of quality, because a copy is simply an exact duplication of the same digital data that were found on the original. Finally, digital recordings offer higher quality sound, as there is almost no loss of sound between the recording and the playback.

The CD-ROM player in your computer is similar to the ones used for music. A laser still reads the CD surface and converts the values there to digital data. The difference is that the digital data are processed as computer data, and not as music. Thus, the computer CD-ROM drive is functionally not much different from a hard or floppy drive. They are all used to transfer digital data into the memory of the computer.

One difference between a CD-ROM and a hard drive is that the data on the CD-ROM can only be read, not written. In fact, the name CD-ROM is an acronym for "Compact Disc, Read-Only Memory." Thus, computer CDs are most often used for distributing software. Thus, rather than install a new program from a series of floppy disks, it is becoming more and more popular to install that new program from a CD.

Anyone who's fed a whole pile of floppies into a computer in a vain search for a single file can tell you it's no picnic. It's a whole lot easier to put all that information on one CD and find it there. In fact, the capacity of a CD is so great that one CD holds the equivalent of two hundred thousand printed pages. This huge capacity has given software companies the ability to ship larger programs that will not consume a lot of space on the user's hard drive.

When a computer program runs on CD-ROM, the usual procedure is for a portion of the program to be installed on the hard drive, leaving the big files that will be needed by the program to stay on the CD. This means that the CD has to be in the drive when you use that program, which is a decided disadvantage to disorganized computer users. But from the standpoint of the program designers, keeping most of the files on CD gives the programmers much more flexibility in terms of what they can do. For example, there is one program that provides a CD containing the names and telephone numbers of all the phone customers in the United States. Users can use the program to search for any person or phone number in the country. This is the kind of program that would not be practical in a world with only hard drives and floppy drives. You would have to send the data on four hundred floppy drives, and the information would consume 600 MB on the poor user's hard drive.

The read-only limitation for CD-ROM drives may soon be a thing of the past. There have always been CD-ROM drives that could be used to create new CDs, but they have been out of the price range of the typical consumer. Technology has advanced to the point where prices are now within the budget of many consumers, so it will not be uncommon in the future for users to buy blank CDs, and then create their own. This will be useful for doing such things as backing up a hard drive. Eventually CDs will be reusable, just as floppy disks are reusable now. To avoid confusion, CD drives that read and write are known as CD-R drives (Compact Disc—Rewritable.)

Although most music CD players can't deal with computer CDs, computers are a lot more versatile than your basic boom box. Most computer CD-ROM drives can handle both music and data, often recorded on the same CD. Some games have both music and data installed on the same CD, and they play music to set the background mood for the game. Most computers with CD-ROM drives also have software installed to allow you to play music CDs while you are working. Some of these are quite sophisticated programs, and provide pop-up control panels that support all the functions supported on a real music CD player, such as volume, pause, and search. A CD that contains both data and music is known as a "Mixed Mode Disc."

Even though most of us haven't even purchased the newest CD-ROM technology, CD-ROM drives may soon be a thing of the past. Eventually they may be replaced with a newer technology known as DVD (Digital Versatile Disc). DVD-ROM discs have a higher capacity for holding information and a faster data transfer speed.

With all these different drives installed in the system unit, you may have wondered how you know which one you are using. How do you tell your program that the file you want resides on a particular hard drive, floppy drive, or CD-ROM? The answer is that the computer assigns each drive a letter of the alphabet. The letters A and B are usually reserved for floppy drives, and the first hard drive is assigned the letter C. If there is more than one hard drive, the second drive starts with the letter D, the third drive starts with the letter E, and so on. The CD-ROM drives are usually assigned letters after all the hard drives are assigned.

Expansion Slots

Expansion slots are unused connection ports on the back of the system unit that may be used to connect new hardware devices. As you may have already conveniently forgotten, your RAM and processor chip are connected to a "motherboard" that resides inside the system unit. The motherboard also has multiple connection points where other electronic cards may be plugged, such as your modem or your CD-ROM drive. In most computers there are also unused slots that are available if you want to customize your computer.

In the future, you may buy a new piece of hardware (such as a scanner) that will connect to your system unit through one of these expansion slots. This usually means you will have to take the cover off the system unit. Inside, near the back of the unit, you will see some slots on the motherboard where additional circuit cards may be pushed into place. The back of the card you insert will also contain some kind of plug or connector, where the new device you purchased will connect to the new card you are installing. The back panel of the system unit will usually have some type of metal or plastic cover that goes over the unused expansion slots, to keep dust out of the system unit. If this is the case, you will need to remove this cover so that the back of the card you just installed will be visible when the cover is placed back on the system unit. When it is all put back together, connect the new device to the newly installed board, and you should be ready to go.

Better yet, if you aren't technically oriented, just take your computer down to the shop where you buy the new hardware and have one of the professionals do the work for you.

From a practical point of view, expansion ports are only an issue when you are buying a new computer. Make sure your machine has at least four unused ports, so that you can install the new devices you will purchase in the future.

Monitor

Now that you know all about the important goodies in the system unit, we can get back to the other parts of the computer. As noted previously, the system unit is the real brains of the operation, so all the other parts we will talk about are simply "Input/Output" (I/O) devices that deliver data to/from the system unit.

The monitor is the device with the screen that looks a lot like a television. Although it is not as common today, early PCs often had the option of using a television as a monitor. Some newer monitors really are designed as monitors, but can also be used as a television when the computer is not in use. As you can see, sometimes the line between a monitor and a television is pretty thin.

The monitor is used by the program or programs that are running on your computer.

It gives you a visual feedback concerning the program you are running. If you run a game, most of the action happens on your monitor. If you run a word processing program, the monitor shows you the document you are composing. To a greater or lesser extent, just about every program displays some kind of useful result on your monitor.

Early PC users were faced with the option of choosing between an expensive color monitor and a cheaper monochrome monitor. The monochrome monitors would only display one color, usually green or blue. Such monitors were fine for most business applications such as word processing, but were pretty useless for anything else. You can still find monochrome monitors, usually on older computer systems such as airline reservation systems and library catalog systems. Fortunately, color monitors have become cheap enough that they are pretty much the standard for PCs. Probably the only choice you will have to make is the size of the screen you want for your monitor.

Early monitors were damaged if a single image was displayed on the screen for a long period of time. This would cause the same image to "burn in" to the monitor screen, so it could be viewed even when the monitor was turned off. To avoid this, programs known as "screen savers" were developed. These were programs that would take control after the computer had been idle for a specified period of time. They would replace the image on the screen with some kind of animated pattern that would rotate, swirl, and change constantly, thus avoiding the problem of burn-in. Although recent monitors have been improved so that burn-in is less of a problem, screen savers are still popular, probably because there are many available, and they are fun to watch.

Keyboard

The keyboard is probably the primary input device into your computer, or the primary means of entering data into the program you are running.

To understand some of the keys on the computer keyboard, you first have to understand the cursor. A cursor is not someone who uses bad language. It is a little box, arrow, or blinking underline that appears on your monitor screen. The cursor is used to identify the current insertion point for any text that is typed on the keyboard. For example, assume you are using a word processing program to write a letter. As you examine a paragraph you wrote earlier, you notice that you left the word "elephant" out of the middle of a sentence. You use some of the control keys on your keyboard to move the cursor to the location where the word should be inserted. Then you type "elephant" and it appears right where it belongs. Now you move the cursor back to the bottom of the letter and continue.

If you have used a typewriter, the keyboard should not look strange to you, although there are some keys you probably have not seen before. An explanation of these keys is as follows. Note that some of these may have slightly different titles on your keys, or may be abbreviated:

❑ **F1–F12**

The twelve keys with the labels F1 through F12 are called "function keys," and are used by some programs to cause certain actions to occur when you press the proper key. The popularity of programs that run under Windows has reduced the number of programs that use these keys, but you will still find some programs that use them.

❑ **Num Lock, Caps Lock**

Numeric Lock changes the keypad on the right side of the keyboard so that pressing the keys will result in number values being transmitted to the program. Caps Lock changes the keyboard so that all letters that are typed will appear in uppercase. When either the Num Lock or Caps Lock key is turned on, a light at the top of the keyboard is often illuminated to remind the user that these functions are in use.

❑ **Esc**

This key is known as the "Escape" key, and is used by some programs to allow you to escape from the current function you are performing.

❑ **Tab / Backward Tab**

These keys are used to tab to the next area on the screen, or to tab back to the previous one. This is used with some programs to move from area to area on the screen.

❑ **Print Screen**

This may be abbreviated on some keyboards. For some programs, this key causes a copy of the current monitor screen to be printed on the printer. For programs running under Windows, this causes a copy of the screen to be copied to the Windows Clipboard (you'll learn more about this later).

❑ **Backspace**

Moves the cursor one character to the left, and erases any character that may be present in that location—just like the backspace on your friendly old typewriter.

❑ **Home / PgUp / PgDn / End**

These keys may be used by certain programs to navigate through data on the screen. For example, Home often takes you to the front of a document, just as

End will take you to the end. PgUp and PgDn will often move the text backward and forward by one page.

❑ **Arrow Keys**

There are usually four keys that point upwards, downwards, to the left, and to the right. These are used by many programs to move the cursor in the direction indicated.

❑ **Insert / Delete**

These keys are often used in word processing programs to allow the insertion or deletion of characters. Delete usually deletes the character at the cursor location, while Insert usually allows characters to be inserted at the current cursor location.

❑ **Alt / Ctrl**

These keys, known as the "alternate" and "control" keys, are important because they are used quite often in programs. Both of these keys are combined with the pressing of other keys to cause different things to happen in the program. For example, pressing the letter "S" in a word processing program will usually just type the letter "S" in the document you are creating. But if you press the "Alt" key, and hold it down while pressing the "S" key, this might cause the program to save the current document to the hard drive. These functions are all under control of the program, so check the documentation that comes with the program for details. If these keys are used, the documentation might say, "Press CTRL-L to load a new document." This means you should press the CTRL key, and while holding it down press the "L" key.

❑ **Return / Enter**

This key has the words "Return" or "Enter" printed on it, or sometimes just an arrow. Some programs wait for you to type some data, and then don't process those data until you have pressed this key. If your program seems to be waiting for something when you type data, press this key and see if that will start things moving again.

Keyboards are all different, and your keyboard may have some keys we did not discuss here. Or, the abbreviations we used in the above description may be slightly different from the ones printed on your keys. If you still have questions about your keyboard, please refer to the owner's manual that came with it.

Mouse

The mouse is a fairly recent arrival on the computer hardware scene, and only started to become popular with the advent of graphical programs such as Windows.

A typical mouse is about the size and shape of a large bar of soap, with a cable running from the back of the mouse into the system unit. Usually your mouse sits on top of a rubber or plastic mat called a "mouse pad." The function of the pad is just to make a smooth surface for the mouse to ride on, because it operates when you move it back and forth and from side to side.

There is a piece of computer folklore about a person who called a computer technical support line to report a problem getting the computer powered up. According to the story, the caller complained that she had "been pushing and pushing on this little foot pedal, but it still won't start." Women who use sewing machines may notice that the mouse indeed looks quite a bit like a foot-operated sewing machine pedal. Even so, the mouse is designed to be operated with your hand, not with your foot.

To operate the mouse, place your hand over the top so that your index and middle finger rest over the two buttons at the back of the mouse (some models have three buttons; just ignore the middle one). When you operate the mouse, you will be moving it around and clicking the two buttons.

If you are running a program that supports the mouse, there will be a little arrow somewhere on your screen called a "mouse pointer." As you move your mouse around on the mouse pad, this will cause the location of the pointer on the screen to change. It takes a bit of practice, but after a while you will become an expert at moving the mouse pointer anywhere on the screen just by moving the mouse. There is no real magic about how this works. If you turn the mouse over and look on the bottom, you will see a small rubber ball sticking out. As you move the mouse, the rubber ball rubs against sensors in the mouse, which cause the mouse pointer to move in a certain direction.

When you get the mouse pointer to the proper location on the screen, you can push the buttons on the mouse to cause the program to respond in certain ways. You will usually click the left button, but sometimes it is the right button. Also, on occasion you will need to do something called a "double click." This means clicking the left button twice. This is often one of the hardest tricks for a mouse novice to learn, and it does take a little bit of practice to click the button twice quickly without moving the pointer.

Usually the mouse pointer is an arrow, but sometimes the program you are running will change it. You might see an hourglass, which means that the program is processing your last request, and you should not click again until the hourglass disappears. When using a drawing program, the mouse pointer will change to a cross, so that it is easier to position your mark exactly where you want it. Sometimes, if you are in the middle of an operation that moves the location of an object on the screen, the mouse pointer will also resemble a double arrow. If the mouse pointer is a hand or a question mark, you can click to learn something about the area where the pointer is pointing. Finally, when used with a program that supports the insertion of text, a mouse pointer that looks like the letter "I" (called an I-beam) means the next text will be inserted after the pointer.

If your mouse suddenly stops working, that usually means the mouse needs cleaning. As small an impediment as a human hair can cause the mouse to stop responding to your movements. Be sure to refer to the instruction manual that came with your mouse before you take it apart for cleaning.

We will talk more about different tricks the mouse can do when we talk about Windows in the software section.

Printer

Without a printer, a computer would be no more helpful for many applications than an Etch-A-Sketch. But with a decent printer, the world is at your fingertips. Fortunately, printers are both reliable and inexpensive. You can purchase a low-end printer that will get your documents on paper, or you can spring for a top-of-the-line printer that will make your documents a work of art. The choice is yours. Printers available today are generally one of three types:

Dot Matrix

These printers form characters and images using a series of small dots that can easily be seen if you look at the letters closely. Dot matrix printers used to be the most common, but they are being used less frequently now that printers using better technologies have come down in price. Output from these printers is black and white only. Although later models double-print the output to make the dots less visible, the result is still inferior to the printing done by the other two types.

Ink Jet

This type of printer features an ink cartridge that moves across the paper rapidly, forming images by spraying a fine jet of ink on the paper. Most printers support both black and color cartridges, so that you may alternate between black and white and color printing. This is the best type of printer for printing color on a budget.

Laser

This type of technology is the most expensive, but produces the best results for black and white printing. It produces images using a laser and a toner cartridge—a very similar technology to that used in copy machines. If you want high-quality black and white printing, this is the technology to choose. Laser printers that do color are still expensive, and the results can't match the quality of most ink jet printers for color printing.

Modem

Although a modem is an optional piece of computer hardware, it is vital if you want your computer to communicate with other computers. You wouldn't be reading this book if you weren't thinking about hooking your computer to the Internet (if you haven't done so already). That being the case, your computer will need to have a modem, and you will need to understand a little about how it works.

The function of a modem is to get data out of your computer, send them down a phone line, and have another computer on the other end of that line retrieve the information. This sounds easy to those of us who have been jaded by the marvels of modern technology, but there is a little bit of magic that the modem has to accomplish. Remember that computers work with digital information, or numbers that are composed of zeroes and ones. But the phone line works with analog information, which is a fancy way of saying it works with sound waves. The function of a modem is to turn the digital information from the computer into sounds that may be sent down the phone line. It might use a high-pitched tone to represent a "1," and a lower-pitched tone to represent a "0." If you have never heard a modem in person, you have probably heard them on television or in the movies. The collection of noises they produce often sound like a fight in a chicken coop, and you wonder what has gotten into your computer that it is suddenly emitting such a collection of whistles, beeps, and screeches.

The process your modem uses to convert digital information into analog sounds is called modulation. When the transmitted sounds get to the other end of the phone line, another modem receives them, converts them back into digital information, and gives them to the receiving computer on the other end of the connection. This reverse process of converting the analog sounds back to digital information is called "demodulation." Thus, the term modem is an abbreviation for modulation/demodulation. All modems perform both modulation and demodulation. In other words, they all function as both the sender and receiver of data.

Your computer may already have a modem and you may not know it. An internal modem may be installed inside the system unit in one of the expansion slots. Look at the back of the system unit and see if one of the slots has two sockets where you can plug in a telephone connector. If you find a slot with these connectors, you have an internal modem installed. One socket is used to connect your computer to the phone line, and the other is used for a secondary phone cord that attaches your computer to the phone. This allows regular calls to pass through the modem and be sent to the phone. If the sockets aren't clearly labeled, you may have to find the manuals that came with your computer and modem.

If you don't have a modem, you will need to go buy one. You can buy an internal modem, but that will require removing the cover of the system unit and installing the modem in one of the expansion slots. Another option is to buy a type of modem known as an "external modem." This modem is built into a plastic case, and sits alongside your computer. It connects to the back of the computer with a cable, and then you run the two phone lines into the modem. An external modem tends to cost more because of the plastic housing, but is easier to install or move to a different computer if you upgrade. Because an external modem usually connects to a port on the back of your computer, you may find that it conflicts with another device, such as a mouse, or that it is harder to configure your computer so that the software can use the modem. If you still have questions about which is best for you, visit your local computer store and ask for some professional advice.

Another thing to consider when buying a modem is its speed. More expensive modems can transfer data much faster, causing less frustration as you wait at your computer for something to happen.

Like all computer technology (this is sounding like a broken record by now), modems have continued to improve in terms of speed, size, and price. The modem that you bought two years ago may be too slow by today's standards, and you may need to upgrade.

Modem speeds are measured in "bps," which stands for "bits per second." Remember that a byte is composed of eight bits, so a modem with an 800 bps rating will transfer 800 bits, or 100 bytes of information per second. Keep in mind that this is the "optimum," or best speed, and that your actual performance may be slowed by such factors as phone line noise. Remember also that your modem will transmit data no faster than the modem on the other end of the connection can receive it. You can have the fastest modem in the world, but if you connect to a computer with an old 800 bps modem, that's the speed that will be used—the speed of the slowest modem involved in the connection.

The most common speeds you will find for modems are 2400 bps, 9600 bps, 14,400 bps, 28,800 bps, 38,400 bps, and 57,600 bps. Note that the faster speeds are often abbreviated, such as 14.4, 28.8, and 57.6.

For any serious Internet work, consider replacing anything slower than 14.4. Anything slower than that will just cause you frustration, because you spend most of your time sitting in front of the computer and waiting for data to transmit. Modems are too cheap—and life is too short—to play that game.

We will talk more about modems in Chapter 1, when we discuss common Internet connection problems.

Other Goodies

We have covered most of the common hardware you will find on a typical computer system, but there are a few other devices that you might find on your system. We will cover them briefly, just for completeness.

Scanner

A scanner allows you to copy pages, photographs, and other artwork or printed material. The scanner then converts these images to a digital file on your hard drive, so the photographs or text can be reproduced in your document or used in other ways on your computer. A scanner is very useful for publishing newsletters or newspapers—or even holiday letters to your friends—because it allows you to include photographs and line drawings in your publication. A scanner is also useful for some of the activities associated with the Internet. We will discuss this more in Chapter 7.

A handheld scanner is a wand-like device that you pass over the item you wish to scan. These types of scanners are usually cheaper, but they are more difficult to use, and they are limited as to the size of the item they can scan. Flatbed scanners are more expensive, but also more useful, because they allow the item you wish to scan to be placed on a platform that will handle larger scans such as pages from a book.

Speakers

More and more new computers come equipped with speakers these days. Speakers allow programs to play music or generate sound effects while the program is running. The speakers sometimes come built into the sides of the monitor, but usually they are two separate speakers that may be positioned around the computer as desired for ease of listening. The speakers connect to a "sound card" that installs in your system unit in one of the expansion slots.

Although computer games were the first programs to really use speakers to their potential, other types of software are now commonly including sounds as well. Encyclopedias have made good use of speakers and sound cards, because now students can actually hear famous speeches or animal sounds, instead of having to imagine them.

We have already mentioned that most computers with CD-ROM drives allow you to play music while working. If you plan to do this, and are a stickler for good sound quality, you need to invest in a good set of speakers.

Joystick

You can always tell a serious game player lives in a home when you find a joystick installed on the computer. Joysticks are needed primarily for "action" computer games that allow users to zoom around and blow things to pieces.

The joystick looks like the "stick" in a small airplane and, in fact, it is often used in games that simulate flight. As you move the joystick from side to side, the program will also cause the plane, race car, or player to move from side to side. There are also buttons, sometimes on the top of the stick and sometimes on the base, that cause guns to be fired, or initiate some other type of action by the program.

External Storage Devices

Computer hard drives have the capacity to store a lot of data, but they have the disadvantage that they are pretty much joined at the hip to your computer. Floppy drives provide the ability to make data more portable, but their small capacity makes them impractical for most applications.

To address this problem, there are many devices available that offer the portability of a floppy drive, but with a higher capacity similar to that of a hard drive. We will refer to these devices using the general term "external storage device." These typically record their data on tape cartridges, or on floppy disks that are somewhat larger than the typical 3 1/2 inch floppy. Once the data have been written, they can be taken to another location for safety, or read by another computer equipped with a similar storage device.

These external devices typically attach to one of the expansion slots, although some of them can just be plugged in between the printer and the system unit. Sharing the printer's cable this way does not affect the operation of the printer.

The most common use for external storage devices is to make backup copies of the data on hard drives. If you value the data on your hard drive, and if it would cause you much pain if your hard drive crashed, you should consider an investment in such a device. Another common use for external storage devices is to transfer large amounts of data between two computers.

SOFTWARE

As we said at the start of this chapter, the hardware and the software work together like a hand in a glove, allowing you to personalize your personal computer. Now that we have given you a quick review of computer hardware, it's time to address the software side of the equation.

Operating Systems

Ask most people to name a common computer application, and they will tell you about their word processor or describe a game that has them hooked. Some of them balance their checkbooks or compute their taxes with software programs. But a critical software program that most people overlook is what is called the "operating system." This program serves as the bridge between the computer hardware and you, the computer user.

The computer hardware responds to a number of different instructions and commands, but these are generally too complex for the typical computer user who doesn't have a degree in computer science or mathematics. The operating system acts as a liaison between you and the computer, giving you an understandable way to tell the computer what you want to do. If you want to explore your hard drive, delete a file, or start a program, you simply request that your operating system do this, and it does the necessary work behind the scenes to cause those things to happen.

This is much like a rich man who has a nice car, but has no interest in learning how to drive or fiddling under the hood. He hires an experienced driver who will respond to his requests and take him where he wants. Your operating system is a similar driver, which navigates you through the unfamiliar terrain of your computer without forcing you to deal with the dirty details of how the motor works or which road is the fastest.

When your operating system was installed on your hard drive, a portion of it was installed into something called the "boot sector." The program in the boot sector will be run automatically by the hardware whenever the computer is started, or "booted." There is just enough code in this little program to bring in other parts of the operating system and start them running. Sometimes you will hear people say they need to "reboot" a computer. This is simply another way of saying that the computer needs to be restarted so that the operating system will be loaded again from the boot sector. Rebooting probably got its name because the operating system pulls itself up by its bootstraps when the computer is turned on.

Once your computer has finished the power-up sequence, not only is the hardware ready, but the operating system has already been loaded and is waiting for your first command.

The remainder of this section will examine the various operating systems that are commonly in use on personal computers.

DOS

When IBM first introduced its personal computer in the early 1980s, it was distributed with an operating system called DOS (Disk Operating System). DOS has continued to improve over the years, with each new version boasting more features and improvements. By the way, the proper way to pronounce the word DOS is to rhyme it with "moss."

Just a little side note here. Software programs tend to be distributed with identifiers such as "Supermath 1.3," which means you are running Release 1, Version 3 of the Supermath program. Minor changes are reflected with an increase to the version number, while major enhancements result in a new release number. Thus, as the Supermath program is improved over the years, you may see numbers like 1.3, 1.4, 1.5, 2.0, 2.1, 2.2, and 3.0.

The same is true for DOS. Most Wintel machines today are running some version of DOS. As of this writing, the most current DOS version is 6.22, although later versions of Windows come with something called DOS 7.0 installed.

Although DOS is an adequate operating system, it is difficult to use because it is "command-line driven." This means that in order to use DOS, you must type a command on the monitor screen. Typing these commands is no easy feat, because DOS doesn't speak English as you know it. Every character or even every blank space means something to DOS, and DOS won't process your command unless you get your request absolutely right. DOS doesn't offer any helpful hints to direct you, either. It just gives you a blank screen and waits for you to type the magic words, much as the genie won't appear from the lamp unless you offer the right incantation.

Most home computer users don't have the time or the interest to memorize the series of commands that DOS understands.

Shown below is a typical series of DOS commands that you would enter to perform some work. You can see that DOS is not the kind of thing a beginning user would jump into without a little bit of reading and practice.

```
C:\>md work
C:\>cd work
C:\WORK>copy a:memo.txt
   1 file(s) copied
C:\WORK>edit memo.txt
C:\WORK>ren memo.txt memo2.txt
C:\WORK>copy memo2.txt a:
   1 file(s) copied
C:\WORK>del *.*
All files in directory will be deleted!
Are you sure (Y/N)?y
C:\WORK>cd ..
C:\>rd work
C:\>
```

For those who are interested, this is what happened above. First, a new subdirectory called "work" was created on the hard drive, and that was set to be the current directory. A file named "memo.txt" was then copied off the floppy drive into the new subdirectory. That file was edited and saved back, although this is not shown in the example. The file was then renamed to "memo2.txt," and it was copied to the floppy drive. All files were then deleted from the new "work" subdirectory on the hard disk, and that subdirectory was deleted also.

Do you want to spend your life memorizing such arcane stuff, when all you have to do to get the same results is click your mouse on a picture? We didn't think so. DOS is a handy operating system for computer professionals, but most PC users would be better off using something else. *Anything* else.

Macintosh

While IBM and Microsoft were changing the world with the IBM PC and DOS, the Apple folks were not sitting still. They had produced a new computer called the

Macintosh that was as different from the PC as, well, apples and oranges.

Although DOS used a command-line interface that was difficult to use, the Macintosh used what was called a Graphical User Interface or GUI (pronounced "gooey"). Despite the fancy sounding title, all a GUI consisted of was an interface based around pictures rather than words. Under the GUI interface, users ran their systems using a group of small pictures, called ICONs, to represent various things. For example, a document that you would create was represented by a little drawing of a page. Subdirectories were shown as file folders. When you wanted to delete a file, you would use the mouse to move the page ICON into the garbage can ICON. When you wanted to save a document you were writing, you would press the button that was an ICON of a floppy disk. Of course, the Macintosh still included a keyboard to allow users to do word processing and perform other functions. But most of the communication between the user and the operating system occurred through the use of the mouse and ICONs.

The Macintosh never achieved the popularity of the IBM PC, partly due to technical problems and partly due to poor marketing decisions. Nevertheless, the Macintosh opened people's eyes to the fact that an operating system could be designed that would be easy enough for even a young child to use.

Windows

While Apple was trying to sell the world on their Macintosh technology, the folks at Microsoft were designing their own application that would bring a GUI environment to the IBM PC arena. This finally resulted in a program known as Windows.

Technically, Windows is not really an operating system, so perhaps it should not be listed here. Yet it is close enough to being an operating system that it would fool most people. PCs that run Windows also have DOS running behind the scenes. DOS initializes itself and then starts Windows. Also, Windows calls upon DOS to do certain system functions. But each new release of Windows makes the line between DOS and Windows a little murkier, and we suspect that Windows may one day be running the whole show.

Early releases of Windows were prone to problems, and didn't really provide a stable or extremely useful operating environment. Starting with Windows 3.1, the system became much better, although there were technical problems that prevented Windows from really exploiting the hardware. Windows 95 was a respectable release, and finally produced an operating system that was powerful and somewhat stable. Windows 98 is basically Windows 95 with some important fixes. Windows NT (also known as Windows 2000) looks the same as Windows 95 or Windows 98, but it is designed to be used in a networking environment (where several computers are connected together over a network).

As we said in the introduction, we assume that you are running one of these versions of Windows, although much of this book will apply even if you are not. If you are running Windows 3.1, it will be almost essential for you to upgrade to a later release if you want to have any success connecting to the Internet.

Frankly, despite all its features, Windows is hardly a stable computer environment. Windows users all know that the system is going to lock up occasionally, requiring the user to reboot and start over. There is much room for improvement in the Windows environment. Still, Windows is the best thing on the market for the home computer user.

UNIX

UNIX is a popular operating system, and many of the computers you will communicate with on the Internet use it. It is not, however, an operating system that is used very heavily on PCs, although several versions are starting to become available that run quite nicely there. One of these is a UNIX-like operating system known as Linux.

OS/2

OS/2 is IBM's attempt to produce a GUI operating system for the PC. Although its fans insist that it is superior to Windows, it has never had the following of Windows, and some suggest it is falling even further behind. IBM has had some success in attracting its business clients to OS/2, but home users have yet to jump to it in any significant numbers.

Applications

Operating systems are all well and good, but the reason you bought your computer was for the "applications," which is a fancy name for the programs you run. Although you are probably already aware of most of these programs, we will spend just a minute to review the various types of applications that are written for the PC.

Business

Whether you run a mom-and-pop business or have thousands of employees, there are many software products designed to help business people.

Word processors are probably the most commonly used software product, not only for businesses, but for education and personal use. They allow you to compose letters, papers, presentations, and other documents.

Spreadsheets are useful programs for anyone dealing with numbers. These programs allow you to create, save, and print sheets containing many rows and columns of numbers. Various mathematical and statistical functions enable you to analyze the numbers in an infinite variety of ways. Once a basic template is completed, you can fill in new numbers and perform a whole series of calculations very quickly.

Database software allows you to keep track of collections of items, whether those be baseball cards, rental trucks, passengers on a plane, or items of inventory on hand. Once items are recorded in the database, they may be selected, sorted, and displayed in a number of different ways.

Presentation software allows you to create materials for business presentations, such as overhead foils and slides. The presentations you create may contain text, pictures, and drawings.

In addition to the general software packages listed above, specialized business software can be purchased to do many business functions, such as managing personnel records, keeping track of payroll information, and printing invoices. There are specialized programs as well as generalized ones, by the way. Whether you run a dental office or are thinking of starting a used bookstore, somewhere a program exists that has been designed just for you.

Financial

Many people use computer software to keep track of their personal or business finances and their investments.

Money manager programs allow you to plan a budget and then use your computer to balance your checkbook and track your expenses against your budget.

Many banks and financial institutions allow you to access and manipulate your accounts "online," and even generate checks on a regular basis to pay expenses. (Online means when you're connected to the Internet, but it is also used in a generic sense to indicate access to a resource through the Internet.)

Those who like to invest can buy software that can be used to keep track of their portfolio of investments. These applications are useful for allowing you to monitor the effectiveness of your investments, and to calculate important tax information.

Tax software is another important software tool, with more and more people each year choosing to replace their friendly accountant with software that will calculate and print their tax returns.

More and more people who buy and sell stocks are doing their trading with a computer, rather than calling their broker. Using this software is usually cheaper, plus it often produces faster trades and more timely information.

Educational

Many parents are interested in software that will help their children learn more about the world, and will give them an advantage in their school studies.

Software for preschoolers generally teaches basic concepts such as numbers and the alphabet. As more and more computers come equipped with speakers, some of this software can also be useful in teaching reading, pronunciation, and vocabulary.

Older children can learn concepts important to them, such as math, science, and English. Some of these programs are done so well that the child does not realize he is learning things while having fun.

Students in high school and college tend to use reference software, such as online encyclopedias and collections of books. Some of these collections include thousands of books that may be read online or searched for selected topics.

No one says that education should stop after school, and many adults certainly use their computers to continue their own learning each day. In addition to the materials already mentioned, there are many software products that can teach us about such topics as movies, music, history, sports, and the arts.

Entertainment

Let's face facts. You might have justified your computer purchase for all the reasons described above, but the *real* reason most people purchase computers is so Dad or Junior can play games. Even though this may not be true in your family, a trip to the local software store should convince you that computer games occupy a large amount of shelf space.

Card games are popular, probably because a version of solitaire comes installed with Windows. But other card games, including group games that allow multiple players, can be purchased. Solitaire games are invaluable to computer users who are stuck on long telephone conversations and need something to do to occupy their hands and their minds when they're allegedly listening to the sales pitch, or getting the details of Aunt Edna's gallbladder operation.

Simulation games are very popular. Thanks to simulators, computer users can practice flying a plane or driving a race car. Other simulation games allow the user to simulate the construction of a city or a world.

Adventure games usually involve exploring a castle or a strange new land. In order to complete the game, the user has to solve puzzles along the way.

Sports games allow the user to manage a football team or play golf on an exotic and challenging new course, perhaps a course of his own design.

Games that parents love to hate are the so-called "action" games, where the goal is to blast the bad guys and save the world, usually with as much blood, and gore, and as many sound effects as possible. The best that could be said for these games is that they do teach hand-and-eye coordination. In fact, people inside the industry call these games "twitch" games, because rapid reflexes are their hallmark.

There have also been some traditional board games that have been adapted to run on a computer. Some of these are pretty good, while others are better if played the old-fashioned way.

Home and Family

Although many of the programs already mentioned will be useful to families, there are a few others we think deserve a mention under the category of home and family.

Medical reference software is becoming quite popular. It helps you to diagnose health problems based on symptoms. Such programs should never replace your local doctor, but they are effective in determining if a problem is severe enough that you should contact a physician. Also, when used with the information provided by your physician, computer programs can make you more knowledgeable about certain conditions. Before you spend too much money on medical software, keep reading for some free Internet resources that allow the same thing.

Many people these days are interested in family history. There are a number of good programs that allow you to keep track of your family connections on the computer.

Want to move out of the old homestead and into that new dream house? There are architectural design programs that help the user design a whole house or just a portion of it.

When you're planning your summer vacation, there are mapping programs that allow you to plan your driving route so that you drive the shortest distance possible. Just enter your starting point and your ending destination, and it will draw and map and print turn-by-turn instructions. Once again, don't reach for that wallet too soon. There are Internet locations that do the same thing for free.

If Mom keeps losing her prize recipes, she may consider a program to keep track of them. Not only does the program keep them secure, but it does useful things such as allowing you to choose several recipes, and then printing out a shopping list for all the ingredients you will need.

Want to design your own birthday cards, or a poster for the garage sale this weekend? Is it time to crank out the annual Christmas letter? There are many publishing programs that allow you to compose and print your own cards, signs, and banners, complete with photographs or artwork and zillions of decorative type fonts to dress up whatever it is you need to do.

Software Development

Perhaps some of the previous discussion about programming has prompted your interest in giving it a try. Maybe it doesn't interest you as a profession, but you might be intrigued to design your own software customized just for you. There are a number of software applications designed for those who want to write their own programs, and then test them and run them.

Most programs are written in "high-level" language. This is a programming language that uses an English-like format to define what the program should do. The program is then run through something called a "compiler," which converts the program into the instruction set that your computer's processor chip understands. You can then test the program, and (assuming it works) start using it on your computer.

There are many different programming languages, and you need to buy the compiler specific for the programming language you wish to use. Examples of common programming languages include COBOL, BASIC, PASCAL, C++, and Java. Before you run out and buy one of them, do a little research to see what programming language best fits your skills and your needs.

Internet

There are many programs designed to run on the Internet, as well as programs designed to develop applications for the Internet. We will mention that they exist now, just to make the section complete. However, more information will be given in later chapters.

The Windows Environment

Because it is a GUI application, most people can learn how to use Windows pretty quickly—perhaps without ever cracking a manual. This is proven by the fact that many children seem to pick it up as if by magic, often running programs during their first session with Windows, as if they were old pros.

But there are some subtle features of Windows that may not be apparent to the new user who just learns by trial and error. Having an understanding of these tricks will allow you to be more productive and save a great deal of time and frustration. So in this section, we will present just a short overview of some of the neat things Windows can do for you.

The explanations in this section assume you are running a version of Windows later than 3.1. If you are running that release, most of this material will still apply, although some of the drawings and explanations will not match. Refer to your Windows 3.1 documentation, or, even better, upgrade to Windows 95.

Point and Click

As we noted earlier when discussing the mouse, much of the work you do in Windows will be accomplished by positioning the mouse pointer to a certain area of the screen and then clicking certain combinations of the mouse buttons. Technically, you can run Windows without having a mouse, and there are keyboard key combinations to perform just about all the mouse functions. But this brings Windows back into the DOS world where you have to remember dozens of obscure commands in order to do your work. You have already invested a lot of money in a computer; don't cut your productivity in half by saving the $20.00 that a mouse would cost.

Moving the mouse will cause the mouse pointer to also move on the screen. You will often have to move the mouse pointer over an artistic rendering of a button that you wish to "push," or over an item that you wish to "select" from a list of items. Once the cursor is positioned properly, you indicate the "push" or "select" action by pressing a button on the mouse, usually the button on the left. Sometimes you press the left button just once, and sometimes you press it twice—one right after the other. This is known as a "double click." When you first start using the mouse, it will be a little awkward, and you may wonder how doing this coordination test will ever be faster than using the keyboard. But trust us. After a little bit of practice, you will be pointing and clicking around the screen like an expert.

ICONs

Like the Apple Macintosh, Windows uses little pictures known as ICONs to make the user's job easier. When Windows starts running after the computer is booted, it usually fills your screen with some kind of background picture or pattern (known as "wallpaper"). On top of this background (known as your "desktop") there should be several ICONs, each of which represents a program that you can run. If you want to run one of them, you simply position your mouse pointer over the ICON, and double-click using the left mouse button.

Not all programs show up on your desktop. Users try to aim for an uncluttered desktop, so only the programs you plan to use most often are visible there. To find other programs, you press the "Start" button at the bottom left-hand corner of the screen, then point to the "Programs" button. This will cause a screen to pop up that may show individual programs, or it may show files of programs with titles such as "Games." Positioning your mouse pointer over the "Games" folder will show you the individual programs in that folder. When you finally find the program you want, just left click it (once this time) and it will run.

Windows uses ICONs in many different ways. For example, your word processor program will have an ICON that you use to start the program. When you're using Windows to browse through your hard drive and look at the files there, you may come across files that were created with your word processor. When this happens, Windows will display the same small ICON next to the name of the file, so that you will know what kind of file this represents.

How does Windows perform this trick? It does it by registering the file extensions it uses. If all the files your word processor creates end in the extension ".DOC," this acts as a red flag to tell Windows, "Whenever you see a file ending in .DOC, represent it with this ICON." This is just another reason to take care when naming your files. If you don't, it won't be as easy for you to identify the files you've created.

Drag and Drop

Remember how the Macintosh operating system will allow you to delete a file by dragging it to the garbage can? Windows will do the same thing, although the name has been changed to the more environmentally correct "Recycle Bin."

This feature is known as "drag and drop," because it allows you to drag things from one place to another and then drop them. You will find a number of places in Windows where drag and drop is supported, such as when you want to move a file from one folder to another. In that case, you simply open both folders on the desktop, grab the file you're interested in, and move it to the other folder. Just as you see on your screen, the file has been deleted from the original folder and moved to the new one.

To perform a drag and drop, position the mouse pointer over the object you wish to drag. Then press down the left mouse button and hold it down. If you move the mouse pointer, the object should move with it. When you get the object to its desired location, just release the mouse button and the object will be dropped there.

Multiple Applications

Many people don't seem to realize the powerful ability that Windows gives them to run multiple applications at the same time. Don't underestimate Windows. It is more than a pretty interface that gives computer users a colorful desktop and the ability to start programs easily.

Assume you are using your word processor to write a letter to good old Aunt Undine. In the middle of the letter, you suddenly remember that she sent you a check recently, and you want to thank her for the gift. You don't remember how much the check was for, because you've already squandered it on riotous living. But being a virtuous spendthrift, you paid tithing on the amount, and you recorded your tithing check in your money management program.

If you were running your computer under DOS, you would have no choice but to save the letter, exit the word processor, start the money management program, look up the amount, exit the money management program, start the word processing program, and reload your letter. Whew! That's a lot of work.

Fortunately, Windows gets rid of most of those intermediate steps. You first "minimize" your word processing program by moving your mouse pointer to the top right-hand side of the screen and clicking on the button that has a single line on the bottom of it. Clicking on this button keeps the program alive but just removes it from your screen. It can be retrieved later by pressing the small button with that program's ICON on the "taskbar" at the bottom of the screen.

Once your word processing program has been minimized, start your money management program, look up the amount of the check, and write it down someplace. Rather than exit the money management program (you might want to come back to it later), minimize that as well. Now there are two ICONs on the taskbar at the bottom of the desktop—one for the word processor, and one for the money management program. Before you go back to work, maybe you want to think about what you want to say when you thank Aunt Undine for the check, so you'll start a solitaire game and play with it for a while. Sure enough, the game gives you the opportunity to think of exactly what you want to say to her—so you minimize the game, click the word processor ICON on the taskbar, and you're back in business. Because you minimized all three programs, you can jump back and forth among them whenever you have a whim to do so.

You will find it handy to be able to run multiple applications when you're using the Internet. As you're writing papers, you may want to do some Internet research or look something up in an online encyclopedia or thesaurus, and then jump back into your word processor. We did that many times while writing this book. We would write something, and then say, "Let's jump out and try that, just to make sure we're telling the truth."

Copy and Paste

Another useful Windows feature allows you to move data between applications. This is known as "copy and paste," because you copy data from one location and paste it somewhere else. There is also a variation called "cut and paste." The difference is that "cut" will delete the material from the original location, but "copy" will only duplicate it.

The copy, cut, and paste functions all use a feature called the "Windows clipboard." The clipboard is a temporary location where you can store something while you are waiting to move it somewhere else. When performing a copy or cut operation, the selected data are moved or copied to the clipboard. Then, when you're ready to insert the information in the new document, you can do a paste operation. Pasting something into a document doesn't delete it from the clipboard, so you could paste it multiple times, into multiple applications. The contents of the clipboard remain there until you exit Windows or replace the data with another copy or cut.

It's easy to select the data to be cut or copied. It is very similar to the drag and drop operation. Position the mouse pointer at the start of the data you want included in the cut or copy. Depress the left mouse button and hold it down. Move the mouse pointer down to include the last character you want included, then release the mouse button. If you have done that correctly, the selected area usually turns a different color, so that you know it has been selected. (This is called being "highlighted.") Once the area is selected, you may cut or copy. We will tell you how to do the actual cut and paste in just a minute.

When we were writing this book, we would often put something in one chapter and then decide it needed to be somewhere else. To correct this, we would open both chapters with the word processor, cut the data from the original chapter, and then paste that section into the chapter where it really belonged. This is an example of using cut and paste within the same application, but it also works between applications. For example, you will often find something on the Internet that you would like to include in a research paper. While using the Internet program, just copy the item to the clipboard, jump into your word processor, and then paste the item into your document. (Be sure to remember the source of your information so you'll be able to give the author credit in the bibliography!)

Window Elements

The reason Windows got its name is because each of the applications runs in its own window. You may move these windows, change their size, and arrange them so that you can see several applications running on the desktop at the same time.

Although it may seem boring to have the same sort of layout for every program you use, the Windows format does benefit you because all applications have the same look and feel, and they all operate pretty much the same. If you've run one Windows application, you can adapt without much effort to any other Windows program that comes along. This standard interface allows you to feel somewhat at home even when you are running a new program for the first time.

In this section we will examine some of the common elements of these application windows, and show you some common tricks you can use with them. Refer to Figure 0-1 to see examples of many of these features.

Figure 0-1

Title Bar and Borders

The top of each window has a title bar, usually of a different color than the rest of the window. This usually contains the name of the application or program you are running, along with other useful information. For example, a word processor might list the name of the word processor, along with the name of the file that is currently being edited. The name of the application in Figure 0.1 is "Netcenter- Netscape."

At the very left on the title bar is a small ICON that is known as the control menu. In Figure 0-1, this is the ICON of the ship's wheel that is to the left of the word "Netcenter." When you click on this ICON, the application will display a control menu of choices you can make. Click on any of those choices to cause that operation to be performed.

There are three important buttons that usually sit on the right side of the title bar:

❏ **Minimize**

The minimize button looks like an underline mark. We talked about the minimize function previously. It makes the window disappear and replaces it with an ICON on the taskbar at the bottom of the desktop. You use minimize to make the window disappear, although it doesn't end the program. Clicking on any ICON on the taskbar will restore that application's window to its former size and location.

❏ **Maximize**

The maximize button looks like a rectangle, or more specifically like a small window. This button increases the size of the current window so that it fills the entire screen, or the desktop. Pressing the button on a window that is already maximized will return it to its original size.

❏ **Close**

The button that looks like the letter "X" causes the current window to close. Depending on the application you are running, there may be more graceful ways to ask the application to terminate.

The title bar has another handy function, which is to allow the user to move the window to a different location on the desktop. Drag and drop the window at any spot on the title bar to do this.

To adjust the size of any window, place the mouse pointer over the side of the border or corner that you wish to shrink or expand. Notice how the mouse pointer turns into a two-sided arrow? Now just drag and drop the border as desired.

Sometimes an application has more data to display than your window can hold.

This often happens with word processors, because only one page of your document is usually visible at a time. When this happens, the application will place a "scroll bar" along the right side of the window, or across the bottom, or both. A scroll bar is a narrow bar that has a "slider" somewhere along the bar, and arrows at both ends. The slider tells you what portion of the document you are viewing. If it is at the top of the bar, you are near the top of the document. To adjust the window so you see a different part of the document, click once on either of the arrow keys, click once on the bar between the arrow and the slider, or drag and drop the slider to a different place on the bar. Scroll bars usually run vertically (top to bottom), but it is also possible to have horizontal scroll bars if you need to scroll from side to side. The example in Figure 0-1 has both vertical and horizontal scroll bars.

Menu Bar

Many Windows programs use something called a "menu bar" to show you the various options they can perform. The menu bar is usually found at the top of the window, often right under the window title bar. The menu bar usually contains words such as File, Edit, and About, along with other words that have unique meaning for each application. In Figure 0-1, the menu bar contains the items File, Edit, View, Go, Communicator, and Help.

When you eat in a restaurant, the menu usually has sections with general titles such as Beef, Poultry, Pasta, Appetizers, and Desserts. Under each of those sections you will find foods specific to that category. Similarly, the menu bar gives you the general categories of functions that the program performs. Selecting a specific category will show you the functions that belong there.

To examine a specific category, move the mouse pointer to the word you want, and single click. This will produce a drop-down list of the specific functions under that category. To select a specific function, point to it and single click. If some of the drop-down functions have an arrow to the right-hand side, it means that selecting that choice will produce yet another drop-down list of choices. This nesting of menu choices can go on for several levels. If some of the drop-down functions have an ellipses (three periods) to the right-hand side, it means that selecting that choice will produce another small window called a dialog that you must complete. We will discuss dialogs below. Finally, if a drop-down item has a check mark on the left-hand side, it means that option is currently in effect. Click that item to disable the option and remove the check mark. Click it again to reverse the operation.

We cannot begin to tell you the specific categories you will see on a menu bar, because they are different for every program. But there are some common ones that you will see on many of the applications you run:

❏ **File**

This category usually contains functions that relate to files. You would use this to load a file from disk, save a new file to disk, or print the current file on the printer. There is also a common function that lets you exit from the program.

❏ **Edit**

This category contains functions that are used to manipulate data within the application. For example, the common clipboard functions of copy, cut, and paste are usually found here.

❏ **Window**

If programs allow you to deal with multiple files at the same time, you will usually find this category. For example, a word processor will allow you to have several files open for editing or viewing at the same time, each in its own window. You would use the functions under this category to navigate between the windows that represent the different files.

❏ **Help**

Functions under this category allow you to learn more about the program or application that you are running. Be warned, though, that help for Windows applications is usually very minimal, and you would often be better to just refer to any manuals that came with the product. One function that is often present is labeled "About..." It usually will tell you the version number of the application you are running. This is useful if you are working with a technical support group who need to know which version of their software you are running. Unless you're interested in learning the name of the program's manufacturer, or the release number of that program, clicking the "About" button is a waste of time.

Tool Bar

One recent addition to many Windows applications is something called a "tool bar." If this is present, it will usually reside just below the menu bar near the top of the window. In Figure 0-1, the tool bar is labeled with the words Back, Forward, Reload, Home, Search, Guide, Print, Security, and Stop,

The tool bar contains ICONs that represent some of the more common functions you will want to perform with the program. For example, a picture of a file folder is often used to allow you to open a file. Similarly, a picture of a pair of scissors is used to cut text to the clipboard. All of the functions on the tool bar are usually found somewhere on the menu bar as well. The idea is just to duplicate the more common functions so they can be requested faster.

Some applications allow you to customize the tool bar, so you can add functions that you use commonly, and remove those that you don't want to be there.

Because ICONs don't always convey the exact meaning of the functions, some tool bars have an option that also tells you, in words, what each button does. Simply point the mouse pointer to a button, and hold it there for a second or two. If your application supports this function, it will pop up a box or balloon that describes the tool bar button's function.

Common Dialogs

Sometimes you will choose a menu bar or tool bar option that requests a function that is quite complicated, such as loading a file. When this happens, another window will be created on top of your application window. When you have completed the items on that second window, and caused the file to be loaded, the window will go away. This type of temporary window is called a "dialog," because the program needs to have a "conversation" with you before it can perform the function you requested. Although some dialogs are unique to your application, others are common enough to be needed by just about every application. For these functions, Windows provides a set of common dialogs that any application can use. Once again, this is a benefit to new users, because it allows multiple applications to operate similarly. Among the common dialogs that Windows provides are the following:

❏ **Open**
Used when you want to load an existing file from disk.
❏ **Save**
Used when you want to save a file to disk that you have changed.
❏ **Save As**
Used when you save a new file for the first time, or when you want to save a modified file under a different name.
❏ **Printer Setup**
Used when you want to select a new printer, or change printer settings.
❏ **Color Select**
Used when you want to choose a color for a graphics application.

Application Elements

Window's dialogs and applications use a common set of elements for communication between you and the program you are running. You will often see these same elements when you invoke a dialog or run a program. Understanding how these elements work will help you understand what you are expected to do when you see them. Refer to the sample dialog shown in Figure 0-2 when reading the explanations below.

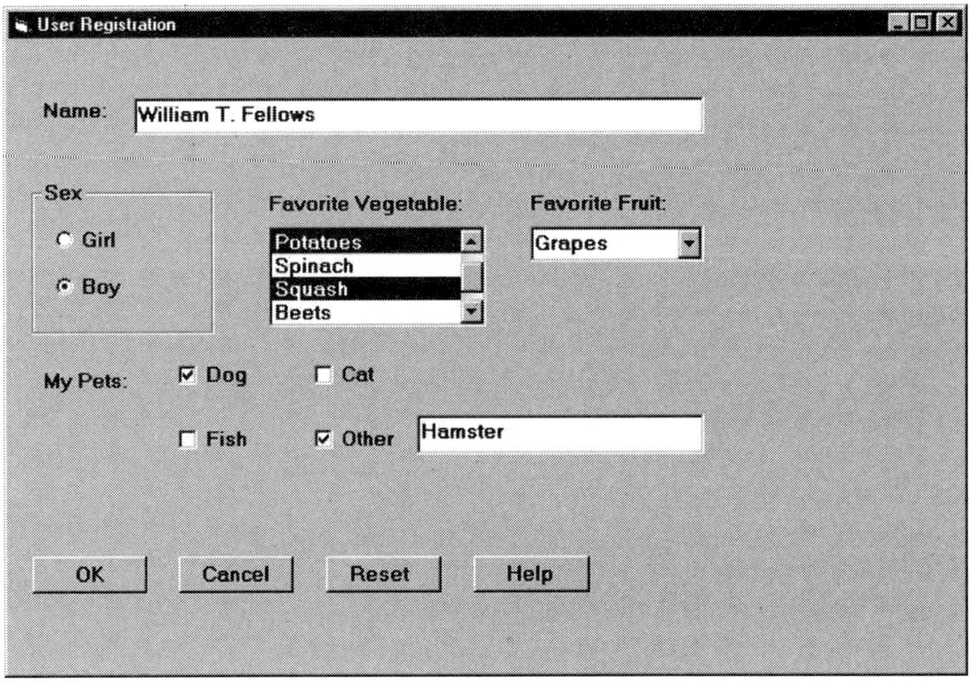

Figure 0-2

❑ **Text Box**

A text box is an area where you are expected to type something. In many cases, the area will automatically be filled in with some value, and you need only change it if you want something different. Text boxes in Figure 0-2 include the areas where the name is typed, and also the word "Hamster."

❑ **List Box**

A list box contains a list of items from which you must choose one or more items. Depending on the application, you may be allowed to choose only one item. You choose one item by clicking it with the mouse. If you can choose multiple items, you select the first one, and then hold down the CTRL key while you select the secondary ones. In Figure 0-2, the area labeled "Favorite Vegetable" is an example of a list box where the user has selected two items, potatoes and squash.

❏ **Combo Box**

A combo box (also known as a dropdown list) is similar to a list box, but is used to save space when there are a large number of items from which to choose. The right side of the combo box area contains a button that points down. When you click on this button, a pop-up screen is displayed that shows you all the items you may choose. Click the item you want, or type it directly into the text area. Unlike the list box, you can only choose one item from a combo box. In Figure 0-2, the area labeled "Favorite Fruit" represents a combo box.

❏ **Check Box**

A check box is a small square box that appears next to an option you may wish to select. The text next to the check box will describe the option being set. For example, in Figure 0-2 the area labeled "My Pets" contains check boxes for many common pets such as Dogs, Cats, and Fishes. The user may check all of these, none of these, or selected ones. Check the box by clicking it once, which will cause a black check mark to appear inside. Click it again to remove the check mark and not select the option.

❏ **Radio Button**

A radio button (also called a choice button) is similar to a check box, except that it is round, you must check one option, and only one option may be selected. It is called a radio button because it resembles the buttons on a car radio. You can only listen to one station at a time; and if you press a different button, then that station will be selected. In Figure 0-2, the area labeled "Sex" asks the user to select the options of "Girl," or "Boy." Usually, one of these will be selected automatically when the dialog is first shown. If you click another option, that button will be selected, and all other buttons in the group will be unselected.

❏ **Notebook Tabs**

When a dialog allows you to set more options than can fit in one window, it is often designed to use a feature called notebook tabs. These tabs really do look like tabs in a book, and they appear usually at the top or the right-hand side of the dialog window. Each tab has writing on it, giving a general description of the options contained within that tab. You use these tabs by clicking on the one that interests you, which should then reveal the options associated with that tab. To move to another section, just click a different tab.

❏ **Buttons**

Most dialogs contain one or more buttons. A button looks like a push button, and it has an ICON or writing on it to explain what pushing that button does. The dialog in Figure 0-2 has four buttons marked "OK," "Cancel," "Reset," and "Help." Press the OK button if you want the dialog to process the options you have set. Press the Cancel button if you want to cancel the dialog and go back to what you were doing before. Press the Reset button to restore the dialog options to what they were when the dialog was first displayed. Press the Help button if you want more information about what this particular dialog does. You "press" a button by pointing to it and single clicking.

*****

Well, that's the end of your remedial computer course. Do you feel confident enough to sit down at your computer and jump onto the Internet? If not, consider reading through this chapter again while sitting down at your computer and experimenting with what you are learning. All the knowledge in the world won't replace a little bit of practice to increase your confidence.

A PARENT'S QUESTIONS

Q. Our son says our three-year-old computer is obsolete. That can't be true, can it?
A. Your computer could very well be obsolete, depending on what you want to do with it. As we have repeatedly pointed out in this chapter, the speed at which computer technology has advanced has been nothing less than phenomenal. One executive at Intel Corporation (the company that makes processor chips) came up with something called Moore's Law. Moore's Law says that the number of transistors that can fit on a processor chip will double every eighteen to twenty-four months. Because the number of transistors affects the speed of the processor, this means that processor speeds will double during that same interval.

So, the computer you bought three years ago may only have a fourth the power of a new model. Similarly, the computer you buy today will only be worth about half as much in a year and a half. This is kind of like buying a new car and having it depreciate twenty-five percent of its value when you drive it off the lot. One could be tempted to not buy a computer until technology slows down, but that could be a long wait. Moore's Law has held pretty much constant over the past ten years, and experts predict the same progress should continue to be made for at least another five years.

It's better to jump into the game with the understanding that obsolescence is just a fact of life.

Although your machine may be a dinosaur compared to current models, it isn't necessarily obsolete. The usefulness of your computer depends on the software you are running. The programs you bought when you got your computer will still run as fast and as well as ever. If you only bought your machine to do word processing, and you never plan to upgrade your word processor, your machine will be adequate until it gasps its last breath.

But as we pointed out in this chapter, software companies tend to push their products to the limits of the hardware. Thus, if most people are buying machines with larger hard drives, new versions of your software will consume more of your hard drive real estate. If most people are buying faster processors, new software versions will tend to be written that eat more processor instructions. Thus, the problem with older machines really occurs when you upgrade the software. Now, all of a sudden, your hard drive is running out of space, or your favorite program runs like a turtle instead of a rabbit.

You will know it's time to upgrade your machine when you cannot install a new version of your software, or when the new upgrades you install run in a way that is unacceptable. Some people like to upgrade hardware regularly just so they can say they are running on the best and newest technology available. Most of us have more sense (and fewer dollars) than those folks, and we upgrade when the pain becomes too great.

Q. We can get an older computer for a good price. Should we do it?
A. That depends on what you want to do with it. After reading the previous answer to see why computers may need to be replaced, you may want to consider that older computers can also be upgraded. You can buy a faster modem for under two hundred dollars and a larger hard disk for slightly more. You can add RAM memory, assuming your motherboard has available slots to hold it. Even processor chips may be upgraded in some cases. You need to make a serious evaluation of what components you will need to upgrade, and the approximate total cost for all the upgrades. Unless you are planning to make the upgrades yourself, consider also what the computer shop will charge you to do the work. Remember that new systems may be purchased for eight hundred to two thousand dollars, depending on your needs. If your upgrade costs approach this range, it may be better to spring for a new system.

Again, much of this will depend on what you are planning to do with the computer. If it is a secondary machine that will only be used for limited functions, it may do the job with minimal upgrades. But if this is going to be the main family computer, think long and hard about it, and evaluate all the costs.

We have an older laptop computer that we use while traveling, mainly for connecting to the Internet and for writing. This machine is significantly slower than our newer machines at home, but it does the job . . . for the most part. The software versions on the laptop are older, so the software doesn't have all the nice features we have come to depend on at home. When we transfer a document from a newer version of the word processor to the old version and then back again, we lose sentence fragments or whole paragraphs along the way. Sometimes the effort of making those conversions and corrections isn't worth the work that is done on the machine when we're away from home. That laptop is only about three years old, but its days are numbered. Even though the laptop is a functional system that will accomplish the work we need to do, it's a pain in the neck to use, and we only use it because it's the only laptop we have. Don't make your family's computer experience miserable just to save a few dollars. Consider the computer to be like any appliance, and get one good enough to really meet the needs of the family.

Q. Where on my keyboard is the "Any" key?
A. Some computer messages, especially those issued by DOS, contain the phrase, "Press Any Key to Continue." According to computer folklore, some people have called technical support centers, complaining that they can't find the "Any" key on their keyboard. Just in case you're so inclined, here is a clarification. There is no such thing as an "Any" key. Any key can be any key on the keyboard.

Q. Did the invention of cheap PCs kill off the dinosaur mainframes?
A. Many people predicted that as PCs became even cheaper, the giant mainframes of the past would end up on the scrap heap. Although it is true that the original giant water-cooled monsters were finally junked, they were replaced with newer mainframes that also benefited from faster, cheaper, smaller processor chip technology. Many large corporations and organizations still rely on mainframes to manage large collections of data. Actually, having the availability of both mainframes and PCs has given programmers the perfect combination of tools to design applications that best fit the needs of the users. Mainframes are best suited for the management of large amounts of data, but PCs are best suited for displaying data to the user.

Chapter 1—The Internet Under a Microscope
• • • • •

Before we even begin this chapter, we have a confession to make. We lied. We told you all the miserable technical information was in Chapter 0, and you wouldn't have to deal with any more of it for the rest of the book. But alas, this chapter is just as technical as the last one was.

In fact, just as Chapter 0 was an introduction to computers for people who had never held a furless mouse, this is the chapter that introduces the Internet to people who have only surfed in the ocean. It's got all sorts of boring technical stuff that is nevertheless information you're going to need before you connect to the Internet for the first time.

If you've already connected to the Internet, you can skip or skim this chapter and only return to it as an occasional reference. It's Chapter 2 that's the first non-technical chapter. . . and beyond that there's even more technical stuff. We can't get around it, alas. This is a technical book.

We love to watch those old movies that contain really bad science. You know—the ones where the seats in the rocket ship roll around on casters and look surprisingly like used office chairs that have been equipped with seatbelts.

Movies about computers are certainly not exempt from bad science. We have lost count of the number of 1950s "B" horror movies where the evil computer learns how to think and decides to take over the world. Usually the villainous computer is thwarted by the brilliant scientist who instructs the computer to divide zero by zero. This always causes the equivalent of an electronic nervous breakdown: Smoke pours out of the machine, its lights blink madly and then dim, and it utters a metallic groan with its last electronic breath. (Actually, Clark has written programs that divide zero by zero, and the results are far less spectacular. You get a nasty error message, the computer throws away your program, and then the processor moves on to do something more productive.)

As the Internet has grown in size and popularity, Hollywood has produced a number of movies about it. But the science in these movies isn't much better than the science in those 1950s "B" movies. If all your knowledge about the Internet has come from such sources, we can see why you are confused and possibly even scared to tackle the Internet on your own. Learning about actual computer operation from watching adventure movies is similar to learning about beach vacations from watching *Jaws*, or learning how to take a shower by watching *Psycho*.

In this chapter we separate the fact from the fluff and give you the true scoop about the Internet. It may not be as sinister as what you see in the movies, but you may find it interesting nonetheless. We will examine both the underlying hardware and software components that make the Internet work. We will also explore the various options available to you when connecting your home computer to the Internet, just in case you have not done that yet. Finally, we will explore common functions or applications that you use once you have an Internet connection, plus the software tools designed to run those applications.

TWENTY WORDS OR LESS

You've finally achieved your lifelong dream of becoming a contestant on *Jeopardy!* You're in the lead as you go into Final Jeopardy. The championship hinges on the question you write. To your relief, the answer is revealed as "The Internet," and you furiously write: "What is a huge assortment of computers, tied together through various communication links, and sharing data via a common language?" Assuming you could write that much on the little slate in a few seconds, you would probably win the big money, go home a hero, and never have to work again.

To be a bit more precise, the Internet is actually a network of networks. You don't need to know what the Internet is to use the Internet, but if you're interested in getting a little background, here it is.

We have two different computers in our home, because we're often working at the same time. But because we often work together (such as when writing this book), it is useful to have our computers be able to share information, such as printers and hard disk files. Thus, our two computers are hooked together into something called a network. This involves installing a network card in an expansion slot on each computer, running cable between the cards, and then using Windows 95 to allow the computers to share files and printers. As a side benefit, we can play network games and send each other messages. This may be the definition of romance in the computer age—sitting twenty feet away in two different rooms and sending messages to each other. Even though we only have two computers, we could follow the same procedure to add many more to our family network.

Now assume we become friendly with our neighbors and find out they have a family network as well. It might be fun to connect those two networks together, so we could share data between their family and ours. We could do this by running some cable between the two houses, connecting it to both networks, and adding some special hardware boxes that route messages to the proper house and the proper computer.

We could repeat this process for all the houses in our neighborhood to form a neighborhood network. We could include not only homes, but businesses and schools that had computer networks. It wouldn't matter if a network consisted of two PCs (like our network), or a dozen super computers—they could all join the neighborhood network.

Neighborhood networks could then form city networks, that could form regional networks, that could form state networks. Then national governments could get involved by installing giant "backbone" communication lines that could carry millions of bits of data per second, and connecting the state networks to them. Finally, backbones between different countries could be connected together to form a truly worldwide network.

Once this network was in place, you could sit at your computer, drink your morning juice, and share information with your next-door neighbor, or your friend living halfway around the world.

WHAT THE INTERNET IS NOT

Perhaps it is easier to explain the Internet by trying to explain what it is not:

The Internet Is Not a Corporation or an Organization

There is no one company or organization named "The Internet." Although there are thousands of corporations, universities, government agencies, military agencies, and individuals connected to it, the term "The Internet" is a generic term that refers to the whole conglomeration of hardware, software, organizations, and data. Think of it in relation to other generic terms, such as "The Entertainment Industry."

There are a few nonprofit groups associated with the Internet, however. These groups help set standards and plan for Internet growth. One such organization is the Internet Activities Board, who manage the assignment of Internet Protocol (IP) addresses, and the maintenance of the Domain Name System (you'll learn about these terms later).

The Internet Is Not a Single Type of Computer

There are millions of computers that participate in the Internet, and probably no two of them are exactly alike. These consist of machines in many sizes and speeds, made by many manufacturers. Some are giant mainframes that belong to universities, and others are individual PCs such as the one you are probably using. All the kids on the block can play, and there is no restriction in terms of size or power.

Granted, having a small, under-powered computer may make your Internet experience less productive than you would like, but it doesn't keep you out of the game.

The Internet Is Not a Single Type of Software

Computers on the Internet run a wide variety of operating system software programs. You will find Internet computers running Windows, Macintosh, UNIX, OS/2, and others we have not even discussed. For example, many large IBM mainframes that are connected to the Internet run an operating system known as OS/390.

Although different types of computers often have trouble communicating, this problem is minimized on the Internet because all the players write their Internet software using the same protocol, or the same set of specifications. We will discuss protocols in more detail later in this chapter.

Once users get connected, a common set of tools allows access to any piece of information, anywhere on the network.

The Internet Is Not Designed to Make a Profit

This may come as a surprise to you, because you may already be paying a monthly fee for Internet access. Actually, that fee you are paying is just an access fee to get you connected to the Internet. Once you get there, everything else is free.

Pretend that you have a big water pipe that runs down the center of your street. You would love to get connected, so that you will have an unlimited supply of fresh, clean water. But the costs of connecting to the big pipe are expensive, so you find a neighbor who is already connected. He will allow you to run a garden hose from your house to his system, and will allow water to flow through that pipe for so many hours a month at a fixed cost. This is roughly what happens when you get an Internet provider.

Once you get connected, most of the costs of sending your data around the network are covered by the other institutions that are also connected. Thus, if you send an e-mail to a friend in Norway, it may travel through computers and transmission links provided by universities, corporations, and government agencies. All of this overhead is provided at no charge, just as the cost of being a good Internet citizen.

Large organizations can connect to the Internet "water pipe" directly, and not have to pay someone else a monthly access fee. Thus, if you are affiliated with a university or a large corporation, you are probably connected to the Internet all the time, and pay no access fee.

The Internet Is Not a Master/Slave Relationship

Some computer systems are designed to use a "master/slave" relationship, where large central computers send data and orders to smaller computers. The Internet is not like that, because any computer is potentially connected to any other computer. Most communication consists of one computer sending a request to another computer, and the receiver answering back.

The Internet Is Not Built out of Concrete

Because new computers and communication lines are being added all the time, the Internet is certainly not an object that has any form to it. It changes from day to day and from hour to hour. Because there is no central management agency over it, no one even knows for sure the exact size of the Internet. Many of the numbers used in this chapter are nothing more than estimates, and even if they are correct today, they will be out of date by next week.

The Internet Is Not Designed to Perform a Single Function

Once you are connected to the Internet, there is not just one thing that you do. There are a variety of different software products you can run that perform many different functions. Think of your Internet connection as being like a pipe. Once the plumbing is in place, you can request water, milk, chocolate milk, eggnog, or motor oil (but we hope you would clean the pipe every time you change selections!).

The Internet Is Not Designed for Those Who Need Hand-Holding

Although it is good that the Internet is not owned or controlled by any one group, there is a flip side to that same coin. You cannot call the Internet toll-free, worldwide hotline, and say, "Help! I'm having trouble!" There is not one central organization that really cares whether or not you're a happy surfer. If you can't figure things out on your own, you're pretty much out of luck.

This does not mean you are alone in the wilderness. If you pay a monthly fee for Internet access, your Internet provider is probably concerned that you stay happy. There are also books, such as this one, that try to make your journey pleasant. There are also a lot of resources out on the Internet itself that are designed to help new users. We hope to show you many of these as you continue reading.

A LITTLE HISTORY

You don't need to know the history of the Internet to use the Internet. Nobody is going to test you. Nobody is ever going to ask you how the Internet got started, unless you have a curious son or daughter who brings up the subject. But if history intrigues you, here's a brief history of the Internet.

Those who think the term "military intelligence" is an oxymoron will be surprised to learn that the Internet originated in a project started by the U.S. Defense Department. In the early 1960s, a military agency known as ARPA (Advanced Research Projects Agency) started a research project related to the connection of computers via phone lines. The first goal of the project was to accomplish this connection using a minimum number of lines. Previous attempts to link computers had resulted in a spider web of lines, with each computer having to have a separate line running to every other computer in the system. The second goal was to design a network that would be able to survive battle conditions, perhaps even a nuclear war. It would not be uncommon during times of war to lose selected computers and communication lines, and the network had to be robust enough to maintain communications in these less-than-ideal conditions.

A solution that would achieve both these goals involved a new idea known as "packet switching." Using this method, messages to be sent would be broken up into smaller packets. Each packet would contain both a return and forwarding address, based on the computer to which it was to be sent. Each computer would be able to determine the location of any other computer on the network, and the possible routes through which a packet could be sent. Packets would usually be sent via the shortest route, but could be resent if there were problems with that link. Because multiple packets from different senders could travel on the same line, packet switching would also accomplish the goal of requiring fewer phone lines.

ARPA's network was designed and completed in 1969, and was called ARPAnet.

Fortunately, there has never been a test of whether such a network could survive a nuclear attack. But the design of the network has made it resistant to less severe forms of mayhem, such as assaults by the backhoe operators who cut through communication lines, and satellites that go off course.

During the 1970s, ARPA realized a second benefit of having such a computer network. The defense budget is spread across many organizations that do military research, including universities, defense contractors, and numerous military and government agencies. It was theorized that perhaps such a computer network would allow all these diverse organizations to better coordinate their projects, by encouraging the timely sharing of information. Thus, ARPAnet was expanded to include these organizations as well. The expansion was so well received by the agencies that eventually two different networks were formed — one for military users, and one for everyone else. The two networks were still connected together, however, so they could still share information. (It was during this time frame that ARPA encouraged the development of network standards, in order to provide some consistency despite the huge differences in hardware and software configurations.)

During the early 1980s, commercial organizations first started to connect to the Internet. These included companies like IBM, who viewed networking as just a portion of their business. Other companies who were among the first to jump on the Internet bandwagon included new types of companies that specialized in providing only Internet services.

In 1986 the National Science Foundation started to build its own fast network, known as NSFNET, which would connect several large supercomputers. Although the project involving the supercomputers was never completed, NSFNET was a success because all the ARPAnet users migrated to it, finally resulting in the shutdown of ARPAnet in 1990. Smaller colleges and public schools also connected to NSFNET, thanks to legislation passed to encourage such connections. Meanwhile, outside the U.S., major Internet networks were also being built, usually by national and local phone companies.

In 1989 the design was completed for the World Wide Web, the component of the Internet that has generated the most excitement over the past few years. (You will read about the web in chapter 6.) Also during this period, commercial services such as CompuServe and Prodigy were getting more pressure from their users to provide Internet services. This finally started to happen in about 1991.

Although commercial Internet users got a late start in joining the Internet, they have since become the dominant users. As of when this was written, it is estimated that there are more than seventy thousand networks hooked together to create what we know as the Internet.

When ARPA encouraged the development of network standards in the 1970s, they referred to those standards as the "internetworking protocols." The Internet's name came from that unwieldy ancient description. Other terms that you will hear include "The Net," "Cyberspace," and "The Information Superhighway." As you might expect, that last term was coined by a politician, and that's why it's too cute for anyone but a politician to love.

HARDWARE COMPONENTS

For all practical purposes, you know enough about the Internet now to be able to use it. In fact, most people don't know—and don't particularly care—about the history of the Internet. (We threw that information in for free.) But if you have questions about whether to subscribe to an online service or dive right into Internet waters, and if you're unsure how to get yourself connected, read on. There's a lot of technical information here, but it's also helpful information—if you can stay awake long enough to read it.

Computers

Because the Internet is always changing, it is difficult to estimate the number of different computers that are connected. As of January 1998, one company estimated there were approximately 29,669,611 unique computers attached.[1] By the time you read this, it is not unrealistic to expect that number to have grown well past 30 million.

As already noted, these millions of machines represent all different sizes and speeds of computers. Small businesses may have computers not much larger than your PC, while those belonging to large organizations would be, well, large computers.

The estimate of computers attached to the Internet at any given time is calculated by sending a message to every possible computer address, and then seeing which addresses answer. But sometimes more than one address may be answered by the same computer, so these duplicates are subtracted from the total number of successful answers received.

We said earlier that every computer connected with the Internet has to have a unique address so that messages will arrive at the right destination. This unique address is known as an Internet Protocol address, usually referred to as an IP address. A nonprofit group called the Internet Activities Board assigns new IP addresses and makes sure no two computers get the same address, although, as previously noted, sometimes an organization will use one computer to service requests from multiple IP addresses.

The IP address is represented by a string of four bytes, or thirty-two bits. Remembering your math from the last chapter, this will give us approximately four billion possible addresses — enough to last for a little while longer.

By convention, an IP address is listed by presenting the values of each of the four bytes, separated by a period. For example, 107.98.211.104 would be a valid representation of an IP address, although we have no idea who would answer if we sent a message there! Remember that a byte has a possibility of 256 different values, ranging from 0 to 255. However, the values 0 and 255 are used for special functions, and are not normally assigned. Therefore, each of the four numbers that comprise an IP address should range from 1 to 254.

Communication Lines

The various computers of the Internet are all hooked together using a number of different types of communications lines. As with water lines, these communication "pipes" vary in size and speed, depending upon the number of people they serve.

As a home user, you will probably use what is called a dial-up line. This means that most of the time your line will not be connected to the Internet, but may be used for phone calls, faxes, or other traffic. When you wish to connect, you dial the organization that provides your Internet service, and you remain connected until you disconnect the call. The opposite of a dial-up line is a leased line, or a dedicated line, that is always connected between your house and the Internet. These are the kinds of lines used by corporations and universities that provide constant Internet connections.

Although a regular phone line will usually provide you with fast enough service, serious home users might consider something called an ISDN (Integrated Services Digital Network) line, which is available in some areas. An ISDN line is quite expensive, and also requires a special modem, but it can transfer data at a speed of up to 128 KB per second (128,000 bps).

Another option for home users in some areas is a cable modem. This is something you purchase through your cable TV provider that allows data to be sent across the cable used by the TV. Although this is quite expensive, it can provide transmission speeds up to one hundred times faster than a regular modem. That's a real plus for users who spend a lot of time on the Internet.

Specialized high-capacity phone lines are used to connect networks with each other, or to connect large organizations to the Internet. For example, a corporation or a university may have hundreds or thousands of users connected at the same time over one high-capacity line. A line known as a "T1" can transmit data at a rate of up to 1.544 MB per second, or 1,544,000 bps. If that is not fast enough, a "T3" line can reach transmission speeds of 44.746 MB per second, or 44,746,000 bps.

The BNS (Backbone Network Service) is the array of large high-speed lines that connect all of the major networks together to form the Internet. These are the fastest of all the lines, and they have continued to be enhanced over time as more speed was required. Currently they transmit data at a speed of up to two billion bps, which is fast enough to send the text of an entire large encyclopedia across the country in less than two seconds.

In addition to the technologies mentioned above, other devices involved in data transmission include fiber-optic cable, microwave links, and satellite transmissions.

Connectors

If a Frenchman and an Italian were going to eat dinner together, it would benefit them to employ a translator to help them communicate. Similarly, specialized connectors are often used on the Internet to smooth the linking together of various computers and various types of communication lines.

As a knowledge of these devices has no bearing upon your ability to use the Internet, we will mention them briefly in this section, just in case you find yourself a contestant on *Jeopardy!* and learn that the Final Jeopardy question concerns Internet connectors.

❑ **Hub**

A *hub* allows groups of computers to link with one another.

❑ **Bridge**

A *bridge* connects local networks together, and routes data between them.

❑ **Gateway**

A *gateway* is like a smart bridge that links unlike networks together, translating data between networks as needed.

❑ **Router**

A *router* determines the optimum path for the transmission of data packets.

❑ **Repeater**

A *repeater* amplifies signals when sent over long distances.

Disk Storage

Once all the other hardware is in place, the object of having an Internet is to be able to move data from one location to another. That implies that some kind of disk storage must be available to store the data that are being moved around. For example, you can visit an area run by the U.S. Senate, where you can see the status of various pieces of legislation, and find information about your senator. But this information cannot just appear on your screen; it must be stored somewhere on the computer the Senate uses to service Internet requests.

Disk space is also needed for more short-term uses, such as for the temporary storage of electronic mail that is being sent from one user to another.

As noted above, the disk storage available on the Internet is not in some magic pool, but is attached to the various computers that form the network.

SOFTWARE COMPONENTS

The computers, communication lines, connectors, and disk storage space comprise the physical parts of the Internet. But now let's turn our attention to the software that makes it all work together.

TCP/IP

As you've already learned, the computers connected to the Internet run a variety of different software operating systems. If you think about that, you should be pretty well impressed—if not downright amazed—that the system runs so smoothly. Anyone who has even tried to create a file on one kind of computer and then read it with another will know that most operating systems tend to think of themselves as being alone in the universe. It's like having a room full of people who are trying to communicate, but who are all speaking in different languages. How is it they can all play nicely together when they're in the Internet sandbox?

The answer is that they all communicate with each other using a common protocol known as TCP/IP. If you want to play the Internet game, you have to speak TCP/IP.

Before we explore that any further, let's define a "protocol." This is a defined set of rules and procedures that everyone has agreed to follow. For example, assume your kids are driving you nuts because they're always asking for treats. So you meet together as a family and define the MDTP (Mom and Dad's Treat Protocol). Everyone agrees (with a little bit of parental pressure) that those who desire to be successful in obtaining a treat must adopt the following procedure:

1. Those who want to receive a treat must meet in the family kitchen between the hours of 8 p.m. and 9 p.m., on any night but Tuesday and Thursday.
2. The requester will sit quietly until a PU (Parental Unit) inquires of him: "And what may I do for you?"
3. The requester must respond, "Please (Mom or Dad), may I have some (name of treat)? I have completed my homework and done all the chores I have been assigned."
4. If the PU responds, "No, we don't have any of those left. The dog ate the last one," the requester should select an alternate treat and restart at step 1.
5. If the PU responds, "No, you've had enough sugar. Go to bed," the requester must terminate all conversation and proceed immediately to bed.
6. If the PU responds, "Yes, I think you deserve that," the requester should accept the treat, say, "Thank you very much," quickly consume the treat at the kitchen table, retire to the bathroom and brush his/her teeth, and then go to bed.
7. Any request that does not follow this protocol will be ignored. Repeated improper requests may caused termination of requester's allowance.

Similarly, computers using the Internet have all agreed to use the common language, or protocol, of TCP/IP when talking to other Internet computers. So, a request coming from an IBM mainframe will follow the same rules as a request coming from a UNIX machine, or a PC running Windows.

Now to confuse things a little more, TCP and IP are actually two different protocols that work together. Transmission Control Protocol (TCP) is used to package messages for shipment. It also unpackages those messages once they arrive at their destination. Internet Protocol (IP) is assigned the task of getting the message to where it's going.

Let's explain with another example. Your family is moving across the country and you want to make sure that your household goods will arrive on time, without damage, and without losing anything. A friend recommended the TCP/IP moving company, run by Thor C. Price and his twin brother Igor.

Thor collects the household goods and packages them carefully in boxes. Sealed within each box, he puts a paper that contains a complete inventory of the contents of that box. Boxes are numbered, such as "Box 43 of 976." Written on the outside of each box is the address of your new house, plus the return address to your old one.

When Thor finishes the packaging, he takes a snooze and lets Igor take over. Igor is an expert at getting your goods to their destination. He knows the shortest routes, and he's careful to avoid the roads that may be congested by heavy traffic. He is so efficient at his job that he may even send some packages by one route, and some via another.

Once the trucks have arrived, Igor can rest in the back of the truck with a bag of Snickers while Thor takes over. Thor unpackages everything, and arranges the contents in your new home. Because each box is numbered, he will know if one is missing. If the contents of a box don't match the inventory, he will know something fell out in transit. If Thor discovers problems, he will ask Igor to find the missing boxes or the missing items, or to send replacements. Thanks to the teamwork of Thor and Igor, you find that everything has been successfully moved from your old residence to your new one—right down to the last paperclip. Thor and Igor may be a little strange, but you have to admit they do good work.

Similarly, TCP/IP works to move a message that is sent over the Internet from one computer to another. First, on the sending computer, TCP breaks the message into multiple packages, known as packets. Each packet is about 1500 bytes, plus some information added by TCP. This information includes the packet number (1 of 3), the addresses of the sending and receiving computers, and something called a "checksum." The checksum can be used to detect changes in the content of the packet, such as words being dropped from the message, letters being changed, or additional letters being added.

The IP on the sending computer then sends the packets to the destination computer. Assisted by something called a "router," it sends the packets over the shortest route on the network, accounting for such things as delay because of message congestion. If conditions change during the transmission of the message, different packets may be sent via different routes.

At the destination computer, the TCP running there rebuilds the messages from the packets. This may be a challenge, because the packets may arrive in different orders. If any packet is missing, or if the checksum indicates a problem with the contents, TCP will communicate with the sending computer (remember, each packet contains the return address), and ask for the missing or bad packets to be sent again.

The requirement for computers to use TCP/IP also applies to your computer when you connect to the Internet. PCs running Windows use a protocol called Winsock that was designed so that Windows applications could talk to other computers using TCP/IP. This is usually installed as part of the Internet software installed on your computer, so it's usually not something you have to install separately or worry about.

Domain Name Servers (DNS)

If you've been reading carefully, you've already learned that each Internet computer will be contacted via its own unique IP address, which will be something like 107.98.211.104. Although this type of addressing system is great for computers, most humans just don't get a warm, fuzzy feeling from a name like that. If you owned the computer in this example, you might wish for something easier to remember, such as "bobs.computer.company," rather than the always-catchy 107.98.211.104.

Good news. Warmth and fuzziness are at your fingertips, because the service you wished for is provided by an Internet service known as a Domain Name Server, or DNS. DNS machines are a special class of Internet computer whose only purpose in life is to convert friendly computer names, such as "bobs.computer.company" into not-so-friendly IP addresses, such as 107.98.211.104.

Technically, the friendly name "bobs.computer.company" is called a domain name. You register your domain name by paying a modest fee to an Internet organization given the assignment of registering and keeping track of all domain names. When you register the name, you also provide the IP address that will be associated with that name. Both the domain name and the IP address will be stored in a disk file that all the Domain Name Servers (DNSs) on the Internet can access.

Now assume one of your pals wants to contact you on the Internet. If he can remember your IP address, he can contact your computer directly, and the DNS does not even get involved. But let's assume he uses the domain name "bobs.computer.company" in his request. Because he specified a domain name instead of an IP address, the name of the requested domain will be sent to the nearest DNS, which will look up the name, and return the corresponding IP address associated with it—107.98.211.104. The message will then be sent to that computer in the normal fashion.

In addition to the obvious advantage of being easier to remember, another advantage of using a domain name is that you can change the IP address assigned to that domain name without affecting the user. Assume that you run a store that sells ten different kinds of products. You want to encourage people to buy using the Internet, so you set up ten different domain names, one for each product. But all of those ten domain names resolve into just two IP addresses, as you use two large computers to service the requests. You may find that some products sell better than others, and so one of the computers is always busy, while the other is just sitting there waiting for work. One solution would be to change the domain/IP assignments, to balance the work between the two machines. You could do this without your customers realizing that a change had been made.

Although the "bobs.computer.company" example is cute, it is also an annoying example if you're fond of apostrophes and want to sneak an apostrophe where it belongs in "bobs." A more accurate example of a real domain name would be the following:

compsci.engineer.mit.edu

To analyze this example, we start from the back and work forward. The last part of the name is the most general, and then you work towards the front to get more specific. The "edu" part of the name is called the top-level domain, and is used to group all domain names belonging to educational institutions. The next part of the name, "mit," identifies the specific institution. The next part, "engineer," identifies this as belonging to a computer in the engineering department, while the final portion, "compsci," identifies the computer science building. Thus, the domain name contains a hierarchy that runs from the general to the specific:

EDU	All Educational Institutions
MIT	Massachusetts Institute of Technology
ENGINEER	Engineering Department
COMPSCI	Computer Science Building

There are a limited number of top-level domains that are assigned. The most common ones, along with the percentage of domain names using that level, are as follows:

28%	COM	Commercial	(Businesses, Corporations)
18%	NET	Networking	(Companies and Groups)
13%	EDU	Educational	(Colleges, Universities, Public Schools)
4%	MIL	U.S. Military	
2%	ORG	Organizations	(Usually Nonprofit)
2%	GOV	Government	

The domain naming system shown above was devised when the United States was registering the vast majority of domains. As other countries started adding domains, it became apparent that the system shown above was too limited. Thus, a second domain name system was developed where the top-level domain was a two-character code representing the country where the name was registered. Thus, you will occasionally see domain names that end in these country codes. Some of the more common ones are as follows:

4%	JP	Japan
4%	US	United States
3%	DE	Germany
3%	UK	United Kingdom
3%	CA	Canada
2%	AU	Australia
2%	FI	Finland
1%	NL	Netherlands
1%	FR	France
1%	SE	Sweden
1%	NO	Norway
1%	IT	Italy

Even though only the most common ones are shown above, these two-character domain names have been assigned to just about every country in the world—even the ones that have no domains to register yet.

Some domain names in the United States have started using the US designation, but the vast majority of domains registered still use the old three-character codes.

All domain names contain at least two parts, the top-level domain, and the host machine. For example, "ibm.com" would be the most simple kind of domain name. If the particular organization has multiple domains, it is common to see names that identify specific locations or machines, such as "usa.ibm.com" and "japan.ibm.com."

As of this writing, there were approximately 2.3 million public domain names that had been registered.[2]

Internet PC Applications

In the previous chapter, we said that PC software consists of the operating system that keeps the computer running behind the scenes, and the application software that does the work you want to do. Similarly, those pieces of software we have discussed thus far (TCP/IP and DNS) are like the operating system of the Internet. They make it possible to address and send data, but they don't perform any of the fun things we can do on the Internet. Just as you buy application software to balance your checkbook or compute your taxes, you buy Internet application software that runs on your PC and performs various functions on the Internet. We will touch on that software briefly in this section. Each of the functions below are discussed as if the function were a separate program. In actual practice, you will most often find that multiple functions are performed in the same product.

Now let's look at the various applications we want to run on the Internet, and the software that allows us to run them:

Mail Reader

Sending and receiving electronic mail (e-mail) is one of the oldest Internet activities, but it remains one of the most popular features. A "mail reader" is a program that allows you to read e-mail from others, and compose and send new mail of your own. E-mail is such an important part of the Internet that a whole chapter has been devoted to it. Look for more detail in Chapter 3.

News Reader

Just as e-mail is typically sent between individuals, "news groups" are public forums where users can place questions and comments about everything from *Astrology* to *Zoology*. A "news reader" is software that allows you to read news groups, and then write your own messages if you are so inclined. You will learn more about news groups when you get to Chapter 4.

Chat Client

Visiting an Internet chat room is like going to an electronic cocktail party, except that you don't have to dress up, and there isn't an open bar. Instead of talking, the guests type their comments. If you want to participate in chats, you need a software program called a "chat client" that allows you to invite yourself to such gatherings. But don't just run out and find a chat room. They're fraught with peril if you don't know how to navigate them correctly. Chat rooms will be covered in all their gory detail in Chapter 5.

Web Browser

The World Wide Web is the newest of the major Internet applications, and it is the one that is attracting a lot of attention. But in order to "surf the web," you will need to have a digital surfboard known as a "web browser." You will learn more about all this in Chapters 6 and 7.

Commercial Provider Software

You don't have to be a computer genius to buy and install and navigate all the different software components that will allow you to use the Internet. As an alternative to all the software mentioned in the previous section, you can obtain your Internet access through something called a "commercial provider." One of the advantages of using such a provider is that you don't need all the other Internet applications mentioned above. You just install the software obtained from the provider, and it does everything for you. It is like buying a complete music system, as opposed to buying it a component at a time. Some people want to select their own amplifiers, tape decks, CD players, and speakers. Others are more concerned with convenience than sound quality, and just want to buy one system containing everything. We will have much more to say about commercial providers in just a few pages. But for now, just remember that it is one option for obtaining the software you need to run Internet applications.

Human Components

Any discussion of the Internet would be incomplete if we talked about hardware and software and ignored the human components. What really gives the Internet life is all the people that use it and contribute to it. Granted, some of these people are only doing their jobs, and providing Internet information is what they do to put food on the table. But as you start exploring, you will become impressed with the thousands of hours of time donated to provide free information and entertainment for others. You will find fans of television shows or musical groups who establish unofficial information sites about their interests. You will find artists and poets who share their work with anyone who drops by to take a look. You will find those who publish and mail free electronic newsletters, just as a public service to others. You will find those who suffer from health problems, and yet share hints for overcoming the disease, or learning to live with it.

You will find those who simply compile their favorite jokes, just so those who visit can start the day with a laugh. The technology of the Internet is quite marvelous, but the thing that gives life to the Internet is the people who contribute and share with others. As you become more of an expert yourself, we hope you will also be willing to share your talents and knowledge.

GETTING CONNECTED

Now that you have a brief understanding of the origins and operation of the Internet, your next question is bound to be, "Great! Now how do I get connected?" That's the question we will try to answer for you in this section. Before you connect there are some decisions to be made, and we need to give you some background so that you will make the most intelligent choices for you and your family.

Direct Connections

You may already be lucky enough to have an Internet connection through your work or school. For these large organizations, it makes sense to link users together on a Local Area Network (LAN), and then to connect that network to the Internet. If you have this type of a connection, it is usually permanent, except for the time the equipment is down for maintenance.

Having a direct connection is quite convenient, as you don't usually have to bother with passwords and other authentication devices that are required with dial-up connections. But even if you have a direct connection at work, you will probably want to have a dial-up connection at home.

Dial-up Connections

The vast majority of users who connect to the Internet from home do so with a dial-up connection. As part of the connection process, the modem dials a local number, connects with a modem there, and then stays connected for as long as you stay online. When you are through, you disconnect and can then use the phone line again for normal telephone use. The number that you call belongs to a service company—the entity that provides your connection to the Internet.

Having a dial-up connection adds a little to the complexity, because it requires you to go through some type of user authentication. The service company you call when you want to connect does not perform this service for free. You will be paying a monthly or yearly access charge for the privilege of letting you connect through them. The only way they can limit their service to paying customers is to make you prove your identity when you request a connection.

This authentication is usually done using two different items—a "user name" and a password. The service company who is providing your Internet connection will either assign you a user name, or will allow you to choose your own. This latter method is the preferred method, because most people would prefer to use an identifiable name (BobJones), rather than a meaningless identifier (DXY123). Your user name is what would be considered your account number—it is what the service company uses to know that a request is coming from you. Because of that, your user name will have to be unique from all the other user names at your service company. This may mean that your first choice will be taken, and you will need to find an alternate, such as "BobJones2," or "BobbyJones." (Note: Although we will use the term "user name" in this book, different service companies may use different terminology. For example, America Online uses the term "screen name." Other terms we have seen include "account name," "user ID," "logon name," and "logon ID.")

Some service companies allow you to have multiple user names on a single account. For example, America Online allows for as many as five different screen names on the same account, at no additional cost. Each screen name is treated as a separate entity that can send and receive e-mail, and can have certain access privileges associated with it. This is an important feature to have for families that will have more than one person connecting. (However, even though the five people who use that online account may have separate online experiences, if one of those five people breaks the rules, the whole account is canceled and everyone is out of luck.)

The second thing you will need is a password. The service company needs this to make sure that it is really you calling, and not someone else pretending to be "BobJones."

It is vital that you use some caution when selecting your user name and your password, because bad choices can cause problems for yourself or your family. Most service companies allow you to change your password regularly, but usually your user name is harder to change once it has been assigned. Read the next chapter before you select a user name, because it will give some suggestions that will safeguard you and your family.

Your wallet is probably happy that you can use the same phone line for calls and Internet connections. But if you find yourself using the Internet a lot, you might want to consider getting a second line. Although you may think now that you'll enjoy the silence of no ringing phones when the Internet is in use, sharing a phone line for telephone calls and Internet use can cause World War III in the most innocent household. Imagine how Dad will react when he's told to get off the Internet so his young daughter can call her boyfriend. Consider the scenario that will arise when Mom is unable to call home and say she's stranded in a broken car because Junior is playing an online game of Shoot-Em-Dead. Even worse are the problems caused by picking up a phone when a modem is sending data across the line. This usually causes the connection to be broken, and may cause you to lose work.

If household harmony is important to you, consider getting a second phone line if you want to spend any time on the Internet.

COMMERCIAL PROVIDERS

There are two general classes of service companies that can provide you dial-up access to the Internet. The first group are the "commercial providers," more commonly called the "online services." Online services came into existence back when most people had never heard the word "Internet," and Internet access was restricted to military personnel. The online services were an attempt to provide similar services (for a fee, of course) to the general public.

Early online services were similar to the ones we have in use today, although the technology was a lot less sophisticated. Subscribers were given a software disk that would install the specialized software onto their PC. Once installed and started, the software would call a local phone number and connect the computer to the online service. It was important that this connection be local, because most users would not be willing to pay long-distance charges in addition to the fee they were already paying. So the online services would lease local phone numbers in all the major urban areas, and would then route all the calls to one or more central computer locations.

The first time they connected, users would be guided through a procedure where they would choose a user name and password. Users would also provide billing information, such as a credit card number. Once they were subscribed, users could play games, search reference libraries, get into discussions with other users, get stock market quotes, and send e-mail. Because they were designed for novice users, most online systems were written using GUI technology, and used a step-by-step approach to guide users through the various services they provided.

Several different online services started during the 1970s and 80s, and they all tried to convince users that they offered better services than the competition. But all of these services were basically closed systems. A subscriber to one service could not access the areas belonging to a different service, nor could he send e-mail to anyone who didn't belong to his own group. Online services were all like private clubs, and subscribers could only associate with the members of their own clubs.

As the Internet became more popular, the online services felt more and more pressure to allow their users access to Internet services. First, the e-mail systems were linked to the Internet, so a subscriber to one online service could send messages to any Internet user, including those on different online services. Then other services were added, such as news groups and web browsers. As the online services added support for these new features, they tried to do it in such a way that all access was still through the same program. Not only was this easier for the user, but it also made sure the user stayed hooked up to the original online service while he spent time on the Internet.

The online services still promote themselves as having three advantages over other Internet services. First, they are easier to use, especially for novice users. Second, in addition to Internet access, they provide other "content." By content, they mean the areas that are still closed to other users, such as game areas and discussion groups. Third, they provide "parental controls," or options that parents can use to limit access to certain types of material, both within the service and on the Internet.

Different online services have come and gone over the years. There are currently four that are large enough to be worth mentioning, and we will tell you just a little about each of those.

CompuServe

CompuServe is one of the older online services. It has many subscribers who are members for business or professional reasons, and who tend to be more computer literate than the users of other services. There are many good discussion groups and technical support forums on CompuServe, sponsored by companies that sell computer hardware and software.

CompuServe has had a reputation of being a little harder to use than some of the other services. It was slow to incorporate a GUI interface, requiring users to remember a series of commands. When Internet services were finally added, they were not integrated very well into the rest of the CompuServe package, and this caused confusion.

Another annoyance was that user names were assigned as a string of numbers, such as "75675,3425." We have heard that recent changes have made the service more friendly, but we have not used it for a couple of years.

If CompuServe software is not already installed on your computer (many computers come with one or more online services installed), call their toll-free number and get a free disk. As soon as you start the program, your modem should dial directly into CompuServe and allow you to pick a local number. Establish your user name, password, and payment options. Then you're all set.

Most online services allow you several hours of free connect time to try things out. If you're not satisfied, contact the service (usually online), and your account will be terminated without any cost to you. But don't just assume the service will contact you when the trial period is up. If you want to cancel, you need to contact the service directly, or the billing will start automatically after your trial period.

Recently CompuServe was purchased by America Online, another online service. At the time of purchase, America Online said it had no plans to force members from CompuServe to America Online, and that things would run pretty much as they had before. Thus far, it appears they have kept this promise.

Prodigy

Prodigy started as a joint venture between IBM and Sears. When it first started, its GUI design made it easier to use than existing services that required users to enter a series of commands. But the Prodigy software was designed for older computers, and it used a larger font that only allowed about forty characters per line. This made the system seem more like a toy than a real computer, and it was extremely hard to compose letters or do any other work on the system. Prodigy was slow to upgrade its software, and this caused a loss of subscribers.

Prodigy advertised itself as a "family" service, and went to great lengths to make sure that inappropriate material was not posted in any of its discussion areas. This was a good idea gone amok, because Prodigy's censorship consisted of software that would reject material that used certain words, even if those words were used innocently. When this happened, your rejected contribution was sent back with a general explanation that it didn't meet their standards, without giving any specific details. This kind of heavy-handed but arbitrary censorship caused us, along with many other users, to abandon Prodigy for the new kid on the block, America Online.

The procedure for subscribing to Prodigy is similar to that of CompuServe, as already described. Like CompuServe, Prodigy used to assign users a meaningless user name, something like DXV276. We have heard that the current version of the software allows you more control over the name you select.

One nice feature of Prodigy is that it allows up to five user names to be created under one account. This allows separate e-mail accounts for multiple family members, and also allows parental controls to limit access based on the user name.

America Online

Is there anyone in America who hasn't received one of those free America Online disks? Until recently, it was difficult to go a week without getting one of those disks in the mail, in a magazine, or in the daily paper. I don't think we've had to buy a floppy disk in years because of the steady supply of free disks that come in the mail compliments of America Online. But their marketing must be effective, because America Online, or AOL, is the largest online service. As of late 1998 AOL claimed more than 13 million members.

AOL is quite easy to use, and the company continually upgrades its software to make it better. There is quite a bit of content unique to service, plus AOL provides the expected Internet access.

Many of the problems associated with AOL are due to its own success. A few years ago, the number of subscribers overwhelmed the system's hardware, resulting in busy signals when many users were trying to connect. AOL software also seems quite prone to problems, and it is not uncommon to have temporary delays in sending or receiving mail. There have also been complaints over billing problems, with people claiming they have been charged a monthly fee after canceling their account.

Those who are experienced Internet users tend to treat America Online users with contempt, because they think of AOL as the service for beginners. Some of this is probably fair criticism, but some is unjustified. With any online service, you get a certain percentage of subscribers who make fools of themselves and annoy others. In any organization that has such a huge base of subscribers, there is going to be a percentage of them who are obnoxious or just plain dumb.

Like Prodigy, America Online allows you to have up to five user names on one account, which makes it easy for families to use. However, parents who join AOL in search of a wholesome environment for their children may be shocked by some of the areas that thrive there. But AOL has much to offer, and if you learn the tricks that we'll teach you in later chapters, your children can have a safe online experience on AOL.

To subscribe to America Online, follow the procedures already explained for the other online services. With millions of members, you might have trouble selecting a user name that is not already in use. Persevere. Your friends will recognize you, even if the only name you can come up with is ASmith7685.

Microsoft Network

The Microsoft Network is the new kid on the block in terms of online services. It was distributed as part of Windows 95, and immediately caused controversy because it came installed as part of the operating system. Other online service companies complained that Microsoft was taking unfair advantage, by installing their own online service as part of a popular software program.

The Microsoft Network supports all the standard Internet features. It does not provide as much content as other services, relying more heavily on services on the Internet that anyone can use. There were also early complaints that the service was slower than other services, and that the parental controls were not as strong as some would have liked.

Subscribing is similar to the procedure for other services, although you will probably find the software already installed on your computer. When you subscribe, you are allowed to select your own user name, although it does have to be unique.

INTERNET SERVICE PROVIDERS

When the Internet opened its doors to commercial users, the doors opened for ordinary folks to get connected for the first time. A number of companies started providing access to small businesses and individuals. These companies are known as Internet Service Providers, more commonly called ISPs, access providers, or service providers.

Unlike online services, ISPs usually do not provide their own content. They do not have games, discussion areas, and services that can only be accessed by the members of that ISP. They just provide you with a door to the Internet—pure and simple. Once you open that door, it is up to you to navigate yourself around and find what you want.

That is not to say you are entirely on your own. When you first connect to a new service, most ISPs provide you with some kind of welcome menu that guides you to interesting or useful places on the Internet. Some of these are so sophisticated that a novice user would have a hard time distinguishing a commercial provider from an ISP. You start the software, it dials a local number, you get connected, you see a welcome screen, and then you follow the menu to go where you want to go. But remember the important difference is that the ISP is not providing its own content—it just opens the door to the Internet and then points you in some interesting directions.

The good news is that as more and more people and companies use the Internet, it has started to provide a lot of good content on its own. If you do a little searching, you can find the same quality of games, reference sites, and discussion groups as you will find on a commercial provider. In fact, many businesses that were once associated with a particular online service have moved onto the Internet instead. This only makes sense, because they can then be accessed by any Internet user, including all ISP users and subscribers of all online services.

Another difference between an ISP and an online service is the software you use to access it. Most online services provide their own software, written by their own employees, and customized for them. Thus, each online service looks different from the others, even though they all do basically the same things.

In contrast, ISPs do not generally have their own software, but expect you to use the Internet application software mentioned earlier. Most ISPs recommend that you use either Netscape Communicator (formerly called Navigator), or Microsoft's Internet Explorer. Both of these programs integrate most of the Internet services you will need (mail and news readers, web browsers) into one product. Many ISPs will provide you a customized version of one of these programs when you subscribe. If not, there is a good chance that one or both of them came already installed on your computer. In fact, at the time of this writing, Microsoft was in the middle of a legal battle with the government, because of a Microsoft contention that Internet Explorer must be installed in order for Windows 98 to run correctly.

Don't use an ISP that provides "shell" accounts. This is an older technology where only the host computer has Internet access, and you have to go through a series of menus to access common functions. This is like asking a friend to watch television for you, and then tell you what he watched. Find an ISP that provides either SLIP (Serial Line Internet Protocol) or PPP (Point-to-Point Protocol) access. That's the technology you need to get full Internet access.

Another advantage of an ISP is that you are usually not subjected to online advertising, at least not from the provider (many Internet sites have ads). Most commercial providers started with no advertising. But competition between the services drove access prices down, so most of them compensated by accepting advertising dollars. These ads range from innocent little buttons you can press for more information to obnoxious pop-up screens that you must click to remove.

Questions to Ask an ISP Representative

If you decide to use an online service, you can count the different providers on one hand. An ISP is more complicated, because there are more than 4,500 of them just in the United States.[3] You will find everything from national ISPs run by the phone companies to small regional ISPs with just a few thousand customers. With such a range of providers available, it is important to find the right one for you, so that your family's online experience is one of pleasure, rather than frustration.

Listed below are some of the questions you should ask about a potential ISP. Don't be shy about asking these questions—better to find out early than when it's too late. Some of these questions have no right or wrong answer. Yet the answer could be important to you, depending on what you want from your access provider.

Will I Have a SLIP or a PPP Account?

Throwing out a few buzzwords at first is sure to get somebody's attention. But make sure the service provides either SLIP or PPP connections. PPP is newer and slightly better, but either is better than shell. If the ISP only has shell accounts, thank the representative and look elsewhere.

What Are Your Pricing Plans?

Make sure you hear about all the pricing plans, and that you understand the options available to you. We will discuss pricing plans in a few minutes.

Are There Any Restrictions on Access Hours?

This is related to the pricing plans. Make sure there are no restrictions on the times you are allowed to use the service. You may be charged more if you connect during certain peak hours or peak periods. Also, ask if there are any times when you cannot access their service because of scheduled maintenance procedures.

How About Local Access Numbers?

It is important to have access numbers in your geographic area. You don't want to be calling a long-distance number. Also, are there local numbers in other locations that you visit frequently? If you spend the summer in Maine and the winter in Florida, find an ISP that can support you in both places. Or, if you travel a lot and connect on the road, make sure there are local numbers in the areas you visit.

If you live in a metropolitan area, make sure the "local" access number you're given really is a local number. We learned this the hard way after an ISP provider hooked us up to a local access number that was in a town about fifteen miles away. It was only near the end of the period that we realized the reason our phone bill had skyrocketed from about $25 per month to about $160 a month was not because the cost of phone service had increased, but because we had been connected to a measured-service number. We were charged money—lots of money—for every minute we were online.

How Large Is Your Network?

If you plan to connect from more than one place, you might consider one of the larger ISPs, including those run by national and regional phone companies. There are several that cover the entire U.S., and some that are even international. Examples of such national providers include AT&T Worldnet, MCI, GTE, Sprint, Mindspring, and Netcom.

What Modem Speeds Do You Support?

This is related to local access numbers. Make sure the access numbers you will use support reasonable modem speeds. If the fastest line in your area only supports 9,600 bps modems, your new 28,800 bps modem won't get much of a workout. Also, if you're planning to pay the big bucks for an ISDN phone line, make sure the provider can support it.

Any Problems with Busy Signals?

This is a tough issue, and it may be hard to get an honest answer. All providers try to provide an acceptable modem-to-member ratio. This is a way to measure the number of total subscribers, versus the ones that can connect at any time. If a service has 100,000 members and 20,000 modems and access lines, their ratio is 1:5. This means that only twenty percent of their members can connect at the same time. This number may seem inadequate, but it is probably better than the ratio used by most ISPs and online services. With most services you will get occasional busy signals during peak periods. It is only when you're regularly thwarted from trying to sign on that it becomes an issue.

How Many Customers Do You Have?

This is a two-edged sword. Small operations tend to provide better support and lower prices, but are subject to problems if they start growing too rapidly. Also, there have been a lot of acquisitions in the ISP area, and small fish are more likely to be swallowed by the sharks if this consolidation continues. Large ISPs have adequate hardware to support the customers, yet they are not as responsive to customers having problems.

Any Problems with Sluggish Performance?

This is also tough to measure. Many users complain of the slowness of the Internet, especially during peak periods of activity. The problem is, due to the nature of the Internet, the slowness could be caused anywhere along the line. It could be your modem, your local ISP, one of the backbone links, or the computer you are connected to at the North Pole. Just make sure the bottleneck isn't with the ISP.

What Software Do I Use?

Does the ISP provide access software, or will you be expected to do that? Most ISPs provide you with a copy of Netscape Communicator, Microsoft Internet Explorer, or a similar product. Often the software is customized for that particular service, and contains either printed instructions or online help. Most beginning users feel lost enough without having to go on a scavenger hunt for Internet application software. Find an ISP that provides this software, or is at least helpful in pointing you in the right direction.

What Kind of Technical Support Do You Provide?

It is important that the company is there to hold your hand, especially when you are just getting connected and learning your way around. Does the ISP provide technical support? Is there any additional cost or limit on the amount of support? What are the hours technical support is available? Is technical support available through a local or toll-free number, or do you have to pay long-distance charges? What kind of help does the ISP provide once you get online? Are there online discussion groups or tutorials? Can you submit a question or problem via e-mail?

How Many E-mail Accounts Can I Have?

The ability to use e-mail is an important part of the Internet, and you want to make sure your e-mail needs are satisfied. How many different accounts will be provided? Are multiple accounts available, and what are the additional costs? Even online services like America Online will only provide five user names per account, and that may not be enough for your family. There are Internet services that provide additional free e-mail accounts (see Chapter 4), but these are not as convenient as having the accounts with your ISP, so get them there if possible.

Do You Provide Web Space?

When we get to Chapter 7, we'll show you how to build your own little corner of the Internet that anyone with a web browser can access. This is called a "web site." If you want to do this, you will need some Internet real estate known as "web space." Most online services and some ISPs provide you with a small amount of this space. If you want to have a web site, ask the ISP if it provides web space, and how much space you will be given. Also ask if you can obtain more, and how much it will cost. Don't reject the ISP outright if it won't provide this, because there are places (see Chapter 7) that provide it for free. Remember, as with additional e-mail accounts, it is more convenient if the ISP provides it. It's always nice to have all your services under one umbrella.

Do You Provide Any Filtering Service?

As parents struggle with protecting their children from indecent material, some ISPs are providing controls over what can be viewed and accessed through their service. In fact, some ISPs offer only materials that are designed for children, or that conform with certain values. We will cover all these issues in future chapters, but for now, just remember you can ask a potential ISP about this if it is important to you. If the ISP does provide this service, ask if it is done on your PC, or on their end of the connection. The latter is better, because it is less available for tampering.

Do You Restrict Access to Any News Groups or Web Sites?

This is similar to the previous question. Some ISPs block access to certain areas on the Internet. Sometimes this is done to protect the subscribers from raw material, but sometimes it is just done to save money for the ISP. If the ISP doesn't provide full access, find out why—and determine whether you consider that to be an advantage or a disadvantage.

Where to Find an ISP

Unlike a commercial provider, ISPs will probably not be filling your mailbox with disks or running ads on the television. In most cases, you will need to contact them.

Try looking in the phone book yellow pages first. Try the headings "Internet Services," or "Computer Access Providers." If your newspaper has a business section that runs classified ads, look under the headings "Internet," "Internet Access Services" or "Internet Providers." In the regular classified section, look for something starting with the words "Internet" or "Computer."

There are also several Internet sites that can be searched to find ISPs in your area. Yes, we realize you can't search on the Internet unless you have access to the Internet. Perhaps you have access at school or work, or have a good friend that will let you use his computer if you whine sufficiently. If all else fails, many public libraries offer Internet access. If you don't know exactly what to do with the names in this list, we will tell you in Chapter 7. You could also plead with an Internet-savvy friend, coworker, or librarian for help. In any case, here are a few places to get you started:

www.yahoo.com

boardwatch.internet.com

www.ispfinder.com

thelist.internet.com

When you visit the Yahoo site, follow the links "Computers & Internet," "Internet," "Commercial Services@" and "Access Providers." Yahoo changes its headings on occasion, so what you see may be slightly different from that listed here.

One final option is to buy an Internet book that includes an access offer. Many of these books have a software CD in the back, with instructions on how to install the software and establish an account with a national ISP. Often, the first month's access is free or discounted. Even if you decide you don't like the service, it will get you started until you can find a better one.

INTERNET PRICING PLANS

Whether you connect with an ISP or a commercial provider, one of the decisions you will have to make is which pricing plan is best for you. Although pricing plans aren't engraved in stone and can be changed later, it will be less hassle if you make the right decision the first time. Most of these plans fall into one of three categories:

Connect Time

The name of this plan says it all. You pay for each minute you are connected to the service. If the fee is $5.00 per hour, and you were connected for five hours last month, your bill will be $25.00. Make sure you understand how the ISP bills for fractional portions of an hour. Does it round up to the next minute, the next fifteen minutes, or the next hour?

Fortunately, these plans are rare these days, because the competition for access providers is so intense that someone is always trying to better the competition.

Unlimited

Again, the title says it all. Unlimited access means just that. You could be connected twenty-four hours a day, seven days a week, and your bill would still be the same. This is probably the most common pricing plan in use today, because most of the commercial services use it, or at least give you the option.

As you would expect, having full-time access also means this is usually the most expensive option, in terms of the fee you pay per month. For a family with several kids that plans to do even a moderate amount of Internet access, it is probably the best option.

Combination

Many providers offer a combination deal where you get so many hours per month for a flat fee, and then connect time charges for every hour beyond that. For example, you might pay ten dollars for up to five hours of access, plus three dollars for each hour after that. So, any month where you had zero to five hours of access you would pay ten dollars. If you let time get away from you, and connected for fifteen hours, you would pay forty dollars.

These plans are actually pretty good for folks who want to use their provider for limited activities, such as e-mail. Most mail-reader software allows you to connect to the service, copy your messages to your hard drive, disconnect from the service, read your mail and answer it, compose new mail, connect again, send your mail, and then disconnect. So while you may have spent an hour reading and answering mail, you might have been online for only three to four minutes. At that rate, you should still come in under the five hour limit, even if you went through this cycle twice per day for each day of the month.

*****

As noted above, we strongly suggest that families find a plan with unlimited access time. You want your children to be able to research papers for school, and learn about new things. They can't do those kinds of things in ten minutes per day, and you don't want Dad going into shock when the monthly bill arrives. We have had several friends who were the happy recipients of $300 monthly bills when their children started realizing the joys of online exploration. One experience like that starts to make an unlimited pricing plan look downright reasonable.

Most providers will also provide you with a better deal if you pay for several months in advance. If your budget will allow it, we suggest taking this option, assuming the plan provides (as most do) a full refund for any pre-paid months if you decide to terminate early.

Even with unlimited access plans, some commercial services are providing games or restricted areas for which there is an additional charge. For example, you might be able to gain access to an area that allows you to track your investments for an additional five dollars per month. In general, we would avoid these kinds of deals, unless they really provide something that would be of particular value to you. There's enough great stuff on the Internet that is free that you don't need to be paying extra for the privilege of being online.

AOL OR ISP—WHICH ONE FOR ME?

If you're still confused about whether you want an online service or an ISP, maybe we can give you one last push in the right direction. Currently, about sixty percent of Internet users do business through a commercial provider, with forty percent using an ISP.[4]

In order to show you where you'd be in that pie chart, let's give you a little test. Don't worry; there are no right or wrong answers. This is like a personality test, and it should reveal which type of provider is best suited for your personality.

Read through the ten multiple-choice questions below. For each question, pick the answer that best reflects your opinion. Each choice will have a point value from zero to two:

1. How comfortable are family members when using the computer, especially when using programs that run under Windows?

We have no fear, and can point and click with the best. (0 points)

We are probably about average. (1 point)

We break into a cold sweat just thinking about it. (2 points)

2. What will be the ages of family members using the Internet?

High-school age and over. (0 points)

All ranges of ages from adults through young children. (1 point)

Mostly younger children not yet in high school. (2 points)

3. How often do you think you will have to contact your provider's technical support group?

Probably just until we get connected and running. (0 points)

No more than the average user. (1 point)

We'll get to know the technical support group so well, they'll end up on our Christmas card list. (2 points)

4. How do family members react when trying to learn to use a new software program?

They enjoy it, and become experts in no time. (0 points)

It's no worse than having to mow the lawn. (1 point)

They'd rather go to the dentist for a root canal. (2 points)

5. Online services claim they are better because they provide additional "content" that is not available anywhere else. How important is this to you?

Not important—the Internet has everything we need. (0 points)

We might use their features on an occasional basis. (1 point)

Those features are even better than the Internet! (2 points)

6. Some services provide "parental controls" that can be used to block access to certain areas and activities. Keeping in mind that none of these controls are foolproof, and none will replace parental supervision, how important are they?

Not important. (0 points)

Of average importance. (1 point)

Very important. (2 points)

7. Online services provide Internet access by integrating the Internet functions into their regular software. Although this makes the Internet easier to use, it usually removes many of the options provided by Internet applications such as Netscape Communicator. Thus, the Internet is less complex, but also less flexible. How do you feel about this?

We're not idiots—give us back those options! (0 points)

Put us in that mysterious group that always says, "No Opinion." (1 point)

Who cares about flexibility? Make it easy! (2 points)

8. How important a factor is the monthly access charge?

We're living on pork and beans now. (0 points)

We're not rich, but we're doing okay. (1 point)

What was the question? I was talking to my broker. (2 points)

9. How important is it for your ISP to also supply you with software to access their service?

It is not important, and/or they do provide the software. (0 points)

Put us down for "No Opinion" again. (1 point)

It is very important that it be provided and/or the ISP does not provide it. (2 points)

10. Is the availability of local access numbers an important issue, and do you travel a lot and expect to connect when away from home?

It's not an issue, or my ISP can provide all the access I need. (0 points)

Either type of provider could supply the needed access. (1 point)

I can find no ISPs that give me the coverage I need. (2 points)

That probably wasn't a very scientific test, but let's look at the results. If you did the math right, you should have a final score somewhere between 0 and 20. If you scored towards the "0" end, consider an ISP. If you scored towards the "20" end, you might be better off with an online service.

If tests make you so nervous that you couldn't hold the pencil, here's the same information in more objective terms:

Advantages of an Online Service:

Easy to learn and use. Good for younger children.

Good technical support, especially for that first connection.

Provides good to excellent features of its own, in addition to Internet access.

Probably has stronger parental controls.

Advantages of an ISP:

Less costly, most of the time.

Provides the most flexible access to the Internet.

Provides access to more Internet areas.

Does not subject the user to advertising while online.

Other things to consider:

Availability of local access numbers, especially if you travel.

For an ISP, whether access software is included.

Availability of online help and tutorials.

Still confused? Subscribe to America Online for a month and see if you like it. Yes, AOL has its critics, but it's the biggest gorilla around, so it's doing something right. Your first month should be free, so you have nothing to lose. If you don't like AOL, try another commercial provider or an ISP.

COMMON CONNECTION PROBLEMS

Whether you use an online service or an ISP, you may have some trouble getting connected for the first time. Connection problems can be frustrating, and you might be tempted to throw the computer through the window. Take consolation from the fact that we have all felt that frustration. The nice thing to remember is that once you solve the problem, it should stay solved—at least until you change your hardware or software again!

Most connection problems are caused by modems. This is because there are minor variations in the way each modem manufacturer follows the standards. It is important you know the model, speed, and manufacturer of the modem you are using. When you install your access software, it will usually go through a process of having you define the modem you are using. You will probably be presented with a menu of about a million different modems, and you need to select the exact make and model you have. If the installation software is smart, it will try to detect this and show you its best guess. If there is a selection that more accurately describes your modem, select it. If you can't find your modem on the list, try a similar one from the same manufacturer, or look for an entry that says something like "generic." Experiment with all the choices that look reasonable, and try to find one that works. Don't spend too much time on this, because your service provider can help you. Technical support staffs are used to working with modem problems, and they can usually find a combination that will work for you.

If you have trouble connecting with your modem, you'll be very glad if you followed our advice and got a second phone line. Otherwise, you'll have to call back every time you try something, and that can get very annoying.

Another common problem is that you can get connected, but then your session disconnects after a short time. This is normal, and happens to all of us. If it happens too often, it could be another symptom of a modem that is not configured correctly for the software. Again, work with the technical support folks. If the modem appears to be fine, you could have "line noise" on your telephone line. Complain to your phone company, and ask them to run some tests. If the phone company finds a dirty line, the company is responsible for cleaning it.

Windows can tell you a lot about the modems you have installed on your computer, and the options that are set for them. Just do the following:

=> My Computer => Control Panel => Modems

We will use the convention shown above quite often when we are having you navigate around in Windows. Here's a translation of the line you just read:

1. Find a button or ICON labeled "My Computer," and double click on it.
2. A folder or selection menu should appear, containing more choices.
3. Find the ICON or menu item labeled "Control Panel," and double click on it.
4. Another folder or selection menu should appear, containing more choices.
5. Find the ICON or menu item labeled "Modems," and double click on it.
6. The item or dialog you wish to see should now be displayed.

All clicks are to be done with the left mouse button. A single-shaft arrow (->) before the choice means a single click, while a double-shaft arrow (=>) means a double click. Note that these directions apply to Windows versions after 3.1. If you're using that version, get out your manuals, or better yet, get upgraded.

AFTER YOU'RE ONLINE

You've selected your Internet connection service, installed the software, solved any connection problems, established an account, and now you're connected for the first time. What are you going to do? No, you're not going to Disney World. You're going to stay right here and learn how you can get the most out of your Internet experience.

Feeling at Home

As with any new neighborhood, it will take you a little while to feel at home. Don't be frustrated if you don't immediately understand everything that you see. If you start to get frustrated, disconnect and come back later for a fresh start.

Exploring can be more fun when you do it with someone else. Get your spouse or kids and make it a family experience. If the kids already know more than you, insist that they share a little bit of the knowledge.

As a newcomer to the Internet, you will be known by the slang term of "newbie." (No, you do not have to use that word.) Being called a newbie may or may not be an insult, depending on how it is used. Your goal is to be a good newbie, and not provoke derogatory comments such as "Boy, that's a real newbie question," or "Pulling a stunt like that certainly qualifies you as a newbie."

You can avoid the "bad newbie" label by lurking. Lurking means just hanging around the different Internet areas, seeing what there is to see, and avoiding the urge to make public comments. America Online has gotten a bad reputation because of all the newbies who jump into everything without understanding what they are doing. They put questions in discussion folders that have been asked and answered a dozen times before, having never bothered to read the previous messages containing the answer. They put questions in the wrong folders, and then become irate when criticized. They respond to honest criticism with crude remarks and profanity. It is easy to see why veteran Internet citizens consider AOL to be the Internet service for the unwashed masses.

Being a Good Citizen

Not only should your family learn about how to use the Internet, but they should learn how to be good citizens of it. Just as in life, there are certain rules and guidelines that good citizens should follow. In real life, these rules are called etiquette. As a clever play on words, the rules for the online world are often called "netiquette."

Much of netiquette is just common sense, and mirrors our behavior in real life. Be kind to others. Watch your language. Tolerate questions from people who don't know as much as you do. Don't monopolize the conversation.

But there are some other netiquette rules that may not be as obvious, that are just as important. We will try to point those out as we go through the remaining chapters.

Just about every access provider, both commercial and ISP, has a set of rules that subscribers are expected to follow. America Online calls these the "Terms of Service" (TOS), and other providers use similar names. You will be provided with these rules when you subscribe, and it is important that everyone who will use the service understands them. The access providers are very serious about these, and they will not hesitate to cancel your account if they find serious or repeated violations. A friend of ours had his America Online account canceled when his son sent an inappropriate message to someone else, and that person complained. There was no warning, there was no appeal, the account was just gone. It didn't matter that four members of the family had behaved properly; misbehavior by one person caused the whole account to be canceled. Most families will consider such rules a benefit rather than a hindrance, because they provide a safeguard against some of the predators you might find online.

No Kids Allowed

Your children are going to hate us for this, but we recommend that you restrict their Internet access until you feel comfortable with the online world and have an understanding of the risks and the things you can do to minimize those risks. This does not mean they cannot explore with Mom and Dad, but they should never be alone, nor should you establish their own user names until you have the rules in place. There are three important reasons why you should follow this rule:

1. If you give them full access now and then restricted access later, you will never hear the end of the complaining. But if you give them no access now, and restricted access later, that will be perceived as an improvement.
2. Having this rule will motivate you to learn what you need to know and establish the rules in a timely manner. If you give your children full access now and intend to establish some rules later, it is likely that "later" will never occur. Decide on a time period of two to four weeks, and promise the kids they will have access at the end of that time. Then force yourself to meet that schedule. This certainly does not mean you cannot modify the rules later, if they need to be adjusted.
3. It will give your children more incentive to teach you. If they know that access will be limited until Mom and Pop understand the Internet, you can be sure that they will evolve from reluctant teachers to enthusiastic tutors.

We will talk more about the general area of rules in the next chapter.

Have Fun

We have covered a lot of material in these first two chapters, and your head may be spinning a bit at this point. So let's end this chapter with a little lighter fare, and remind you that the Internet can be useful, educational, entertaining, and just a whole lot of fun. Don't let all these details weigh you down to the point where you are no longer having fun. Having fun should be one of your goals as you explore your new online world.

Our computers have become indispensable household tools, as valuable as the vacuum cleaner or the washing machine. Let us just share a few examples of how we use the Internet on almost a daily basis:

- Kathy has friends that she exchanges e-mail with from all over the world. Some of these were people she met online in discussion groups. Others were neighbors who moved to other states that we still keep in touch with. They exchange jokes, recipes, inspirational stories, and just news about life.
- Clark had a bad attack of sciatica this past summer, to the point where he was eating aspirin like candy. But searching the Internet turned up lots of advice about treatments, exercises, suggestions about doctors, and ways to relieve the pain.
- Kathy needed to go visit a new person who lived in our neighborhood. She had the address, but had never heard of the street before. She visited an Internet map service, and typed in the person's address. Not only did it print a map to the new neighbor's house, but it also provided step-by-step driving instructions from our door to the neighbor's.
- We used to live out West, and still maintain an interest in some of the news from our former state. Not only do many of the newspapers have versions that can be read online, but some of the radio stations have Internet sites as well. Clark visits these sites, and plays the radio program through the speakers on his computer.
- Kathy loves to read books, but the local bookstore doesn't always carry what she wants. She shops at an online bookstore that allows her to search for books by title, author, or subject. When she is ready to check out, they discount the books, charge them to her credit card, and ship the books so they arrive in two to three days.
- Clark was driving to work and heard a piece of classical music he'd never heard before. The radio station had an Internet site with an online playlist, so it was easy to get the name of the song and the artist. Then, a visit to an online music store not only found the album, but revealed that it was on sale. Within a week, it was in his hot little hands.
- Kathy has a mania for type fonts that is almost an addiction. When she first started collecting fonts, each new font cost about a zillion dollars. Kathy gave up her collection in despair until a friend recently sent her the address of a web site that had hundreds of beautiful and unusual type fonts that could be downloaded for free. Kathy spent a week playing with fonts instead of working on this manuscript, delaying the delivery date of the completed book by several days in the process. She had a lot of fun doing it, even though Clark spent the week grinding his teeth.

Experiences like this aren't unique to us. As you start learning more, you will start getting more benefit from your online time. Just always remember that you need to have some fun in your life as you are learning.

A PARENT'S QUESTIONS

Q. I read something about an Intranet. Was that a misprint?
A. No, many businesses are replacing their Local Area Networks (LANs) with something called an Intranet. This is the same technology as the Internet uses, but restricts access to only those allowed by the company. This access control is provided by a "firewall," which sits on the connection between the company's network and the outside Internet. It can control requests in each direction, so that outsiders are kept out, and insiders are kept in—or are at least restricted to certain areas outside the firewall.

Q. I live five hundred miles from my nearest neighbor, and none of the commercial providers or ISPs have a local number in my area. Am I doomed?
A. No, but you need to expect to pay more for your service. Providers such as America Online have a toll-free number that has a lower rate than many long distance services. But keep in mind you are still charged by-the-minute long distance fees, in addition to the regular monthly access fees. If you use tricks to limit your connect time, such as reading mail offline, you should be able to keep your bill within your budget.

Q. Buying the computer trashed the family budget. How can I get free access?
A. If you are determined to get a bargain, there really are places that allow you free Internet access. Unfortunately, most of these aren't very good for families. Most public libraries offer Internet access on a limited basis. We will tell you later how to get free e-mail and free web space, even if you don't have a permanent provider account.

Running up to the library each night isn't very practical, but there are free services you can get at home, assuming you have a computer and a modem. There is an older technology known as "bulletin boards" that will often provide you with a free guest account, and a certain amount of online time each day. These usually don't provide unlimited Internet access, but will provide you access to some features.

Some colleges or communities run services called "freenets" that provide free accounts, sometimes with a nominal one-time setup charge. These are usually "shell" accounts, which are an inferior technology. But they do usually provide e-mail access, and access to a few Internet services. Remember, however, a free service is often worth what you pay for it. Many freenets are often overloaded, and it is not worth even trying to connect during peak times.

There is a service called Juno that provides free e-mail access, to those with a computer and a modem. See Chapter 7 for more information.

Q. What is this about "text only" mode for Internet access?
A. If you only want to pay $300 for a computer and modem, you can get an old, slow computer and access the Internet using "text only" mode. This prints just the text from the Internet, and ignores all the pictures, sounds, and other stuff that really makes the Internet fun for kids. This is about as much fun as sitting around and watching the TV with the picture turned to black. Don't give your kids that kind of experience. Save that $300 as the down payment on a real computer.

Q. I still don't understand the difference between an ISP and an online service. Help!
A. Think of the online service as being like a big department store. Everything is under one roof. Their prices are higher, but they have a lot of employees there to help, and you don't have to travel too far to find what you want.

Think of the ISP as a local shopping mall. You have to look around for what you want, often traveling to several stores for different items. There are fewer employees, so you have to know what you want and how to find it. The selection of items is also greater, and the prices are usually cheaper, because the overhead is lower.

Notes

1. Network Wizards Web Site; www.nw.com
2. *Inter@ctive Week;* September 14, 1998
3. *Wired*; August 1998, p. 94
4. *Wired;* August 1998, p. 95

Chapter 2—Not So Fast There, Kids!
● ● ● ● ●

IF YOU'VE BEEN OVERWHELMED BY TECHNICAL details until you don't want to hear another bit (or byte!) of computer information, you can relax. There's nothing in this chapter that will take any technical knowledge whatsoever. In fact, this is the chapter you've been waiting for because it focuses on the relationship between your children and the Internet. After all, that is the reason you bought this book.

Despite the lack of technical detail, this chapter will be a real eye-opener for you. We're going to tell you the potential hazards that exist if your children are not taught to use the Internet correctly. Some of them won't surprise you, because you've read about them in the sensational stories you've seen in the newspapers. But there are other threats you probably have never considered that are more likely to cause you grief. We're going to give you a road map to those pitfalls, too.

It's important that you have discussions with your children and set some basic rules before you let them loose on the Internet. If your kids are connecting even as you read this, you may have an uphill battle on your hands, but you should still be able to bring the situation under control. We will suggest some general ground rules, and explain why those rules are important. These are rules that should be in place and understood even before you make that first Internet connection, and penalties for breaking those rules should be strictly enforced.

Once a set of rules is established, your job won't be over. You'll be the law enforcement officer who will make sure your family rules are being followed, and who will administer warnings and punishments when necessary. If you're not used to being a law enforcement officer, don't worry. We'll suggest some ideas to help you when you're wearing that policeman's badge.

The final section will suggest some other safety precautions that apply to your children's behavior when they are connected to the Internet. These are things that will keep them safe while connected, and will minimize the chances of them running into trouble. Primarily, these guidelines will make children less likely to attract the attention of those who are up to no good. But equally important, if your children are approached by unscrupulous characters, these rules will ensure that the bad guy gets frustrated and goes on to bother someone else who is less savvy to his tricks.

This is not the only chapter where we give rules and suggestions for avoiding trouble. Other chapters will give advice related to specific Internet functions that are covered in those chapters. The advice in this chapter is more general in nature, and will apply no matter where your child goes on the Internet, or who he meets when he is connected.

UNDERSTANDING THE DANGERS

The media are full of stories about the dangers that exist online. Some of these are real, and some are exaggerated. Let's take a few pages and summarize the dangers that really do exist.

Loss of Innocence

You may think that kids in America are so jaded that they don't have any innocence left to lose. And to an extent you're right. Children are regularly exposed to profanity and sexual innuendoes in the situation comedies they watch during "family hour" on television. They play graphic video games where the object is to dismember their opponent before he dismembers them. They know the names of prominent serial killers, and they hear of improprieties by sports heroes, musicians, and politicians. They know by the time they're in grade school that advertisements are misleading and deceptive, and they learn not to trust those ads or the corporations that sponsor them. They've probably already been approached by other children who want to sell them drugs, and they know that they're not necessarily safe from being shot to death when they're sitting in their desks in school. The few years they've lived have already shown them that there is little in life that is either sacred or safe.

By and large, your children will probably see more of the world by the time they're ten years old than you did by the time you were thirty, and that's a frightening thing to contemplate. However, if you think your children don't have any innocence left to lose, think again. The things your children have experienced in the normal course of life can seem like a Sunday School picnic when compared to the stuff they may be exposed to on the Internet. They may not even have to go anywhere to be exposed to this sleaze. Predators go looking for children, and they can easily find your child right in your own living room.

The very e-mail box where your son or daughter receives letters from Granny can also contain graphic depictions of sex in all its variations. Photographs and videos are so easy to access that they can be viewed simply by clicking the mouse on the highlighted blue text. And these aren't just "girlie" pictures, such as the ones you may have peeked at as a kid when you found a copy of *Playboy* in the gutter. Back when we were growing up, magazine editors at least used an airbrush to cover the naughty parts. Today the naughty parts are the focus of the photographs. Your children can see graphic color photos of men having sex with women, with other men, with children, or even with animals. They can see pictures of women or children being held in bondage or even tortured, and they can see pictures of urine and feces being used as tools for sexual pleasure.

If these things disgust you, just think of the effect they'll have on your ten-year-old son or daughter. Your children can learn things about sex that you may not even know exist, and they can become addicted to pornography before you're even aware there's a problem.

In order to exploit your children, predators first have to find your children. They do that by uncovering your child's screen name in any one of a number of creative ways. Later in this chapter we'll show you how your child can avoid those situations. Until then, be aware that every time your child uses a search engine or posts a message in a public place or visits a chat room or even adds his name to an innocent-looking "member's profile," he's opening himself up as a potential target to predators.

Loss of innocence isn't always a sexual issue. The Internet is a fountain of information in every realm of human interest. Your child may be subjected to racism, to religious discrimination, and to sexism. He may read enough tales of criminals and murderers who never got caught that he'll begin to believe he could commit those same acts and get away with them. He may be exposed to extreme political philosophies that are presented in such a sophisticated way that he can easily be brainwashed—and children who are brainwashed at an early age are often lifelong converts to whatever group reeled them in.

Maybe the worst thing that will happen to your own child is that he'll meet up with a group of kids his own age who'll tell him that only dummies obey their parents. But if your child believes those other children, your family may be damaged all the same.

Loss of Money

Just like in the real world, there are all kinds of Internet schemes designed to separate you from your hard-earned money. Although there are outright scams such as chain letters, most money-making schemes are usually just offering opportunities that are too good to be true. For adults, junk e-mail regularly offers hot stock tips, or ways to make money with your computer by working at home or stuffing envelopes. What person wouldn't want to give up a full-time job if he could make the same amount of money by working on a computer at home for a few hours a week? But those who fall for such offers find they have been fooled by updated versions of the same scams that have been around for years. Another common way to lose money online is to order a product or medicine that offers more than it delivers. There are legitimate places online where you can spend money and get quality merchandise, often for good prices. But you must use the same caution when shopping online as you would when shopping in a regular store.

For some reason, the Internet seems to give credibility to scams that would never reel you in if you got the same offer via a phone solicitation. As you will learn later in this book, anyone with a little time and a few dollars can design an impressive Internet advertisement, but that doesn't mean the product or service is any more legitimate than those offers you get on cards placed on your windshields in parking lots.

Fortunately, dangers that cost you money are more of a threat to Mom and Dad than to the kids. Most of these offers require a credit card number or a check, which should keep most children from being entrapped. But parents should still take advantage of teaching opportunities, so that children won't fall for such things when they do get into a position that they can pay for them.

Loss of Privacy

Most of us would slam down the telephone if a stranger called us and started asking all kinds of personal questions. Yet many people have no reluctance about disclosing such personal information to people they meet online. The Internet is such an informal medium that we need to remind ourselves that the same privacy concerns we have in real life should apply online as well. You may feel as though you're just talking to another computer, but you're actually communicating with a real, live flesh-and-blood human being who can be just as dangerous as the obscene telephone caller or the flasher in the school playground.

Sometimes children don't understand that giving out seemingly harmless pieces of information can jeopardize your whole family. Even the name of a school, or a friend, or a favorite vacation spot can be clues to someone who is determined to uncover your child's identity.

If family members are not careful about what they reveal online, they expose themselves to a number of potential problems. At the very least, they will probably get on a lot of junk e-mail lists, and start receiving advertising for questionable goods and services. At the worst, they could have people stalking them, or doing various acts of mischief against them.

Physical Harm

These are the kinds of online horror stories you often read about in the news, and that make any parent's blood run cold. A child makes a friend online, which eventually results in a face-to-face meeting, which then results in molestation or physical harm.

Parents can take comfort from the fact that such tragedies only apply to a very small percentage of children who venture online. Most of the people they meet online will be friendly and harmless, some will be rude but harmless, and a small number will be out-and-out dangerous.

No one should ever underestimate the cunning and patience of those who would prey on children. They are willing to build trust and friendship over long periods, and will devote considerable energy, time, and money to the process. They will buy the friendship of children with compliments, kindness, attention, and even presents. They will be quite knowledgeable in regards to children's interests, such as music, movies, and television programs. They will always be willing to lend a listening ear, to sympathize, or to give advice. Gradually, they may slowly introduce sexual references into their communications, in an attempt to spark a child's curiosity about such matters. If this behavior is allowed or encouraged by the child, it may lead to ever more frank discussions, including the exchange of child pornography. As children get deeper and deeper into this trap, they not only feel close to their new online friend, but get excited by having someone that will help them explore such forbidden topics. This may then escalate into the worst possible scenario—a face-to-face meeting.

Parents can take comfort from the fact that just a little time and attention on their part can usually prevent these kinds of tragic situations.

Emotional Harm

When children get online, they leave the controlled, secure environment of your home to enter the cold, cruel world. Yes, they will probably meet lots of nice people, and it would be lovely to think they'll have only positive experiences, but they could also meet some people who will display the negative side of human nature. Not all of these negative influences come from evil people—many of them come from regular people who have different backgrounds and different sets of values from yours—in short, the kind of people your children will meet when they grow up and venture out into the real world. As a parent, you should take every precaution to make sure your children can handle this sort of public exposure. Your children should be warned ahead of time that people they meet online may be rude, impatient, and abrupt. These online strangers may insult them, and they may use bad language or make suggestive comments.

Some parents try to use online access to expand the world of a child who is moody or depressed, or who feels isolated from the rest of the world. This plan is not without some merit. Online activity appeals to introverted people who are more comfortable typing at a keyboard than talking face-to-face. But parents should use caution when they steer their quiet children toward the Internet. Online friendships can give some children more confidence, self-assurance, and self-worth. But other children can have a different experience, retreating into that online world and leaving the real world behind. Children who immerse themselves into online access may eventually feel even more remote and isolated than they did before they discovered the computer. Make sure all family members have some balance in their lives, with their online life being only a small part of that experience.

AN OPEN DIALOG

Any parenting manual will tell you that the best parenting is done where there is a two-way channel of communication between parent and child. This same rule should apply to supervising the activities of a child who uses the computer. If you as the parent engrave a set of rules in stone and give them to your child without explaining them, you'll end up with a hostile child who may break the rules just because the rules are there. If the child—particularly an older child—understands the potential dangers that are involved with Internet access, you can then set guidelines that the child will follow.

Start the process by having some discussions with your children, telling them about some of the online dangers, and explaining why certain rules are necessary. Ask your children what they can do to make sure they don't fall in the traps and snares that are being set for them by unscrupulous characters they could meet online. Perhaps you can even involve your children in setting the rules that will apply to them.

Continue to keep the process open as your children venture online. Use trial and error, allowing that the rules may need to be adjusted a bit as your children become more sophisticated in their online activity. You may also wish to relax the rules as your children become more mature, especially if they have done a good job of honoring the previous rules that have been established.

The key is to regularly emphasize the point that these are not arbitrary rules dictated by Mom and Dad, but rules developed by the family, for the protection of the entire family. This means that the parents must follow the rules also, although they will probably be granted more privileges than the children.

Setting the Ground Rules

In an ideal situation, you're reading this book before your children have ventured online for the first time. If that's the case, consider exploring the Internet yourself for several weeks before establishing the rules and allowing access to your children. Granted, your children may scream and call you the worst parent in the world, but this is one time when you shouldn't back down. You can't very well set rules unless you understand what needs to be controlled. This doesn't mean that you need to find every sleazy spot on the Internet, but you should become familiar enough with the Internet environment that you will encounter some of the same things your children are bound to find. If your children complain about you having all the fun while denying them access, invite them to come and explore with you so that you may both learn together.

Another suggestion is that you finish reading this book before you make your family rules, so that you fully realize the scope of the dangers that exist. Your forays into the Internet may not expose you to all the potential dangers that will face your children, and you'll want to get a good idea of what those dangers are before you set your children loose in the Internet environment.

Once you're familiar with the Internet and its potential dangers, explain those dangers to the children and involve them in setting the family rules. You may wish to call a formal family meeting at which the topic will be discussed and the rules will be established. Most rules go down better with refreshments, so be sure to add milk and cookies as part of the process.

As a reminder of the rules that will safeguard your family, print them out and post them next to the computer. You might even consider writing the rules as a contract, and having family members sign their names at the bottom to indicate that they agree to abide by the rules. Children should understand that even though the rules are posted next to the family computer, they apply to all online access. Just because your children may happen to be at a friend's house or at school doesn't mean the same family rules are not in effect.

Connection Is a Privilege

When teenagers first get their driver's licenses, many parents emphasize with them that driving is a privilege, not a right, and that driving privileges will be revoked under certain conditions. This same attitude should be applied to online access. No family member has the right to be online—not even the child who was given a personal computer as a birthday gift. Your children earn the privilege by following the rules that have been agreed upon by the family. Make sure your children understand this before they venture online. You may even want to include this reminder in the contract or set of rules that you post by the computer.

What Is Prohibited

Every set of rules should probably contain a section of things that are not allowed. This list will obviously vary based on the age of the children, but consider including one or more of the following:

- I will never disclose personal information to strangers without my parents' permission. This includes my last name, my street address, my city and state, my telephone number, my age, and the name of my school.
- I will not disclose personal information about my parents or other family members without permission. I will not disclose where my parents work, or when they work, or tell anyone their occupations.
- I will never agree to meet an online acquaintance in person, unless I have permission.
- I will never make or receive phone calls from online contacts without permission.
- I will never mail anything to an online contact without permission. Similarly, I will not open anything I receive in the mail from an online acquaintance without getting permission first. (This refers to regular postal mail, not e-mail.)
- I will not give out my e-mail address to anyone unless I have permission.
- When sending e-mail, I will not send any attached or embedded files without getting permission. Similarly, I will not download any such files I receive from others without permission.

- When someone asks me to send a picture of myself, either through the mail or attached to an e-mail, I will not do so until I get permission.
- I will not respond to any message I receive that is rude, suggestive, or harassing, and I will report all such messages to my parents.
- I will not stay online if someone starts to annoy or threaten me, but will disconnect immediately, and contact my parents.

In general, don't allow younger children access to Internet newsgroups or chat rooms, unless they are groups or rooms that are designed for children and are strongly supervised. These are Internet resources designed for older users anyway, and most young children will find them quite boring. We will discuss newsgroups and chat rooms in Chapters 4 and 5. After you read about chat rooms, you may want to decide to ban participation in chat rooms altogether!

Also, as a general rule, children under twelve years of age should never have unsupervised online time, but should always have a parent with them when they are exploring. This does not mean they can't do other computer functions by themselves, but they generally lack the maturity needed for unsupervised online activities. And even children who are older than that magic age should be carefully monitored.

What Is Allowed

Now that we have covered the negative side, let's accentuate the positive, and discuss the things that should be allowed or even encouraged.

When children reach their teenage years, they are probably mature enough to start spending small amounts of time online without adult supervision. Before starting to do this, it would be a good time to again review the dangers associated with online access, the family rules that have been established, and why those rules are important. Then start allowing some unsupervised time, gradually increasing that time if the rules are being followed and the child is having an enjoyable experience.

As children approach their later teenage years, most are responsible enough that they can function with general guidelines, rather than specific rules. But make sure they understand that more freedom does not imply less responsibility, nor will it prevent punishment if the rules are broken. Explain that all family members, even Mom and Dad, are expected to follow the rules.

In later chapters, you will learn ways to customize your Internet software so that you can tailor the online experience to your children's particular areas of interest. You can establish address books containing the e-mail addresses of friends and relatives.

You may subscribe them to certain newsgroups that may be appropriate for them. You may provide a list of areas for them to visit on the World Wide Web. Rather than establishing a lot of rules related to where your children can't go, it might be better to build a list of places where they *can* go. If you customize their environment so that they can only see the good stuff, and then limit them to that environment, you can avoid a lot of hair-splitting as your children try to determine exactly how far they can go. As your children mature, and as their interests broaden, you can regularly review their online activity, and grant access to new places.

The online experience should be one where the entire family can grow as they learn new things. If your kids want to spend all their time in chat rooms, perhaps it's just because they don't know about the other interesting things that are available for them to do online. As you find exciting new things, share them with your children if they are appropriate for the child's age. Encourage your children to also share things with you that they discover. Take some time to sit down and explore together as an entire family, or as a parent with one or two of the children at a time.

You should also teach children the proper way to behave while online. Just because some people they meet will be rude and crude does not mean they should be. Teach them to be polite and courteous to others they meet online. In later chapters we will teach you some of the rules of etiquette related to the online world. You should also share that information with family members, so they can learn early how to be good Internet citizens.

Hours of Access

Any set of rules you make for your family should include some provisions about the times that online access is allowed. In general, avoid letting children connect at times when other family members are not present. Be especially cautious of times that are late at night, or when parents are not home. Also keep in mind that the evening hours are the busiest times, and that is when children are most likely to run into unsavory characters online. If you live in a family where only one parent works, it is more reasonable to insist that online access is only permitted when a parent is home. If both parents work, perhaps you could allow younger children to connect only if their older siblings are home.

Your rules should also control the amount of time that any one family member can spend online. Some Internet activities can be quite addicting, and you don't want children ignoring schoolwork or other relationships for their online world. Your household rules will not only prevent unhealthy amounts of access, but will also reduce the number of arguments between children about who can use the computer.

Location of Computer

This seems like a minor issue, but it is really quite important. The family computer may clash with the decor of your home, but your children will benefit by using the computer in a room where the family spends most of its time. The more chance there is that others can see what your children are doing, the less opportunity they'll have to yield to temptation and break the household rules.

The best place to put the household computer is in a common area with a lot of traffic, such as a family room or living room. The worst places to put a computer are in a child's bedroom, or in an area with little activity such as a basement.

The best way to position the computer is to place it so that the monitor screen faces out into the room. This way, others can see what is displayed as they go about their household tasks. If the monitor is placed in the open, it will be less likely that your child will use the computer for improper activities.

There is a second advantage of following this rule. Some studies have shown that girls tend to be less computer-literate than boys, causing them to lag behind in school and in the workforce. Part of the reason for this is that household computers are often dominated by the boys in the family, giving girls little opportunity to learn by using them. Locating the family computer in a common area will give all family members equal opportunity to use this valuable tool.

Letting Friends Connect

You may want to establish some rules regarding the computer behavior of other children who may use your household computer. If you have an account with a common online service, many of your children's friends may have accounts on the same service. If they do, they can connect from any computer that will access the service—even your computer, and even in your own home.

If you decide to allow access to non-family members, make sure they use their own identities, and do not borrow a user name that belongs to your family. More than one innocent parent has had an online account canceled because a child let a friend use a screen name—and the friend got into trouble while using that identity.

Another thing to keep in mind is that your children's friends may have fewer restrictions on their accounts than your child has on his. Using their own screen names, they may be able to access information that that is off-limits to your child. Because screen names are tied to an individual rather than to a computer, a neighbor child who has no restrictions on his account can use your family computer to open a whole new world to your children—a world you don't want your children to enter.

Before you let your children's friends use your family computer, they should understand the access rules that exist in your house, and be willing to follow them. If the kid next door wants to use the Internet to look for pictures of scantily-clad babes, that's one thing—but you don't want him doing it in your household. In fact, it may be a good idea for you to contact little Damien's parents to see if they have established any access rules, because those rules should also apply in your house while Damien is visiting.

We all know that children tend to get into more mischief when they are with their friends. Also, most children tend to want to impress their peers by teaching them something they don't know, especially if what they're showing them has a hint of the forbidden. These circumstances combine to form a potentially dangerous situation when friends are exploring online together. Be especially attentive when your children are in this situation, and make sure they understand that the rules still apply. On the other hand, being too obnoxious about this may just cause your children to go elsewhere, perhaps to a place where the rules are even more lax and unenforced. So, allow them to explore together at your home, but be especially alert for problems.

Following the Rules

Once the rules have been decided and established, take advantage of every opportunity to remind family members of your rules. Print them up and post them near the computer. Better yet, print them as a contract, with a space at the bottom where each family member can sign his name after he agrees to abide by the rules. If you hold regular family meetings, take several opportunities each year to review the rules and explain why they are needed and why they are important. If you see stories in the media where people are harmed because of Internet activities, relate those stories to your children, and use them to reinforce the importance of having and following family rules. When you see minor infractions, warn the child and remind him of the rule again. If the child continues to break the rules, some sort of punishment should be meted out.

The Element of Trust

Just as you do in other areas, it is important to trust your children to follow the rules until they have proven that they cannot. Give them the benefit of the doubt, but keep your eyes open at the same time. You don't want to act suspicious, but you also don't want to be naive. Try to establish and enforce the rules in a cooperative setting, and not in a hostile environment. You want to learn with your children, and be their copartner in discovery. You don't want to play the part of the policeman or the censor unless you have no other option.

Seeing the Danger Signs

There are certain behaviors that can be a clue that a child is not following the rules, or that he has attracted the attention of a sex offender. Although none of these things by themselves prove that such activities are taking place, be suspicious if you start seeing a number of these warning signs:

- The child starts to spend an excessive amount of time online. Although some of this is normal as children learn about the wonders of the Internet, a sudden excessive desire to be online should arouse suspicions.
- The child is online at unusual times of the day, especially late at night or when other family members are not at home. Most sex offenders are online during the evening, so you should take extra care to control evening access.
- The child spends most of his time in chat rooms. This is where sex offenders usually contact their victims. It could be that your child just doesn't realize how many other resources may be enjoyed online. If so, you need to teach him.
- The child looks guilty or acts startled when you enter the room containing the computer. He might turn off the monitor, or cause it to switch to another screen, so that you can't see what he has been viewing. When he uses the printer, he removes the printed material immediately and puts it away so that you cannot see the printed side of the paper.
- The child gives evasive answers when you ask questions about his online activities.
- You find pornography stored on the computer, especially child pornography. Child pornography is often used by sex offenders to get children curious about such activities.
- The child starts to save files on floppy disks, which he then removes and takes with him. Although there are legitimate reasons for using floppy disks, the use of removable disks may also indicate that improper files are being sent and saved.
- The child starts to receive phone calls from strangers, particularly long-distance phone calls.

- The child starts making unusual long-distance calls, even though no charges may appear on your bill. Some sex offenders tell children to call them collect, or even establish toll-free lines.
- The child receives unusual mail or packages that are unmarked or are from people you don't know. Sex offenders often send pictures, gifts, or even plane tickets through the regular mail.
- The child suddenly becomes withdrawn from the rest of the family. He may be hostile to family members or uninterested in family activities. Some sex offenders try to disrupt family harmony to build a closer relationship with the child.
- You suspect the child might be accessing the Internet through someone else's account. Sex offenders will often supply an alternate user name and password that bypasses the controls you may have in place on the child's regular account. Your child might also be using such an account away from home, such as at school or the public library.

Don't make the mistake of thinking of a sex offender as the "dirty old man in a raincoat." A sex offender may be any age, of either sex, and may come from any social class.

Parents who have a good relationship with their children will often have a sixth sense that tells them when the child is having problems. These feelings should not be discounted, especially when some of the warning signs in the above list are present.

Looking for Evidence

If you suspect your children are breaking the rules, there are ways to check your computer to see where they have been spending their time. As a parent, you can track down clues in much the way that Sherlock Holmes looked for clues at the crime scene. We will talk about some of these in the following chapters.

Children should understand and agree that their parents always have the right to access their online accounts and check their activities. Some children will probably not like this, and some parents themselves may not be too keen on it. After all, it goes against the rules of trust, and it's the electronic equivalent of going through your child's dresser drawers looking for bad things. But just as Mom and Dad set the rules for using the family car, they should also set the rules for using the family computer. Although most parents will not need to access their children's accounts often, they should still maintain the right to do so when necessary. Many times, just the fact that children know they could be monitored will cause them to behave properly. But if you do suspect the worst, you need to be able to access the child's account and look for evidence. Even though we will show you ways of doing this that are less intrusive, you should still maintain the right of unlimited account access.

Check your phone bills regularly to check for long-distance calls that can't be explained. If you have a separate line for computer and personal use, check both bills.

If you have a problem with unexplained incoming or outgoing calls that don't appear on your bill, contact your local phone company and ask about different options. With features like Caller ID, you can monitor the calls you are receiving. You can also block any unexplained outside calls that are being made to your home.

Giving Warnings

For the first violation of online rules, you may consider giving a warning. This is especially true if the violation was a simple oversight, or was motivated by ignorance or curiosity. Some children are so embarrassed to be caught doing such things that they only need to be caught once before they repent and follow the rules thereafter.

If you catch your child exploring improper material, don't immediately assume he is doing it on purpose. Many Internet sites, particularly the ones that feature pornography, go out of their way to make sure they can be easily found. As a result, children may stumble upon such material while looking for harmless information.

As a parent, it is your responsibility to determine how many warnings your children should receive. As a general rule, warnings should be given while rules are still new, but should be replaced with punishment when the child knows he is breaking the rules.

Punishment

After an appropriate number of warnings, violations of your household rules should result in punishments. *Those punishments should be strictly enforced.* Each subsequent violation after the first should result in increasingly severe punishments.

One common punishment is the loss of online privileges, or the imposition of stronger parental controls. (See the explanation of parental controls later in this chapter.) If you take away online privileges, don't rely on your child's word that he won't get online. After all, he broke his word when he broke the rules he'd agreed to follow. Instead, make sure you use the software to lock him out of the system. One way to do this is to change the password used to access the child's user name, and don't reveal the new password or change it back until the probation period is ended. During this probation time, make sure your child is not spending time with friends who are going online. You might require the child to remain at home (be "grounded") for the duration of the punishment period.

If these punishments seem harsh, remember that a child who exposes himself to pornography is in danger of becoming addicted to pornography. A child who exposes himself to pedophiles is in danger of losing his life. And a child who obtains and uses your credit cards can run up thousands of dollars in charges before you even realize you have a problem. Penalties for violations of your in-house computer rules should be stiff, and they should be rigorously applied. If your child whines about the stiffness of the rules, this is no time to take pity on him. The safety of your family is at stake. If he pays the price this time, he may learn his lesson.

GENERAL SAFETY GUIDELINES

Here are some general safety guidelines that will apply to all your online activities. In later chapters, we will supplement these with more specific rules related to particular Internet topics.

Selecting Your User Name

Because most of you will connect to the Internet through some type of dial-up connection, it will be necessary for you to identify yourself, not only with some kind of user name, but also with a password. If your service provider will allow you to choose your own user name, choose one that will reveal little about yourself to others. In particular, avoid user names that reveal details about your age or your gender. Choosing names such as "HotBody," "TinyAngel," or "CuteBabe" is just asking for trouble. Women and girls are more subject than males to online harassment, so they should take particular care in selecting a user name.

You should also avoid user names that reveal your true name, particularly your last name, as these make it easy for someone to find you using one of the people searching services we describe in Chapter 7. For example "BillShatner" would be a bad choice, "WilliamS" would be better, and "BeamMeUp" would be the best of all.

Parents should also make sure that all user names selected by their children will meet these guidelines. User names such as "TopDog" and "WittyOne" may not be as impressive as the child's own name, but they will cause fewer problems. Surely Mom and Dad and Junior can reach a compromise that will be acceptable to all.

Selecting Your Password

Your password is a critical item of information, because it is the sentinel that keeps others from accessing the Internet through your account. Anyone who knows your password can connect to the Internet through your user name, causing all kinds of problems for you. It is hard to emphasize too much that family members need to keep passwords secret from everyone with the possible exception of you, the parent.

Assume your child sends an e-mail to a friend who is a little bit mischievous, if not downright dishonest. From the e-mail, the friend can determine the user name of your child, and the name of the online service that he uses. There is a pretty good chance that the friend has access to the same online service, or can find a computer where the software for that service has been installed. Now the password is the only piece of the puzzle that prevents the friend from connecting as your child. If your child has revealed his password, or selected one that is easy to guess, the bad guy is in.

Although this may appear far-fetched, it really is not. There are groups of very serious pranksters and criminals who spend a lot of time trying to guess passwords so they can get online using a stranger's account. There are also "password cracking" programs that are written just to try and guess passwords. Once outsiders gain access, you can be sure they'll cause trouble. After all, if their purposes were honest, they wouldn't need to steal someone else's identity.

When choosing a password, following these guidelines will make it difficult for your password to be guessed by a person or a password-cracking program:

- Use at least six characters.
- If your online service recognizes both uppercase and lowercase characters, use a mixture of each in the password.
- Use a mixture of letters, numbers, and other symbols that are allowed.
- Do not use any word found in any dictionary, and do not add a number to the front or back of a dictionary word. Password-cracking programs try such combinations.
- Make sure your password has no relationship with your user name. Avoid the obvious trick of spelling the user name backwards.
- Do not use any item that makes up part of your personal identification, such as

your phone number, address, Social Security number, any of your names or the names of family members—including the trusty family pet. Avoid backwards spellings of any of these items as well.

If children have trouble remembering complex passwords, consider using some type of memory device that will remind them. For example, the nursery rhyme "Sing A Song of Six Pence . . ." could be used to remember the password "SASO6P."

Try to avoid writing down your password. If you must write it down, store it away from the computer, such as in a drawer, or in a book. Writing the password on a sticky note and placing it on the computer monitor is a bad idea.

Some services, such as America Online, allow you to store a password on your computer so that you don't have to enter it when connecting to the service. This only works on your own computer, so a neighbor could not connect using your user name from his computer unless he had the password. You may want to consider this option for your children for a couple of reasons:

- If you establish the password for your children, they will never need to remember a password to get connected. They just need to select their user name from the list of family names and hit the Enter key to connect.
- Because they don't know their own password, your children will not be able to connect to the service from another location, such as a friend's home.

Of course, there are some disadvantages to using stored passwords. Because no password is needed to sign on, anyone with access to the computer can connect using that user name. Family members could connect with the wrong user name, or even outsiders visiting your home could connect. This could be a problem if you have different names defined with different levels of access authority. (For example, eight-year-old Horace, who has been firmly restricted to eight-year-old subjects, might get a real education if he signed on using Dad's user name.) But there's nothing to stop you from using stored passwords on some user names but not others. For example, the kids can connect without passwords, but Mom and Dad still need to enter theirs.

Under no conditions should the master user name (the first one that was specified when the account was opened) be allowed access without a password, because that is the user name that controls the access levels for everyone else.

Online Profiles

Commercial services such as America Online often allow you to build an online profile that can be displayed by others who want to learn more about you. An example of such a profile is shown in Figure 2-1. Although on the surface the profile looks quite innocent, you can see that there could be potential for problems. If someone gets annoyed with a message you write or something you do online, he can easily display your profile and find out about you. Using some of the people-searching services that are described in Chapter 7, this person could easily locate your address and home phone number.

If you must use an online profile, follow the rules about privacy that have already been discussed. Profiles will usually allow you to leave items blank, so you need not reveal anything about yourself that you don't want known. Services that support profiles also usually allow you to search for profiles that match certain characteristics. For example, I could search for others who lived in my state, or who were interested in my hobbies. Such features are commonly used by sex criminals and scam artists to recruit potential victims.

One final reason for avoiding online profiles is that they expose your e-mail address to the world. There are people who compile lists of e-mail addresses and sell those lists to those who send junk e-mail. Once they get your user name from an online profile, they can also determine your e-mail address (we will explain more about this in the next chapter). Anyone could find the online profile shown in Figure 2-1 by searching for all profiles containing the word "the." More specifically, someone starting an online dating service may want to have a more exclusive mailing list, and may search for any profile with a marital status of "single" or "divorced." In any case, building an online profile is like throwing open the doors to the world and saying, "Please send me some junk e-mail!" As we will learn in the next chapter, junk e-mail is something you definitely want to avoid.

Parental Controls

All the popular online services have "parental control" features that allow you to limit some of the activities of family members. If you access the Internet through an ISP, there are also software packages you can buy that control access. These packages are known as blocking software, and they will be discussed more in Chapter 6.

In order for parental controls to work, each family member needs to have his own user name, because access privileges are defined by user.

For an example we'll use the parental controls provided by America Online, because they are fairly typical. The first user name you define when you subscribe to the service is called the "master screen name." Although other screen names can be changed at will, this one never changes. It is the name that is responsible for all other names on the account. Passwords are changed and parental controls are assigned through this user name, so only Mom and Dad should be able to access it.

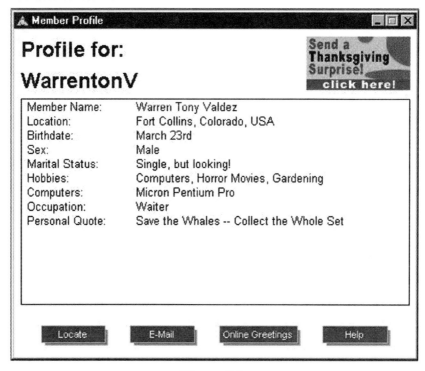

Figure 2-1

Under the America Online system, each user name can be assigned to one of four categories, with various permissions, as follows. (If terms such as "chat rooms" and "instant messages" are unfamiliar to you, there will be chapters covering them later in this book.)

Kids Only (recommended for age 12 and under)
- Can use the "Kids Only" channel (games and activities for kids)
- No instant messages may be sent or received

- No access to member-created or private chat rooms
- No web site access
- No newsgroup access
- No access to premium (extra cost) services
- Can send text-only e-mail (no attachments)

Young Teen (recommended for ages 13-15)
- No access to member-created or private chat rooms
- Some web sites blocked
- No access to premium (extra cost) services
- No access to newsgroup messages with file attachments

Mature Teen (recommended for ages 16-17)
- Some web sites blocked
- No access to premium (extra cost) services
- No access to newsgroup messages with file attachments

Adult (age 18+)
- Full access to all areas and services

Once you have selected one of these categories of access, there are custom controls that can be used to further restrict access. For example, you can block access to premium services, even to those who have adult access.

You may not understand some of the terms and restrictions described above, but by the time you've finished reading this book they should all make sense. For now, just remember that there are certain categories of access that are already defined by the online service, plus some custom controls that you can fine-tune for even more flexibility.

Don't think that just because you have implemented parental controls you have no further obligation to monitor safe online behavior. For one thing, all category systems rely on the opinions of others, who may have different ideas than you do about what is appropriate for different ages of children to access online. A little investigation is in order before you blindly accept somebody else's decision of what your ten-year-old daughter can handle. Also, parental controls aren't foolproof. There was recently a story in the news about a boy who made extra money by charging his friends ten dollars each to deactivate the controls on their home computers. Make sure to check the access on a regular basis to make sure the controls are working and are still in place.

A Wolf in Sheep's Clothing

Constantly emphasize to children that they cannot always believe everything they learn about the people they will meet online. People can lie about their age, their sex, their marital status, and just about anything else. The six-year-old girl who is a pen pal with your daughter might in reality be a 40-year-old divorced man who gets his thrills by talking to young girls. Some people exaggerate their attributes while online, or tell minor lies. For example, a thirty-five-year-old married man might say that he is five years younger and single. A more dangerous type is the person who takes on a completely different persona while online. Often such a person develops elaborate characters, and then plays those characters while online.

Fortunately, most people have a small circle of online friends they regularly contact. These are often the same people they interact with in person, such as relatives and school friends. Allowing your children access to these people should usually present no problem. You should become involved when a child is establishing a new friendship with someone he has never met in person. Keep a close eye on the relationship, until you're convinced the new friend is really a sheep and not a wolf.

Trust No One

This is a difficult principle to teach, because it probably goes against everything you want your children to be. Parents usually want their children to be outgoing and willing to trust and help others. But just as you must teach your children to be wary of strangers in cars, you must also teach them to be careful of strangers online. This does not mean they have to be rude—just cautious. All communications with strangers should be brief and unrevealing, at least until you are convinced that the person represents no threat. Children should always be taught to consult with their parents when they start receiving communications from a stranger.

Disclosing Personal Information

This is a rerun, but it bears repeating. Teach all family members to be suspicious of any request for personal information, especially if the request comes to you unsolicited. About a year ago, many America Online subscribers started receiving e-mails from people who claimed to be America Online employees. These e-mails claimed that in order to solve a system problem, the employee needed to know your password immediately. Sometimes the letters said that if the password wasn't given within two minutes of receipt of the letter, the member's account would be canceled. This scam became so prevalent that warnings appeared on many screens to tell users that real employees would never ask for their password, nor would they ever contact a customer unsolicited. If you ever receive a similar request, not only should you ignore the message, but you should report the incident to your service provider.

Online Commerce

Children should always contact their parents when they wish to purchase something from an online store, and parents themselves should also exercise caution when spending money online. Despite what most people think, the real danger is not in getting your credit card number stolen. Most online businesses support "secure transactions" that scramble any data you send and then unscramble it on the other end. Leaving a carbon copy of a charge slip on a restaurant table probably exposes you to more threat than using a secure online transaction.

The biggest risk from online commerce comes from dealing with companies that may not be honest. You should make sure you know something about the company you are using, and make sure it has a good reputation. Use only online businesses that were recommended by friends or other sources that you trust.

Look for more information about online commerce in Chapter 7.

A PARENT'S QUESTIONS

Q. Is any one online service safer than the others?
A. There are some smaller service providers that claim to provide only content that is appropriate for children or other conservative groups. Although having the content filtered by the service provider eliminates almost any chance of circumventing the controls, such systems still may not exactly meet your needs. For one thing, you are still relying on other people to determine what is appropriate for your family, and their opinions may differ from yours. Also, with millions of Internet resources to evaluate, most companies will not have the staff to do the kind of thorough checking that is necessary. This means that either bad resources will slip through, or that good resources will not be accessible.

If you use a commercial online service, all of them provide some kinds of parental controls that allow you to determine what your children see. Because all of these services offer temporary free memberships, subscribe to one and see if it meets your needs.

If you connect through an ISP, you should expect to pay extra for blocking software that will limit what your children can access. Some ISPs will include this software automatically when you subscribe. If not, include the cost of the blocking software when deciding which service provider to use.

As noted in this chapter, the way you connect to the Internet is less important than the procedures you have in place to protect your children. Use the proper blocking software or parental controls, combined with open discussions and regular monitoring of their online activities to keep children safe.

Q. With all these dangers, wouldn't it just be easier to forbid my children from going online?
A. Keeping your children off the Internet would avoid the problem, but it would make as such sense as preventing them from going outside, or talking on the telephone, or watching television. It would also put them at a distinct disadvantage in terms of learning the things they will need to be successful in school, in their careers, and in life.

There certainly are dangers online, just as there are dangers in many of the things we do on a daily basis. The key lies not in prohibition, but in educating children to the dangers, and then taking the proper steps to protect them.

Q. What should I do if I think laws have been broken?
A. Contact your local law enforcement office, your local FBI office, or the National Center for Missing and Exploited Children at 1-800-843-5687. Keep in mind that many of the offensive things you will find online are not illegal. For example, sending a child an e-mail advertising a pornographic web site is probably not illegal, unless you can prove the sender knew the recipient was less than 18 years of age. The things that are illegal include sending child pornography or making sexual overtures to someone known to be under 18 years of age. If you have any questions, it's better to call the experts and get their advice.

Q. I cannot believe my child would ever become involved with a sex criminal. Why are you so cynical?
A. Even good children will sometimes become involved with shady characters out of curiosity or a sense of adventure. As children mature they become curious about their sexuality and sexual topics. They are also moving away from the control imposed by their parents and are seeking to build friendships with others. Although such a child may be embarrassed to discuss his sexuality with his parents, he may find no such

inhibitions about discussions with others—especially the faceless and nameless people who inhabit the online community. Such children may even seek out such material online, by searching for adult chat rooms or pornographic web sites. Curious children are easy targets for sex criminals.

Some activities that start out as simple curiosity may spiral out of control until they turn obsessive and dangerous. As children get more and more involved, increased feelings of guilt will make them even more secretive and less likely to talk to their parents. If you are aware of the signs, you can anticipate the problem and stop it from getting out of hand. If you think your children are good kids, they probably are. But you still need to stay in tune with their lives, and be objective about the behavior you observe.

Chapter 3—Neither Rain, Nor Snow, Nor Sleet
• • • • •

THE CHARMING OLD CUSTOM OF SITTING DOWN with pen and paper to write a letter and then address an envelope, find a stamp, put the letter in the mailbox, and wait for a reply two or three weeks up the road went out of style with muttonchop sideburns and bell-bottomed pants. People are learning that if they want their relatives to communicate with them, they'd better buy a computer and get an e-mail address.

Most colleges offer free e-mail to students, most students are quick to adapt to its usage, and most parents are wise enough to know they will receive more letters if they don't have to rely on "snail mail." (Snail mail is a derogatory term used to refer to letters that are not e-mail—old-fashioned paper letters that are stamped, sent, and delivered by a postal employee who may or may not be disgruntled.)

Once you get e-mail, you won't be able to understand how you ever lived without it. We've found that the friends and family members we stay in touch with are the ones who have e-mail. We communicate with many of them on a daily basis. Clark exchanges jokes with people in half a dozen states. Kathy is sharing an exercise program with a friend in North Carolina, and the two of them write daily to keep each other informed of their progress. We send and receive recipes, forward news items, and tell friends who've moved away about the goings-on at home. Our e-mail letters can act as our journals if we keep logs of what we send. E-mail is a huge part of our daily lives.

We have friends and family members who are just as dear to us, but our usual contact with them consists of a Christmas card, or maybe one letter a year if we are lucky. There is no difference between these two groups of friends and relatives, except that the first group can be reached through e-mail.

Our unconnected friends think we're real snobs because we don't write more often. But people who learn to use e-mail quickly get spoiled by the ease of instant communication. Although it may seem easy to you to sit down and write a letter, stamp it, and put it in the mail, e-mail is so much easier and faster that doing those things becomes an insurmountable burden. If you don't believe this, just wait until you get a little experience with e-mail. Within a year your handwritten letters will be a thing of the past. You will soon be asking your friends for their e-mail addresses.

When your aged relatives or technophobic friends refuse to convert, you will pity them for living such a crude existence—and you may find yourself being slightly annoyed that they expect you to accommodate their backward ways.

The first part of this chapter will explore the basics of e-mail, including a lot of really nice features that many e-mail systems provide.

Even when you are a wizard, and know every e-mail feature backwards and forwards, you can still brand yourself as a newcomer by not following certain rules of e-mail etiquette. There are certain courtesies that should be followed when composing e-mail, and failure to follow them will annoy the people who receive letters from you. But these rules are easy to learn, and by the end of this chapter you'll understand all of them.

We will also explore a variation of e-mail known as a mailing list, which allows you to automatically receive information via e-mail on a wide variety of topics. An e-mail list is a valuable tool for keeping you informed.

Once you know your way around the e-mail system, you will be ready to be taught about the ways in which e-mail may be abused or incorrectly used by your children. This chapter will give suggestions for avoiding such problems, as well as some suggested rules that your children should follow to avoid most of the pitfalls. We will also suggest ways in which your computer can be used to assist you in monitoring adherence to the guidelines you have established.

E-MAIL BASICS

E-mail is just like old-fashioned mail, only easier. Whenever you are connected to the Internet, you can open your mailbox. Inside you will find letters that others have sent to your unique mailing address. You can receive these letters from anyone in the world. You can also subscribe to electronic magazines and newsletters that will arrive magically in your mailbox on occasion. Sadly, you will also get your share of "junk" mail that you will soon learn to discard without reading.

Not only is e-mail a great replacement for the old-fashioned custom of writing letters, but you'll also find that e-mail is superior to your telephone in many aspects. You can compose mail when it is convenient for you, be that midnight or 6 a.m. You can reach your recipient without playing "telephone tag" to find a convenient time for him to receive your message. Since your recipient can open your mail whenever he wants, it is less inconvenient to have a friend in a different time zone than it would be if you were relying on the telephone. E-mail conversations also eliminate a lot of the misunderstandings that are associated with telephone calls, because once a friend or business associate reads your letter, he'll have a copy of it to use as a referral so he can remember exactly what instructions you gave in your message. Last, but certainly not least, there are no long-distance charges for sending e-mail. It costs you no more to send a message around the world than across the street.

Common Features

Before looking at the most common features of Internet mail programs, let's review some of the more common e-mail programs that you will find being used:

Commercial Providers

If you use a commercial provider such as America Online or CompuServe, the mail program will be included as part of the software, and you usually will end up using their mail program just by default.

Netscape Communicator

If you use an ISP, you will likely use Netscape Communicator as your Internet application software. If so, it comes with a mail program that supports all the regular mail functions. Netscape has a forwarding function that will forward all the e-mail received at your Internet address to another box. Thus, if you have e-mail coming to your Internet address and also to your address at America Online, you can set the Netscape mail preferences so that your Netscape mail is forwarded to your AOL account and you only have to look in one e-mail box.

Outlook Express

Microsoft's Internet Explorer is also commonly used to access the Internet through an ISP. If you use Internet Explorer, it comes packaged with a second program called Outlook Express that will handle mail.

Eudora Light

Many ISPs will allow you to use different mail programs once you get connected. One of the most powerful and popular ones is called Eudora Light. Eudora Light has the advantage of being free of charge.

Eudora Pro

This program is the big sister of Eudora Light, but this one is not free. The idea is to get you hooked on the free version, and then sell you the more expensive. The Pro version has some nice features, including the ability to automatically filter out the mail you aren't interested in reading. If you have children who receive e-mail, this feature may prevent them from receiving X-rated material in their e-mail boxes.

Pine

This is an older UNIX mail system that is frequently found on systems with the older kinds of "shell" accounts. It is menu-driven, text-based (not a GUI), and looks pretty ugly, although it will perform most of the standard mail functions.

Reading Mail

One obvious feature that all mail programs must provide is the ability to read mail. In order to understand how a letter arrives in your mailbox, it is necessary to understand a little about e-mail addresses. Each Internet user has a unique e-mail address, and anyone in the world who knows that address can send e-mail there. Any resemblance in this book to any real e-mail addresses is unintended; as far as we know, we're making all these addresses up. Keeping that in mind, a sample e-mail address is shown below:

EarWig@aol.com

This e-mail address comes in two parts. The first part, "EarWig," is called the mailbox, and the second part is the domain name. In this case, the user is a subscriber to America Online, whose domain name for e-mail is "aol.com." (The domain name usually reflects the name of the ISP or the commercial provider.) The mailbox name is separated from the domain name by the @ character, which is called the "at" sign. Thus, the e-mail address is an abbreviated way of saying "Send this to Earnest Wiggin at America Online."

Usually, the mailbox name will be the same as the user name used when connecting to the Internet. Thus, when Earnest Wiggin connects with America Online, he will use the user name of EarWig, and his mail will also be sent to the mailbox named EarWig. Although America Online does not support it, some e-mail systems allow multiple "aliases," so perhaps you could send letters to "EWiggin," "Earnest W," or "Ear_Wig," and they would all arrive at the same mailbox.

Now let's assume your parents, Mr. and Mrs. Wiggin, were so overjoyed over the prospect of your birth that they named you Earnest without considering the nickname possibilities. Nevertheless, your name is Earnest Wiggin, the whole world knows you as EarWig, and you own the e-mail address shown above. Your brother Philip (FlipWig@compuserve.com) sends a letter to you at that address. The mail message is sent across the Internet to the domain called "aol.com." When it arrives at America Online, it is given to a program called the mail server. The server first looks to make sure there is a mailbox named "EarWig." Sure enough, there is, so your letter is saved in that mailbox (which is actually a location on a very large hard drive). The mail server is then done with that request for a while.

Eventually, you're going to wonder if anyone has been writing to you. You'll connect with America Online to receive your mail. America Online is one of many systems that will check for new mail automatically when you connect. (Other systems will not check for mail until you specifically tell the program to do so.) And sure enough, almost as soon as you've connected with your AOL account, an obnoxious computerized voice chirps, "You've got mail!" (If this computerized voice annoys you too much, you can turn it off. You'll still be able to see if you've got mail because AOL displays an ICON of a mailbox prominently on its toolbar. If you have mail in your box, the red flag goes up.)

If you want to read your mail, you usually need to take some kind of action, such as clicking on the mailbox ICON with America Online. This causes the mail server to check your mailbox and build a summary screen that will show you all the mail in your box that is still unread. The end result is a screen that might look something like this:

09/28	FlipWig@compuserve.com	Dinner Friday Night
09/28	EBunRab	Re: Weather Up Your Way?
09/29	horatio@musicworld.com	About Your Order # 12734
09/29	Debbie	Fwd: Jokes About Cats

According to the screen there are four unread messages. The column on the far left shows the date each message was received. The middle column is the e-mail address of the person who sent the message. Notice how two of the messages have no domain name. This usually means that the letters originated from the same service provider. Thus, if Earnest Wiggin is using America Online, then these messages are from two other America Online users with user names of EBunRab and Debbie.

The third column contains the subject of the e-mail. The second message, where the subject line starts with "Re:" is probably a reply to a message that Earnest sent. For example, Earnest sent EBunRab a message asking him about the weather in his area, and EBunRab responded to that message. The fourth message, where the subject line starts with "Fwd:" is probably a forwarded message. Perhaps someone sent Debbie some cat jokes, and knowing that Earnest likes cat jokes too, she passed them on to him as well.

Once you determine which letter you want to read, you usually just click (or double-click) on it. Assume in this example Earnest wants to read the third letter. If he clicks on that, the mail server will have to go out to the mailbox and get that letter. The mail program will then display that letter on the screen, probably in its own window:

Subj: About Your Order # 12734
Date: 9/29/98 4:45:57 PM EST
From: horatio@musicworld.com (Horatio Hornpipe)
To: EarWig@aol.com

Dear Mr. Wiggin:

We have received your music order, "Great Opera Arias For Accordion and Bagpipe," and have assigned Order Number 12734 to it. If your shipment does not arrive in two weeks, please e-mail me back and mention this number.

Thanks for your business.

Horatio Hornpipe
Music World

<PREV   DELETE   FORWARD   REPLY   FILE   NEXT>

Notice that the subject and the date are the same as from the summary screen, except that the date has been expanded to include the full date and time, including the time zone. The "from" information is also duplicated, except that a different name, Horatio Hornpipe, is also listed in parentheses. Some mailer programs allow the user to specify an alternate name that is sent and displayed along with the e-mail address of the sender.

Notice the last line displayed in the example above. These are all commands that allow you to do various things with this message. These functions are as follows:

- ❏ **PREV**

  Read the previous message in the mailbox.
- ❏ **DELETE**

  Remove the message from the mailbox.
- ❏ **FORWARD**

  Send the message on to someone else.
- ❏ **REPLY**

  Send a reply back to the sender.
- ❏ **FILE**

  Move this letter somewhere else.
- ❏ **NEXT**

  Read the next message in the mailbox.

We will discuss most of these functions in the next few pages.

Sometimes you will get a message that contains some really strange text, usually at the start or end of the message. An example is shown below:

```
————————————————————— Headers ———————————————————————
Return-Path: <crackup@goodboy.com>
Received: from relay99.mx.axl.com ([172.31.155.66]) with SMTP;
Received: from goodboy.com (goodboy.com [207.198.169.1])
    by relay99.mx.axl.com (8.8.8/8.8.5/AXL-4.0.0)
    with ESMTP id RAA19181 for <BobSmith@aol.com>
    Thu, 13 Aug 1998 17:24:26 -0400 (EDT)
Received: from localhost (crackup@localhost)
    by goodboy.com (8.8.8/8.8.5) with SMTP id OAA08163
    for <EarWig@aol.com>; Thu, 13 Aug 1998 14:28:27
```

These lines are called the "headers" of the e-mail message. As an e-mail message is sent on its way across the Internet, various statistics are kept and recorded as part of the message. This information includes the IP addresses, domain names, and times associated with each leg of the journey. Some mail readers have options to show full headers, show partial headers, or show no headers. Other mail readers may behave differently depending on whether the message was an internal (same domain) or external message. Although headers are interesting to try to decode, you can usually just ignore them, or set the option so they don't display.

Sometimes you will read a message that looks like it has been through a blender. Clark recently received a message that contained this portion of text:

It does have to do with how much is internalized; how much the person
embraces and struggles with the different values. If you=A2re only fo=
llowing
a belief because of conformist reasons, just doing what is expected of
you and it hasn=A2t penetrated very deeply into one=A2s conscience, th=
en it
doesn=A2t have the long*term effect we=A2re talking about. =20

The problem here is that there are all kinds of computers and operating systems that are sending mail across the Internet. You may receive mail on a PC that someone composed on a Macintosh, or on an IBM mainframe. Although the code that translates mail between different systems is pretty good, it is not perfect. The example shown above is pretty typical of translation problems across different systems. Notice that punctuation characters are not handled well, nor is line wrapping. When this happens, just be patient and try to decipher what was being said.

Another thing that may lead to strange-looking messages is the problem of different type faces, or "fonts." Sometimes someone will send you some columns of numbers, but they are all smashed together and difficult to read. This may be because your mailer is using a proportional font, which varies the distance between letters. Try changing to a "fixed font," which is a font where every letter is spaced the same distance apart. (Courier is a great example of a fixed font. It is hideous, but you can always read it.)

One nice feature of many mail readers is the ability to download new mail to your PC for later reading. This is a good technique if you are connected over a long-distance line, or if you have a pricing plan that limits your access per month. When you do a "flash session," you stay connected just long enough for the mail server to copy the mail from your mailbox to the hard drive on the PC. After transmission is complete, the modem disconnects but the software remains displayed so that you can continue reading your mail and can write responses for later delivery, even though you aren't connected. Many mail readers support this feature.

Sending Mail

Although it is more fun to receive e-mail than to write it, e-mail works just like regular mail in that if you don't send any, you won't get any in return. But writing e-mail is a simple process—so simple that young children can easily master the technique.

No matter what Internet interface you use, there will be some prominent ICON or menu selection at the top of your screen that will allow you to compose letters to others and then send them. When you select this option, it will usually display a Compose Mail screen that will look like a blank form. You will need to use the mouse and the tab and arrow keys to navigate around the form and fill in the proper data. The areas you will need to complete will be the following:

❏ **Address:**
Fill in the e-mail address of the person to whom this message should be sent. If you want to send the letter to more than one person, you can often do that by entering a list of e-mail addresses, separated by commas.

It never matters whether you capitalize letters in the domain name portion of the e-mail address, and it almost never matters for the mailbox names (there are a few old systems that require proper capitalization of the mailbox name). In other words, our friend Earnest Wiggin can be reached at EarWig@aol.com, EarWig@Aol.Com, or EARWIG@AOL.COM.

❏ **CC and BCC:**
Back when all letters were written on typewriters, the notation "cc: Earnest Wiggin" at the bottom of a letter indicated that a carbon copy of the letter was being sent to Earnest Wiggin. Carbon copies were made using carbon paper, which was the ancient equivalent of blue fingernail polish. Carbon ink seemed to get everywhere except on the sheet of paper where it was supposed to go. Often, at least one page of a multiple-page letter was printed with the carbon paper upside-down, so that the page in question could only be read by holding it to a mirror.

In any case, the "cc:" notation is still used in most mail programs to allow you to send additional copies to other e-mail addresses. There is really no difference between "To:" and "cc:"—both notations still route your message to all the people in both lists. The difference is in the intent. The primary recipients are usually the ones who have to take some action, while the other folks are just included for informational purposes only. The rules for coding the e-mail addresses are usually the same as were given above for the "To:" area.

A "bcc" means a blind carbon copy. If you want to send the same letter to Uncle Theron and Uncle Lloyd and Uncle Jethro, but you want each uncle to assume it was a warm personal letter just for his eyes alone, a blind carbon is your ticket. A mail program that supports this feature will send a copy to everyone on your list, but without letting the recipients know that other copies were sent. On America Online, blind carbons can be sent by putting the address of the recipient in parentheses—such as (EBunRab@aol.com).

❑ **Subject:**

Use the subject area to type a short description of the content of your e-mail. This is the text that will appear in the summary window when your recipient opens his mail, so it should be meaningful.

Some mailing programs require you to provide a subject, but others make a subject optional. Even when a subject is not required, putting a subject on your letter is a courtesy that makes your letter appear more appealing.

❑ **Text Area**

All mailing programs will provide a text area where you can type the body of the message. This usually has a vertical scroll bar, and allows you to type more text than can fit in the area. Use the scroll bar to scroll back and review the first part of the message. Some programs have a limit on the amount of text you can type, and will stop you when you get to that point.

Some mail programs have become quite sophisticated, and allow you to change the font type and size. Occasionally the user can even change the color of his type, or the color of the background "paper." A common feature of many mail systems allows different typesetting features, such as bold, underline, and italics. Keep in mind that these formatting tricks will probably only work in your same domain. Thus, if you are an AOL user who sends a pretty colored message to a bunch of people, other AOL users will see your artistic genius, but non-AOL users will just see plain text, and will wonder if you've had your prescription checked lately. In addition, it doesn't make any sense to use a beautiful type font if the person who will receive your letter doesn't have that type font on his machine. If you're a serious letter writer, you'll soon learn that letters that are written with a plain typefont and on a white surface are easier to read.

Because of the differences in mail systems, some of your typing habits don't always give the same results for the recipient of your letter as you might intend. A tab key is a big example of this. Because of this, it's better to just leave a blank space between paragraphs, rather than trying to use the tab to indent.

*****

If your mail program runs as a Windows application, remember that you can use Windows tricks such as copy-and-paste. This makes it easy to copy e-mail addresses or paragraphs of text between one message and another. You can also transfer data between any Windows applications, such as from your mail reader to your word processor, or vice versa. You can usually paste into any area on the form, and not just the text area.

As with reading mail, many programs allow you to compose mail when not actually connected to your service provider. Thus, you can write a batch of messages offline, then connect and send them all within just a few seconds, and then break your connection. Another advantage of offline composing is that you can go back and modify or cancel previous messages any time before you send them. This is a nice feature if you've written a nasty letter to the boss and then think better of it.

When you have completed the message you are writing, there should be a button labeled "Send" somewhere in the Compose Mail window. This is the button you should push to cause your mail to be sent. That will get the mail server involved again, when it determines whether to save the message in a local mailbox or send the message to another domain on the Internet.

Occasionally even the best typists will misaddress a letter that is sent via e-mail. Computer e-mail systems are not as friendly as your local postal carrier, who will try to deliver a letter no matter how your name is garbled on the envelope. If a letter that should have been addressed to EarWig is mistakenly sent to "EarWag," the letter will be delivered to any user who happens to have the name that was typed. It doesn't matter if Earnest Wiggin lives in Utah and Earn Wages is a company out of Melbourne, Australia. If the name you type is EarWag, that's the address where your letter will go.

Suppose there is no EarWag on the system. In that case, the letter will be kicked back to your e-mail box as an electronic "return to sender." If you send a misaddressed e-mail message within your own domain, you'll get the error back so quickly that the letter might never even go out. Sending a message to a bad mailbox in another domain is a little more complicated, and causes something called a "bounce." When the mail server on the remote domain gets the message, it will determine there is no such mailbox on its system. Because it knows from the headers who sent the message, the mail server will then build an e-mail message documenting the error, and send it back to you. These error messages will usually have a subject line something like "Unable to Deliver," or "Mail Delivery Error." Reading the message should give you a pretty good indication of where the error was detected. If the mailbox name is bad, then the domain name is fine, but you just need a different mailbox name. Perhaps you just typed the name incorrectly, or perhaps your friend moved or canceled his account. If the error says something about not being able to resolve the domain name, check the spelling of the domain name. If it looks fine, then perhaps the computer running that domain is not currently active. If that is the case, try sending the message later.

Here's a suggestion that may save a lot of time. Before you hit that Send button, review the message carefully—not just the address, but the content itself. E-mail is designed to be a fast and informal communication mechanism, but some people take that to extremes. An excessive number of typos or incomprehensible sentences will send the message to your readers that you are either dumb or just plain sloppy. This reminds us of the story about the coach who asked one of his players, "Son, are you ignorant, or just indifferent?" The player replied, "Coach, I don't know and I don't care!"

Reply

One of the nicest features about most mail reader programs is the ability to reply to a letter as you're reading new mail. If someone sends you a message that needs a reply, you press the reply option, type a reply, request that it be sent, and then the program will take you back to the original message you were reading.

When you press the Reply button, the mail program will jump into the Compose Mail screen, just as if you were writing a new message, but it will automatically fill in some of the data from the original message. For example, the "To:" area will be filled in with the "From:" address in the original message, so that the reply is directed back to the person who sent it. Also, the subject area is filled in with the original subject text, except for a prefix of "Re:" that is added to the front. This tells the user that this message is *regarding*, or *replying* to, the subject of the message he sent.

Most mailer programs also allow you to quote all or part of the original message in your reply. This is a dubious enhancement. Some people think that throwing your own quotes back to you makes it easier for you to understand what they're saying, especially when they're replying to a complicated message with multiple parts or questions. Other people know full well what they said, and think these huge quoted blocks of their own text are a pain in the neck. (The authors of this book are divided as to which way is better, with one of us being a quote boomerang and the other preferring to write a letter using standard English.)

If you feel constrained to throw somebody's quotes back at him, use the "copy" feature to block out and copy the text you're interested in throwing back at the hapless reader. Start at the first thing you want to quote, and block all the way to the last thing you want to quote. Then hit the "Reply" button. The mailer program will usually insert a comment, followed by all the lines you wish to insert from the original message. These lines will often be prefixed with a special character, such as ">" so that you can tell the quoted lines apart from what your response is. All these lines will be in a block, but you can delete the stuff you don't want to quote and insert your own responses in between the quotes.

For example, look at the letter our friend EarWig sent to his pal Bill, together with two optional replies:

Subj: What about lunch?
Date: 9/30/98 9:02:17 AM EST
To: BillBonz

Bill,
We keep saying we should go to lunch. How about today?

You decide on the time and the place. Anything is fine,
but I prefer a buffet.

Earnest

Here is Bill's response, which was done by quoting Earnest's letter back to him:

Subj: Re: What about lunch?
Date: 9/30/98 9:45:38 AM EST
To: EarWig

In a message dated 9/30/98 9:02:17, EarWig writes:

> Bill,
> We keep saying we should go to lunch. How about today?

That sounds good to me. I'd like to tell you about a
new project I have been planning.

> You decide on the time and the place. Anything is fine,
> but I prefer a buffet.

There is a place by my office that will stuff you for $5.
Why don't you meet me here at 11:30?

Bill

Now look at the same message as a normal human being would write it, without using the "feature" of quoted blocks of text:

Subj: Re: What about lunch?
Date: 9/30/98 9:52:36 AM EST
To: EarWig

Lunch sounds good to me. I'd like to tell you about a
new project I've been planning.

There's a place by my office that will stuff you for $5.
Why don't you meet me here at 11:30?

Bill

Perhaps after looking at the simple, clean readability of the second letter, you'll decide you prefer the old way better. But if you want to use the new and "improved" version that we showed you first, let's review how it was done. Bill highlighted the whole original letter that EarWig had sent to him. Then he hit the "Reply" button. The text that begins "In a message . . " was inserted automatically by the mailer program. Then the mailer program pasted the entire original message onto the reply form, with a ">" prefix to identify each line. Bill then inserted his own comments between the quoted lines, and at the end. (When the same message has been exchanged several times, it is not unusual to see four or five ">" marks prefixed to the front of a line.)

If you receive a letter that was sent to a whole list of people, most mailer programs also give you the option of replying to everyone on the list. "Reply to All" will send your reply back to everyone who received the original message, where using the regular "Reply" option will just send the reply back to the original sender.

Just because the reply function automatically fills in certain areas on the address or subject area doesn't mean you can't change them. In fact, one rule to always remember when using the reply function is to check addresses of people who will be sent your reply. There are a couple of reasons for doing this. First, some people have their mailer options set incorrectly, so that the "From:" area doesn't really contain their e-mail address. Trying to reply to such a message will just copy the bad data into the "To:" field on the reply, and then your message will bounce.

Second, it's a good idea to review the data just to make sure you're doing what you really want to do. For example, perhaps you used the "Reply to All" option when you meant to use "Reply." Just about everyone who uses e-mail in an office can tell you an embarrassing story about how the reply he intended for one person was actually sent to the entire company.

Forward

When reading a message, most mailer programs also give you the option of forwarding the message to someone else. When you use this option, the Compose Mail window will appear. You will need to complete the "To:" and "cc:" sections with the addresses of the persons to receive the message. The subject line will be copied from the original message, usually with a "Fwd:" prefix added, to indicate this is a forwarded message. You may also optionally add text in the text area if you want to make some comments about what is being forwarded. The message you are forwarding usually doesn't appear in the text area, but will be added to the back of the message when you send it. An example of a forwarded message is shown below:

Subj: Fwd: Great New Recipe
Date: 9/30/98 6:45:57 PM EST
From: EarWig@aol.com
To: Jill@prodigy.com

Jill,
With your cooking skills, I'm sure you'll enjoy this!
Earnest

Subj: Great New Recipe
Date: 9/27/98 9:34:07 AM EST

From: Sally@compuserve.com
To: EarWig@aol.com

Mix one can of tuna fish with one jar of chunky peanut
butter. Microwave for 10 minutes. Serve cold. Enjoy!
Sally

Some mail programs allow a specialized kind of forward called a "redirect." This is used when you have received a message that really should have been sent to someone else. A redirect will usually place the original sender's name in the "From:" area, so any reply sent will go back to the proper person, and not to you.

To be a good e-mail citizen, you should avoid messages with long chains of forwarding information. You will notice from the above example that each time the message is forwarded, another set of informational lines is added at the front. Once a message has been forwarded twenty times, there is more junk than message. It's common to receive jokes where you have to scroll down through six pages of junk just to find five lines of joke. If you get one like this that you want to forward, use the old copy-and-paste trick to extract the good stuff, then build a new message with it. Those who receive your message will thank you.

Address Books

A handy feature of most mailer programs is the ability to build and maintain an address book. This contains the e-mail addresses you frequently use, so that you don't have to keep them written down on a piece of paper somewhere.

Address books usually support features such as "add," "modify," and "delete." The entries you create usually contain a description, and one or more e-mail addresses. For example, you could have an entry called "Uncle Buck," that would contain the e-mail address "BuckoCuteo@aol.com." A more complex entry might be "Sewing Club," which would contain the addresses of all the ladies in the club. Many mailing programs allow you to create a new address book entry from the e-mail you are reading. Thus, if you are reading an e-mail from a long-lost college buddy, you can add him to the book for future reference.

When you are composing a message, you can open your address book and use it to fill in the address portions of your message. Sophisticated mailers will also allow you to define shortcut names, and use them when addressing messages. Thus, when you compose a message you might address it to "Mom." Before sending the message, the mailer will find that entry in the address book and replace the shortcut name with your mother's real e-mail address.

File Folders

Most mailer programs allow you to maintain a series of file folders to better keep track of your mail. Sometimes messages are moved from one folder to another automatically, such as when you read messages. Other times, you may manually move a message from one folder to another. The names assigned to the file folders will vary from one mailer to another, but you will typically find a series of folders with names similar to the following:

❏ **New**
   Contains incoming mail that you have not read yet, or mail that was read and then "kept as new."

❏ **Read**
   Contains incoming mail that you have previously read.

❏ **Sent**
   Contains copies of mail that you have sent to others.

❏ **Drafts**
   Contains outgoing messages that you are still writing.

❏ **Trash**
   Contains mail you have deleted. Letters are usually not deleted until you exit the mail program. Prior to that, you may change your mind and move a letter to a different folder to keep it.

❏ **User**
   Some systems allow users to create their own folders. You could create folders with names like "Jokes," "Recipes," and "Family Letters."

You will find that commercial providers are usually the least flexible in terms of the file folders they support. For example, America Online only supports the first three folders listed above, and messages in the "Read" mail folder can only be kept for one to seven days. You can't blame AOL for doing this, because old messages take a huge amount of space on corporate disk drives. Nevertheless, it can be frustrating to look for an old message, only to learn it has disappeared. (America Online does support an option called Personal Filing Cabinet that allows messages to be stored on a permanent basis on your hard drive. This is not only useful for finding old messages, but is a handy tool for monitoring the e-mail activity of other family members. This will be discussed in more detail later in this chapter.)

Some sophisticated mailer programs allow you to apply filters to incoming mail, and to file it in a specific folder based on the sender or the subject. For example, any incoming messages with the word "joke" in the subject line might automatically be filed in a "Joke" folder (or the "Trash" folder if you have no sense of humor).

Delete

All mailers allow you to delete a message you don't want. This usually just moves it to the "Trash" folder, only actually deleting it when you exit the mail program or when you empty the trash. Most mailers also allow you to delete from the Summary screen, so you can delete messages without even opening them. You will find this to be an important feature when you start receiving junk e-mail, as you can safely delete any message with a subject like "Make $100,000 Working at Home!!!"

Unsend

America Online offers a nice feature that allows you to retrieve and erase a message that has been sent to another AOL subscriber, provided the recipient has not read it yet. This only applies to messages sent to other America Online users, and not to addresses in other domains.

Show Status

Some commercial providers allow you to check on the status of a message that you sent. If the recipient has read the message, you can see the date and time the message was read. This feature is only available for messages that were sent within the same service, and not to messages sent elsewhere on the Internet.

Return Receipt Requested

This is similar to Show Status, except that it returns you an e-mail message when the recipient(s) has read the message. This feature is also only available for messages that were sent within the same service.

Signature Files

Many mailers allow their users to put a "signature file" at the end of every message that is sent by that user. This is a small file that contains the name of the user, to save the user the burdensome task of actually having to type his name at the end of every message he sends.

Many who use signature files tend to get carried away with them. They include their name, address, home and work phone numbers, e-mail address, plus a clever quote or saying. If you use a signature file, please be considerate to other users and limit it to no more than five lines of text.

Another abuse of signature files is to include "ASCII art" along with the signature and/or quote. This is a picture that is composed using the characters on your keyboard. ASCII art may be clever the first time you see it, but it quickly gets tedious. Hapless readers who print out your letters may be annoyed when they have to waste an extra sheet of paper to print out the art that you've so cheerfully appended to the end of the letter. Another drawback of ASCII art is that people who use different machines or different screen sizes are unlikely to see the same pretty picture you so carefully composed with your own keyboard. Here is a sample of ASCII art from a signature file:

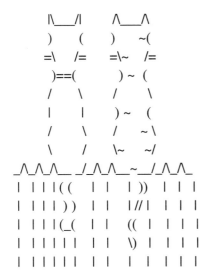

It just warms the cockles of your heart, doesn't it?

File Attachments

The ability to attach files to messages is one of the finest features of e-mail. Assume that you are using your word processor to write the Great American Novel. In the process of sending an e-mail to your mother, you wonder if she would like to read your masterpiece. You simply click the button on your Compose Mail screen that says "Attachments," or "Attach Files," or something similar. The program will bring up a standard Windows "Open" dialog, which will allow you to go through your computer files and select the file you wish to attach. Send the message, and away it goes—carrying with it the word processing file you appended.

Here's what happens on the other end. When your mother receives her mail, she will see an indication that a file attachment is present. There may be an ICON on the Mail Summary screen with a picture of a floppy disk or a file folder, which will tell her a file has come with your letter. Or the text of the letter itself will have a notation that there is a file attached that may be downloaded.

When reading your message, your mother can select an option on her mail reader that will download the file for her. When she clicks on the "Download" ICON or option, the software will open the standard Windows "Save As" dialog, to allow her to specify the file name and the location for saving. After the file is downloaded, Mom can fire up her word processor and read your pearls of wisdom. Mothers being mothers, she might even correct your spelling and grammar, and send the file back to you.

If you think about it, you can come up with nifty uses for file attachments. They can allow you to work at home, by transferring files of your work across town or across the country. They can offer you the opportunity to send pictures of the new baby to everyone you know who has e-mail. If you're a writer who is paranoid about losing your work if the computer crashes or the house burns down, you can upload chapters of a book to yourself on the computer. That way, the chapters will be accessible to you no matter what computer you use at a later date.

Sending file attachments is a terrific feature, but it is also a feature that causes a lot of frustration for new users. Some of this frustration is because of different software versions and operating systems. For example, you might be using version 7.0 of your word processor, but your mother is only using version 6.0. Thus, it is possible she will not be able to read your document, even though she is running the same word processor on the same operating system. Most software is "downward compatible," meaning that it can process earlier versions of its own files, but not "upward compatible," meaning that it cannot handle later versions. Once you are aware of this problem, you can avoid it if you remember to save your document in version 6.0 format, instead of in the version you would normally use.

A larger problem is caused by the fact that most e-mail systems just were not designed to send files. Recall that a byte is composed of 8 bits, and can therefore represent up to 256 different combinations. The problem is that some mail systems are designed to ignore the first bit of each byte. When this is the case, the mail system can only represent 128 characters. That is fine for representing the keys on your keyboard, because they all have values less than 128. But when you throw a file into the mix, especially something like program files or graphics files, then it's pretty certain you will have a lot of bytes where the first bit is used, and, therefore, dropped when the message is sent.

Early e-mail users got around this problem by writing a couple of programs called "uuencode" and "uudecode." If Alphonse Twiddlethumb wanted to send a file to his brother Farfel, he would first process it with the uuencode program, which converted the original file into multiple lines of characters that could safely be sent through an e-mail program because all the byte values were less than 128. After the program was converted, he would then paste those lines into his message and send it.

If you ever see some lines like this in an e-mail message, it is probably a uuencoded file:

```
begin girls.gif 587
MKIWJDHSSKD-WEEUSJDKSI[-SKLKIS97654TE77D6EDJDN
M3KIS983049SKSNU8467583-KKS:SKIEKS,SJHDHGDH787
MOSJDHYE6483HLD]SLKD084773-SJJDJ65SKDJI,9873KJ
MSJKEUJSOIE83U3883-WIJSJJHD-SS87367L
end
```

Once Farfel received the file from his brother, he would run the saved message into the uudecode program. It would find the lines of encoded characters in the message, and convert them back into a file in the original format. This was a pretty complicated way to send a file, but it did work with only minor problems. Even today, many mail readers still have an option where the user can run uudecode against the message he is reading.

Most mail readers have been upgraded to support a newer standard, known as MIME (Multipurpose Internet Mail Extensions). Like its earlier cousin, uuencode, MIME converts files into characters within the message that can be safely transmitted over the e-mail system. On the other end, MIME then converts those lines back into the original files. MIME can handle multiple files in one transmission, and can handle just about any kind of file.

The main problem you find with MIME is that not all e-mail systems have been upgraded to support it yet. You are pretty safe when sending an attachment to someone in your same domain, but could run into trouble when sending it to someone using a system with an older mail system.

When sending files via MIME to another user, one of three things will happen:

1. If the user's system supports the same version of MIME, he will be able to decode and download all the files.
2. If the user's system is ignorant of MIME, he will get a bunch of strange garbage lines included at the end of the message.
3. If the user's system supports an older version of MIME, it may recognize that you have sent a MIME file, but may not know how to decode it. It will give you the option of saving it as a MIME file, and you can then run an external decoder program to break it into the multiple files.

Although older mailer programs usually limited you to one attachment per message, some of the newer versions are allowing multiple attachments.

If someone sends you a file and its extension name is ZIP, it means you have been sent a "compressed" file. Compression programs are useful when sending file attachments, because the sender can combine multiple files together and compress them, usually reducing their original size by fifty to ninety percent. This means the message can be sent faster, because only one small file is being sent, rather than multiple large ones. If you receive a zipped file, you need to uncompress it and extract the original files.

Some commercial providers, such as America Online, have options to automatically uncompress such files after you download them. Otherwise, you will need to get and install some of the compression software you can download from the software sites listed in Chapter 7.

If you are trying to attach a text document and not having much success, you do have the option of doing a cut-and-paste from your word processing program into your mailing program, and sending the message as plain text. One problem with this is that some mailers don't like long messages and will either cut them off or will convert them back into attachments, leaving you with unreadable text.

Users new to e-mail often have trouble understanding file attachments. If you're sending a file attachment to a new user, you may want to include detailed step-by-step instructions in your message, telling them exactly what to do to retrieve your file. If you're the one on the receiving end, go to the "help" area of your client server or Internet provider.

MAILING LISTS

There is an Internet feature called a "mailing list" that expands upon e-mail technology to send regular mailings to a group of people with similar interests. For example, Clark has a friend who sends out a list of jokes every Friday morning. All the people on the list find a new set of jokes waiting for them when they check their mail on Friday. Anyone who likes the jokes and wants to receive his own copy can send a request to the jokester, and he will add the new name to his list. On the other hand, if someone decides he doesn't have time to read the jokes, he can send a message and get removed.

Mailing lists may not use the most sophisticated technology, but they use e-mail in a way that turns a letter into something that is more of a newsletter than an e-mail message. Remember at the start of this chapter how we said that e-mail was a lot like postal mail, and you could even subscribe to magazines and newsletters? Well, we're about to teach you how to subscribe to more newsletters than you could ever read in a lifetime.

Newsletter Versus Discussion

The joke mailing that we just mentioned is an example of a newsletter mailing list. The members who subscribe to the list don't really contribute to it. Instead, they are the recipients of someone else's work and opinions. A mailing list is a one-way communications medium, in the same sense that a newsletter would be. People who are interested in the subject of the "newsletter" are welcome to subscribe, just as they would subscribe to a newsletter that they received in the mail. There are thousands of these newsletter type mailing lists, focusing on everything from UFO sightings, to stock tips, to gardening hints.

The second type of mailing list is called a discussion list, because it features ongoing discussions among the members of the mailing list. Unlike a newsletter, which reflects the efforts of one or two people, it is the members themselves who provide all of the content in a discussion list. Assume there is a mailing list used to discuss the music of the Beatles. Perhaps the e-mail address of the mailing list is "beatles@xyz.com." If you have a comment to make about the music of the Beatles, you can compose an e-mail message and send it to the address of the discussion group. But instead of going to just one person, it will go to everyone who subscribes to the mailing list, whether that be one hundred people or one hundred thousand people. Likewise, whenever anyone else sends a message to that group, you will also get a copy of their message. As you can see, if you subscribe to a large, active group, you will certainly get practice reading your e-mail.

Moderated Versus Open

Sometimes a discussion mailing list will be "moderated." This means that all new messages will go to a moderator, who will filter the messages and only send relevant ones to the rest of the list. So, using the example given previously, perhaps you will send a comment to the Beatles list. The moderator will read your message, and determine whether it would be of interest to the other members. If so, he will forward it to the rest of the list and it will be sent out to everyone. Moderated lists are usually the best option, provided you have a good monitor who is fair. His job is to keep out the junk and the duplicate information, not to suppress comments just because he happens to disagree with them.

The open, or unmoderated, list is just what it says. All postings are forwarded to all members of the list with no editing or filtering. This is fine for a small list, but it can cause problems when you get too many members, or when you get a few members who insist on dominating the list or being rude to other members.

Digests

Some mailing lists support a digest option, which means that user contributions will be grouped together and sent in one e-mail message. Unless you want to see each message as it is sent, this is usually a better option, because you can end up getting one or two large messages a day, rather than forty to one hundred small ones.

One danger of the digest option is that large messages may not be handled well by your mail program. It may break one large message into several smaller ones, or it may turn a long message into an attachment that you will have to download and then view with another program after you read the rest of your mail. Although neither of these options will lose your messages, both of them defeat the convenience of the digest option if you have to work harder to read it.

Sometimes a digest version will be maintained as a separate list. For example, you would subscribe to "beatles" if you wanted the regular list, and "beatles-digest" if you wanted the digest version. Other times, the list only has one name and you use an option of the mailing list manager to enable or disable digest mode.

Finding a List

At the time we were writing this book, there were just under 85,000 different mailing lists in various stages of activity. With that many different lists to choose from, you can be sure they cover the gamut of topics from A to Z. In fact, just for fun, we sampled five lists from the A group:

- An open, unmoderated discussion list about playing the acoustic guitar.
- A list to discuss issues of importance to families with the surname of Abernathy.
- A list for adoptive parents, to discuss the everyday life experiences and challenges.
- A discussion of the Appalachian Trail, including long-distance hiking.
- A list for people who are interested in and will try to get Perpetual Adoration of the Eucharist set up in a Roman Catholic parish.

Then we jumped to the other end of the scale, and selected five from the Z group. Our choices were fewer here, and most of them were related to music:

- A list discussing Trevor Horn's UK record label Zang Tuum Tumb and the bands that have appeared on it over the years.
- A list for the discussion of the legendary rock and roll band "Led Zeppelin."
- A broadcast list from a publishing house named Zondervan that specializes in Christian publications.
- A forum for the music of John Zorn and other artists/musicians from the downtown NYC avant-jazz-improv scene.
- A list for fans of the blues rock band ZZ Top.

One of the most common ways to find out about an interesting list is to hear about it from a friend. Perhaps your friend will find something interesting on a list and forward a copy to you. If you like what you see, often the instructions for subscribing are right in the message you were forwarded. Or, you can contact your friend and ask him for more information.

An updated list of many groups is published regularly in the Newsgroup *news.lists.misc* (see Chapter 4). There are also several web sites that allow you to search for interesting mailing lists. We know we haven't talked about web sites yet, but we will in Chapter 6:

www.egroups.com
www.escribe.com
www.liszt.com
www.neosoft.com/internet/pam1
www.reference.com

The last two listed above are interesting, because they store the postings from many mailing lists on their web sites. Rather than having to subscribe to the lists and read them in your mailbox, you can read them at these sites using your web browser (again, if this all sounds like Greek, read Chapter 6).

The last site also gives you the option of creating your own mailing lists.

Joining and Leaving

When you find the mailing lists that look interesting to you, there should also be information about how to go about subscribing to them. For small mailing lists, sometimes this is a manual process. When you send an e-mail request to subscribe, a real human being reads your request and adds your address to the list.

Because a major mailing list can sometimes get dozens of new subscription requests per day, many lists use an automated subscription process. This means that the e-mail request you send to subscribe is not read by a human, but by a program that processes your request. This type of program is called a mailing list manager, and there are three different ones that will most commonly be used. We will discuss them in a moment.

Because your subscription request will be handled by a program instead of a human, it is important that you follow the directions exactly, and don't make any spelling errors, or your request will fail.

Once your request has been processed by the mailing list manager, it will send back one or more e-mails with the results of your request. If you made a mistake so that the program couldn't determine what you were trying to do, it will tell you so. If that happened, just send a new message without the mistake and try again.

Sometimes you will get a message back that the program is processing your request, but that you need to send back another message to confirm the request. This is done because sometimes pranksters will subscribe on behalf of other people. Asking for a confirmation is just one way to make sure you are not the victim of a prank. If this happens, and you do want to subscribe, then follow the directions and send back your confirmation.

Once you are subscribed, you will get back a confirmation message telling you so. That message will also usually give directions on how to unsubscribe if you decide you want to leave the list. Print out those directions and keep them in a safe place. If you don't, you may have to jump through all kinds of hoops when you want to leave and can't remember how.

Stay on the list for a couple of days, and see how you like it. If you receive too many messages, or the content of the list was not what you had in mind, feel free to unsubscribe. After all, your requests are handled by a mailing list manager, and you won't hurt its feelings.

Using Mailing List Managers

As we noted previously, there are three common programs that are used to manage requests for mailing lists. You will know you are using one of these if the mailbox to which you send your request is one of the following:

- Majordomo
- ListProc
- ListServ

For example, if the instructions for subscribing to a list specify that you should send your message to "majordomo@bradley.edu," the "majordomo" mailbox indicates you are using the Majordomo mailing list manager program.

All of these programs work quite similarly. You send a message to the mailing list manager at the domain name where the mailing list resides. The subject line in your e-mail is ignored by the mailing list manager, so leave it blank or just put anything there. Each line in the message text contains a new command for the mailing list manager to process. For example, here is a sample request to subscribe to a mailing list about the music of the Beatles:

```
Subj: x
To: majordomo@bradley.edu
```

```
subscribe beatles
end
```

The commands accepted by all three mailing list manager programs are similar, and yet slightly different. Below we will give examples of some of the common commands you might find useful with each program:

Majordomo

❑ **subscribe beatles**

Subscribes you to the named list.

❑ **unsubscribe beatles**

Stops the subscription for the named list.

❑ **info beatles**

Returns information about the named list.

❑ **index beatles**

Returns an index of available files for the named list.

❑ **get beatles charter**

Returns the named file associated with the named list.

❑ **who beatles**

Shows who is subscribed to the named list.

❑ **which**

Shows the lists at this domain to which you are subscribed.

❑ **lists**

Shows all the lists available at this domain.

❑ **help**

Provides help about the Majordomo commands.

❑ **end**

Stops processing — use this when you have a signature file.

ListProc

❑ **subscribe beatles John Doe**

Subscribes the indicated person to the named list.

❑ **unsubscribe beatles**

Stops the subscription for the named list.

❑ **information beatles**

Returns information about the named list.

❑ **review beatles short**

Returns a short description of the named list.

❑ **review beatles description**

Returns a longer description of the named list.

❑ **recipients beatles**

   Shows who is subscribed to the named list.

❑ **set beatles conceal yes**

   Hides your name and e-mail address from other users.

❑ **which**

   Shows the lists at this domain to which you are subscribed.

❑ **lists**

   Shows all the lists available at this domain.

❑ **help**

   Provides help about the ListProc commands.

ListServ

❑ **subscribe beatles John Doe**

   Subscribes the indicated person to the named list.

❑ **signoff beatles**

   Stops the subscription for the named list.

❑ **info beatles**

   Returns information about the named list.

❑ **confirm beatles**

   Confirms your subscription request to the named list.

❑ **stats beatles**

   Returns statistics about the named list.

❑ **set beatles dig**

   Sets digest mode on for the named list.

❑ **set beatles nodig**

   Sets digest mode off for the named list.

❑ **set beatles conceal**

   Hides your name and e-mail address from other users.

❑ **lists**

   Shows all the lists available at this domain.

❑ **help**

   Provides help about the ListServ commands.

If you are having trouble with one of the options above, use the "Help" option to get an updated version of the mailing list manager instructions. It could be that your program is a different version from the one described here, and the commands are slightly different. It is useful to play around with help anyway, as you may find some options we didn't cover in the above summary.

Posting to a Mailing List

When you subscribe to a mailing list, don't jump in with both feet. "Lurk" for a while, reading posts from other members to see what sort of conversations you can find in the group, as well as the tone of that particular group. If you take this precaution, it will save you the embarrassment of jumping right in with both feet and making a fool of yourself. Many mailing lists maintain a FAQ (Frequently Asked Questions) file. If your mailing list has such a file, be sure to read it. This is the place where you can find answers to common questions you may have about the list itself, or about the subject that the list addresses. Use some of the commands listed above to see what information is available about the list, and then request and read the information. This will keep you from making statements or asking questions that are out of place, or that have already been answered a dozen times.

Before you attempt to post a message, you need to understand the different addresses that are available for a mailing list. Using the hypothetical Beatles mailing list, there will usually be three e-mail addresses associated with it:

majordomo@bradley.edu
beatles@bradley.edu
owner-beatles@bradley.edu

The first address is the administrative address, or the address of the mailing list manager program. That is where you send requests for administrative functions, such as subscribe, and unsubscribe. The second address is the list address. Mailing to that address will send your message to everyone on the list, or to the list moderator. The third address will direct your message to the person designated as the manager of the particular list. Keeping these lists straight will spare you a lot of grief.

Everyone who has subscribed to a unmoderated discussion group mailing list has had the experience of seeing a message posted to the list saying something like:

Dear Sir,
I hear you have a nice list.
I would like to subscribe.

My e-mail address is DumbBunny@aol.com
Thanks,
Norman Neophyte

This is obviously a person who has no understanding of how a mailing list works, and who thinks you subscribe by sending a request like this to all 50,000 people who are already members of the list. Letters such as this one usually result in a flood of angry e-mail, telling the poor neophyte that he's an idiot. If he's lucky, a couple of people will take pity on him, and send him instructions for subscribing the right way. Of course, now that you've read this section, you would never make a mistake like that, would you?

MAIL ROBOT

One final interesting application of e-mail technology is something called a mail robot. This is similar to the technology used in the mailing list manager programs. A mail robot is a program that responds to commands by sending data back to the requester.

For example, a government health agency may have a large number of research papers available to the public on health-related issues. The agency could set up a server to handle requests to mail those documents to interested citizens. People would make a request by sending an e-mail message to the robot, containing commands much like those used in the mailing list manager programs. For example, a person could first request an index of all available papers, and then make requests for individual papers by order number. The mail robot would retrieve the requested paper from the hard drive, format it into an e-mail message, and send it back to the requester.

An interesting adaptation of this technology is used by America Online for something called a "news profile." A subscriber who is interested in building a news profile can ask to see news items related to specific topics. For example, if you had a deep and burning interest in UFOs and Elvis Presley, you could create a profile to have the program search for the words "UFO" and "Elvis." Every time a news release or news story gets sent to America Online, the mail robot would compare the story against your profile. If either of the words in the profile is found in the story, the story will be e-mailed to you so you can see what the UFOs are doing these days, and whether there have been any Elvis sightings. (If Elvis is ever found on a UFO, you'll hit the jackpot.) This is a valuable service for keeping track of topics that are important to you, without having to read a dozen newspapers each day.

E-MAIL ETIQUETTE

As you learned in Chapter 1, all communities have their rules of behavior, and this applies to the Internet community as well. Following these rules will make your Internet experience more enjoyable, and will also benefit those with whom you interact. Here are some rules to keep in mind while using e-mail. Most of these are just common sense, but they're listed here anyway—just in case you haven't thought of them.

General Guidelines

Keep in mind that e-mail is usually not as formal as a letter you would send through the mail. In tone, e-mail messages are often more like spoken communication. Because e-mail is so easy that you can fire off letter after letter until an issue is clarified, e-mail letters tend to be shorter than letters that would go through the mail system. Thus you can have a conversation via e-mail that consists of such terse statements as, "Dinner tonight?" "Sounds good." "When? Where?" "The Rio Grande, 7 p.m." "Okay." Needless to say, the conversation would not be held in these brief bursts if the letters were being sent via a letter carrier.

When we meet new people in person, part of our impression is based upon their appearance, their actions, and their mannerisms. None of these things are present with e-mail communication. When you communicate by e-mail, you are known to others only by your words. This can be a two-edged sword. On one hand, people will not factor your age, your sex, your appearance, or your race into what you have to say. Your message will be judged by the message alone.

But on the other hand, when you're judged only by your words, every word counts. If you don't use proper spelling and grammar, people will think less of you. After all, they can't judge you on anything other than what you say and how you say it. They won't know you have a PhD in physics, or that you were voted Miss Congeniality in the Miss America pageant. All they see is that you either don't know or don't care when an apostrophe should go in "its," and when to use "their" instead of "there." That makes you either ignorant or sloppy—neither of which is a ringing endorsement for you.

If you can't spell to save your life (and a lot of smart people can't), that doesn't mean you can't communicate online. Most mailing programs have spell checkers these days. It won't take you more than a few moments to spell-check your document before it goes out, making your thoughts more legible to those who read them.

Another problem with e-mail is that written words convey little emotion. When we talk to others, we communicate through gestures, facial expressions, and tone of voice, as well as through our words. All of these visual cues are missing from e-mail. This means you must be extremely delicate in the way you write things. Sarcasm doesn't translate to the written word—it just makes you come across as hostile and obnoxious. The written word comes across as being so much colder than face-to-face conversation that if you write a letter that is so obsequious that you feel as though you kissed the feet of the recipient, your letter will probably be interpreted in the same way that the recipient would interpret your normal face-to-face conversation.

Even if your correspondence is always calm and gentle and kind, this does not mean that people will necessarily extend the same courtesy to you. Some people who would never raise a voice in a person-to-person conversation are capable of turning into raging maniacs when using e-mail, and especially when using mailing lists. It's not uncommon to express an honest opinion in a discussion, only to open your e-mail the next day and find a nasty, vile response from some stranger who may insult your intelligence, your parentage, and your family dog. The very fact that there's a name for these red-hot letters (they're called "flames," for obvious reasons) tells you that this is a common problem on the Internet. The best thing to do is to just ignore the message, fighting off the urge to send your own flame back in response. In many mailing lists, particularly those that address subjects such as politics and religion, a large percentage of the message traffic consists of "flame wars" between members of the list. Life is too short for this aggravation. Don't allow yourself to be sucked into hostility and contention.

Another thing to remember when using e-mail is that you shouldn't assume that anything you write is private. You may send a piece of private correspondence to someone, assuming that what you say will be treated in confidence, only to find that your message has been forwarded to several states. And the recipients of your e-mail are not the only offenders. If you use e-mail at work or at school, many companies and government agencies have the right to monitor your mail if they choose. If you want to share a secret with someone else, do it face-to-face and in private, but certainly not via an e-mail message.

Capitalization

When you communicate via e-mail, try to use proper capitalization in your written messages. For some reason, many people who are new to the Internet tend to want to turn on the Caps Lock key, AND TYPE ALL THEIR MESSAGES IN

UPPERCASE. This is considered to be the Internet equivalent of shouting. If you want to make people angry, writing your messages in all-caps is a sure-fire way to do it. Save your Caps Lock key for telegrams. Regular e-mail messages consist of both capital and lowercase letters.

By the same token, don't write your messages in all lowercase letters. This is a common problem with teenagers, who have been exposed to e.e. cummings in junior high and think his idea of writing in all lowercase is just too cool for words. Only a child would be so pretentious as to refuse to type the personal pronoun "I" in uppercase, but there are tens of thousands—perhaps hundreds of thousands—of teenagers who show us their individuality by typing in exactly the same way.

The same teenagers who shy away from capital letters also seem to be attracted to alternate spellings of common words. A lovely example of a creatively and ungrammatically constructed sentence is "itz kewl cuz i sez so." These messages are annoying to read, but they're more than that. It's extremely dangerous to let your child write like this in a public forum because this kind of writing is a dead giveaway that the author is a young person. You and your children should always keep in mind that there is a small percentage of predators online who are trying to find young people for sinister purposes. Allowing your children to act in a way that identifies them as children is like hanging a "fresh young meat" sign around their necks! Teaching them to write like adults will teach them the skills they need to be adults, and will also give them some level of protection.

Abbreviations

One of the things that might puzzle you when you start using e-mail and mailing lists is the appearance of strange abbreviations in some messages. The official reason given for this is that online people type a lot each day, and they want to save time and avoid medical problems such as carpal tunnel syndrome. We suspect the real reason is that the use of such abbreviations makes them part of the "in group," and confuses all the newcomers.

In any case, below is just a sample listing of some of the abbreviations you will see online. We would urge you use them sparingly, if at all, in your online conversations.

AFAIK	As Far As I Know
AFK	Away From Keyboard
ASAP	As Soon As Possible

BAK	Back At Keyboard
BBL	Be Back Later
BRB	Be Right Back
BTW	By The Way
CU	See You
CUL8R	See You Later
DH	Darling Husband
DW	Darling Wife
FAQ	Frequently Asked Question
FYI	For Your Information
F2F	Face to Face
G,D&R	Grinning, Ducking & Rolling (on the floor)
GMTA	Great Minds Think Alike
GTRM	Going To Read Mail
HTH	Hope This Helps
IMHO	In My Humble Opinion
IMNSHO	In My Not So Humble Opinion
IMO	In My Opinion
J/K	Just Kidding
LOL	Laughing Out Loud
MorF	Male or Female?
OIC	Oh, I See
OTOH	On The Other Hand
PMJI	Pardon Me (for) Jumping In
ROFL	Rolling On the Floor Laughing
RTFM	Read The Friggin' Manual
TIA	Thanks In Advance
TNX	Thanks
TTFN	Ta-Ta For Now
TTYL	Talk To You Later
WB	Welcome Back
WTG	Way To Go
YSR	Yeah, Sure, Right

Emoticons

As noted earlier, sometimes it is difficult to determine a person's feelings just from his written words. Because of this, some people add little symbols to their messages to try and convey their state of mind. These are called "Emoticons," which is a combination of the words emotion and ICON. Sometimes they are also called "Smileys." The idea is to turn your head sideways, to the left, and the Emoticon will look like a face expressing various emotions.

A few of the more common Emoticons are shown below. As with abbreviations, please try to use them in moderation—if you feel as though you have to use them at all.

:)	little smile
:-)	regular smile
:^)	regular smile in profile
;-)	smile and a wink
:>	a little happy
:D	very happy
:*	blowing a kiss
*<;-)	clown in a pointed hat
:(	sadness
:<	pouting
:/	disappointment
:|	mild disgust
>:(	anger
8)	person wearing glasses
B)	person wearing sunglasses
:X	my lips are sealed
:o	mild surprise
=:o	big surprise that raises your hair
:~(	crying
0;^)	angel with halo
};^)	devil with horns
:9	licking your lips
:6	sticking out tongue, sad
:p	sticking out tongue, happy
:<>	yawning
<g>	grin
<grin>	grin
grin	grin

<bg>	big grin
<vbg>	very big grin
<eg>	evil grin
<xeg>	extra evil grin
<s>	smile

WHERE DANGER LURKS

Now that you are somewhat familiar with the concepts of e-mail, we can turn our attention to potential problems that it may cause. Once you start to understand the dangers, you will better understand the measures that can be taken to minimize the damage that can be done by e-mail abuse.

Junk Mail

By far, the worst danger associated with e-mail is found in the unsolicited advertisements that arrive in your mailbox each day. Most of these are certainly not meant for the eyes of children—unless you want your children to be subjected to pornography, moneymaking schemes, questionable health products, hot stock tips, and other dubious items. This electronic junk mail is often called "spam." Why it got this name is unclear, although many speculate it relates to an old Monty Python skit about Vikings who ate nothing but Spam.

The flood of spam is a major problem for most service providers, because it consumes a huge amount of resources to deliver mail that most people just delete, and it also wastes the time of employees trying to locate and terminate the accounts of "spammers," or those who send spam to others. America Online has estimated, for example, that of the 30 million messages that pass through its system each day, thirty percent of those are spam.

Most legitimate companies advertise in other more traditional ways, leaving the spam arena to those small-time hustlers trying to make a fast buck with little or no investment. This is obvious from the content of their messages, which often contain embarrassing spelling errors that no marketing department would ever let through. In the thousands of spam messages we have received over the years, we have yet to buy a product or service that has been pitched to us via spamming.

When we were researching this book, Clark decided to do some informal research, so he tabulated all the spam that arrived in his mailbox during the month. During that time, he received 168 junk messages, or slightly more than five per day.

This does not count several duplicates of some messages. The breakdown of these 168 messages by category is as follows:

Online Pornography (56%)

Invitations to visit Internet sites that display all kinds of pornography. Featuring college girls, cheerleaders, preteenage children, older women, couples and groups, amateur photos, straight sex, gay men, and lesbians. Spam caters to all preferences and perversions.

Make Big Money Fast (24%)

Offers to make you rich through chain letters, selling toys, government auctions, hot stocks, gambling tips and low-cost phone service. Lots of multi-level marketing (MLM) schemes, and ways that you can make money at home with your computer.

Buy This Product (8%)

Offers trying to sell different kinds of health products, insurance, pagers, investment property, novelty items, and even a drug to cure hangovers.

Solve Credit Problems (6%)

Offers to help you obtain loans, qualify for credit cards, get a copy of your credit report, or fix a bad credit rating.

Internet-Related (6%)

Companies that show you how to advertise on the Internet, and how to accept credit cards when you do get orders. Invitations to visit other Internet sites to purchase what they are selling. Offers for software that allows you to send your own spam to others, making the problem even worse.

Before you get too alarmed at this flood of junk mail, we need to state that we have had the same e-mail addresses for nearly ten years, and we are probably on every junk mailing list in the world. Because we got our e-mail addresses before the advent of spam, we failed to follow a lot of the advice we are giving you in this book about avoiding junk e-mail. Thus, hopefully you can benefit from the mistakes we made when we were new to e-mail.

Hypertext Links

As if the spam for pornographic web sites weren't bad enough, many of these messages contain something called a "hypertext link" that will take you directly to the site, without any effort on your part beyond one click on the underlined word. At the risk of making you lose your lunch, shown below is one of the e-mails that Clark received when he was tabulating junk e-mails. We hope you won't be offended by the advertisement printed below, but we need to emphasize that this is no-holds-barred marketing, and many of the creeps who are peddling pornography have no reservations about sending such trash to millions of e-mail addresses, many of which may belong to children.

THE WEB'S BEST HARDCORE!!

Hot Oral & Anal Sex, Lesbo Action, Gang Bangs, Bestiality...
We've got it ALL!
Over 2,000,000 Pix, Video, and Stories to Drive you Wild!

Click Here for Some Free Hardcore Pix.

Your Search for the Ultimate Hardcore Site has Ended!

You notice how the next to last line is underlined? It also appeared on the computer screen as a pretty blue color, as opposed to the black typeface of the rest of the message. The blue line is a hypertext link. Clicking on that line would have started up Clark's web browser (see Chapter 6), and taken him immediately to a site that displayed all different kinds of pornography. Most of these sites have opening screens that warn the viewer what he is about to see, and advise him that he should only continue if he is eighteen years of age and is not offended by such material. These screens are added purely for legal reasons; you can imagine that few teenage boys are going to be stopped by such a warning. Another thing that may not stop your teenage son is the fact that most of the "good" stuff is hidden until the customer gives a credit card number and becomes a subscriber. Many unsuspecting parents have received credit card bills where hundreds and thousands of dollars were charged to one porno site or another by a teenager who gained access to the card just long enough to get the card number and the expiration date. But even if your child would never use your card, he can still see enough raw material during the sneak preview to singe his eyebrows. Even the free preview usually contains material much more raw than you would see on the pages of a typical girlie magazine.

Unsolicited Mail

Although spam is always unsolicited, the usual intent of spam is to make money by having you buy a product or service. There are other categories of unsolicited e-mail that are usually not designed to make money, at least not directly. Although these are not as annoying as spam, they can be an irritation, and they can be dangerous. Most of these unsolicited requests fall into four categories, which we will describe briefly:

Letters from Strangers

This doesn't happen very often, but occasionally you will receive a letter from a total stranger. Sometimes a friend has given your e-mail address to someone else, who is writing with some kind of legitimate question or request. Clark will occasionally get letters from people researching their genealogy, asking him about the Kidd family. This is because his surname is part of his e-mail address. He could probably avoid these letters if he changed his user name to something less specific, like "Big-Bunny." But then he would probably get questions from rabbit farmers!

Letters from strangers are usually pretty innocent, and most adults can handle them with no problem. The real danger comes when children start to receive such letters, because they can just as easily be sent by people with sinister intent. Child molesters and pedophiles will often spend time in various online areas, just looking for children to approach. As noted earlier, the writing and spelling habits of young children will often betray their age, and possibly their sex. Once the pedophile has the user name of the child, it is a simple process to send an e-mail and try to start a friendship. Many of these characters will assume roles, often pretending to be other children, and wanting to be friends and exchange personal information with your child. Because children are less cynical than adults, they will often take these requests at face value, and play along with these schemes. That is why you need to teach them differently.

Chain Letters

Many of the same silly chain letters that have been going through the mail for years have now found new life on the Internet. Some want you to send money to those ahead of you on the list, but many just want you to pass on the letter to ten other people for "good luck." You'd be surprised how many otherwise intelligent people who would never waste a stamp on such a letter will gladly send it to ten online friends, probably because e-mail is just so easy to use. If you really want to do your friends a favor, use your Delete key.

Hoaxes

A few months ago, a friend forwarded an interesting letter. According to the letter, Microsoft was testing a new e-mail tracking system, and somehow the company would be able to test the progress of this letter as it was forwarded all over the world to different people. In order to thank those who participated, the first one thousand people who got the letter would be given $1000, plus a copy of Windows 98.

That same day, we got a similar letter from another friend who lived clear across the country from the first friend. This version was pretty much the same, although the first one thousand people were going to be given the money, plus a trip to Disney World.

Both of our friends had been victims of e-mail hoaxes. Many of these stories, or "urban legends," have been around for years, passed verbally from one person to another. But the Internet has given life to some of these same old stories, often updated to add new details. Many years ago there was a recipe being passed around for a red velvet cake, and there was a story that went with the recipe. It seems a woman really loved a red velvet cake that was served in a hotel restaurant. When she asked how much the chef would charge to give her the recipe, she was told "two-fifty." Thinking the charge was $2.50, she bought the recipe, only to find out when her charge card bill came that the charge was $250.00. She was determined to get even with the chef by sharing the recipe with everyone she met. There are two versions of this old chestnut that regularly circulate around the Internet. One is for Mrs. Field's chocolate chip cookies, and the other is for Neiman-Marcus chocolate chip cookies. Other online hoaxes that have been popular within the last few years are the boy/girl who is dying and wants to collect cards/letters; the "Good Times" virus that destroys your computer; the "modem tax" the FCC is going to levy on new modems; and the scuba diver scooped from the ocean and dropped on a forest fire.

All these stories are fun to read, but take them with a very large grain of salt before forwarding them on to any of your (former) friends.

Scams

Among the most dangerous unsolicited messages you might receive are scams designed to cheat you out of goods or money. America Online regularly has a problem with people sending e-mail and claiming to be AOL employees. These letters will claim that there is a problem with the account, and AOL needs the user's password to correct it. Another version is that there is a billing problem, and AOL needs a credit card number or the account will be deactivated. Obviously, both of these are just scams designed to use your AOL account or your credit card number. These scams are apparently so popular that many of the AOL areas have been updated to include warnings such as, "An AOL employee will never ask for your password or billing information."

It's amazing how many human beings who are normally intelligent can fall for one or another of these scams. Many of these e-mail requests have grammatical and spelling errors, and are obviously the work of really dumb criminals or really young kids. But even if the request looks as though it was designed by a pro, treat any such request with suspicion until you can verify the facts.

Mailing Lists

Mailing lists are a wonderful way to bring information into your mailbox, but they do present some risks as well, especially for those lists that support unmoderated discussion groups. When you consider that anyone can send any message to all the recipients of the list, and there will be no censorship or editing, you can easily see the potential for trouble. Your family may be exposed to profane or obscene language, racism, sexism, and people whose ideas and values are far different from yours. Newsletter or moderated discussion lists are usually safer, although even there you are allowing an editor or moderator to be your filter as to what is proper.

Posting to a mailing list can also generate problems. Although personal e-mail you send is limited to a small audience of acquaintances, messages sent to a mailing list may reach an audience of tens of thousands. Thus, you expose your ideas and opinions to many others. Even if all the messages you post are so vanilla that no human being could possibly take offense to what you say, people can—and will, especially on lists dealing with controversial topics. Hostile responses are pretty common occurrences. Many people are not shy about sending flame mail to others, so you might generate some replies that are pretty blistering. This is even more traumatic if the flamer chooses to post his response to the entire list, leaving you open to further ridicule. Adults and older teens can usually weather this kind of storm, but it can be a bit much for younger children or even adults who have fragile egos.

Another danger of posting is that it exposes your e-mail address to the world. If all you send are private e-mails to others, you pretty much have control over who knows your e-mail address. But if you post to a mailing list, your address is fair game for anyone. Predators and other people who have less-than-honorable intentions make a practice of monitoring various mailing lists and trying to start up private e-mail conversations with those who post to the list. If the person who is targeted for a private e-mail exchange is a teenager or a younger child in your home, there may be trouble down the road.

There is some danger in subscribing to a mailing list, even if you never post to it. If you'll remember, the mailing list manager programs have commands that will show you the subscribers to a given list. Unscrupulous persons can get your name and e-mail address even if you lurk silently and never post. (Some mailing list managers have options to prevent this, and we will discuss these later.)

Even if your family members are never targeted by predators, another reason to keep your e-mail address private is that going public will subject you to even more spam. Most spammers have programs that read through mailing lists and other public forums and "harvest" the e-mail addresses found there. Once spammers have a mailing list, they often trade it or sell it to other spammers.

File Attachments

Although it is handy to be able to send a file as part of an e-mail, such attachments may also be the source of potential problems. The biggest problem is from viruses, which are programs intentionally written to cause some kind of damage to your computer. These programs usually present themselves as being a useful or fun tool, such as a game. When you run the program, it may or may not perform as you would expect, but it also infects your system with the virus, which usually doesn't appear until later. While the virus is lying dormant in your system, it is probably spreading itself to other files, or to floppy disks that you create. Those disks may then infect other computers, before you notice that you have a problem. When the virus finally starts to act, the results can range anywhere from annoying to catastrophic. Some viruses simply clear the screen on occasion, or produce an unexpected message. Others will damage files, or possibly erase all the files on your hard drive.

There is much misunderstanding concerning the nature of viruses and e-mail. One of the hoaxes mentioned above, the "Good Times" virus, caused a lot of fear a few years ago when it was making the rounds. According to the hoax, the virus would infect your system when you opened an e-mail with the subject line of "Good Times."

As a general rule, you cannot damage your computer or catch a virus just by opening an e-mail, even if there is a file attachment included with it. Even if you download a virus-infected file, you are usually safe from the virus until you actually run that file as a program, or open it in some way.

Attachments are often used to send pornographic images. Such images are created by processing a real photograph with a scanner, or by using a "digital camera." Once the image is in digital format, it is stored in a graphics file that can be used to record any type of photograph or line drawing. There are various types of graphics files, but the two most common usually have the extensions JPG or GIF. Refer to the appendix for more details.

We'll learn in Chapter 6 how a web browser can be used to visit pornographic web sites and save copies of the photographs that are there. Once a copy is made, it is a simple matter to attach it to e-mails and send it to other friends who are interested in such material, or even friends who may not be interested. Many pedophiles use e-mail attachments to trade copies of their favorites with their like-minded friends.

Another variation of the attachment is a feature that is provided by some commercial services, in which the user is allowed to imbed pictures and send them as part of an e-mail message. This usually works only when sending mail to someone within the same service. The imbedded pictures are sent with a technology similar to that used for attachments, but instead of having to download them and view them outside of the mailer program, the mailer program makes the pictures available to the view of anyone who reads the mail.

File attachments aren't just problems when they come into the home. If your children don't understand that some things are not designed to be shared, one of them could unwittingly undermine your family's security. Any file on your computer could be a target for being sent to others. Is there anything stored there that could cause you embarrassment? Do you really want Junior sending copies of your latest tax return or your personal journal to his friends?

Outgoing Mail

As a general rule, incoming mail has a great potential for nuisance, but outgoing mail can invite more of a threat. If you and your children are scrupulous about following the rules in this book, you may never find any pornography in your e-mail box. Instead, most of the potential for real problems occurs when you start sending things in the other direction.

Sending e-mail is fun, and it's also increasingly necessary in our highly technical world. But you should make sure that every member of your family follows the rules of sending mail. It's always a good practice for your children to pause for just a second over that "send" button, giving them time to make sure they are not doing something that would expose them to later trouble.

AVOIDING PROBLEMS

Now that you have seen the threats, let's make some suggestions that should help you avoid most of the problems mentioned above. If some of those problems do occur, we will also try to show you some ways to fight back.

Establish Some Rules

You should establish some definite rules about the use of e-mail, and should make sure all your children know them and agree to them. Review the general guidelines we gave in the last chapter, particularly the ones about disclosing personal information to others. As you read through this chapter, particularly the previous section about potential problems, there should have been some warning bells going off in your head. You should have been formulating some ideas about the kinds of rules you feel are proper for your family.

Here are some suggestions to get you thinking about some rules for your family. Your family situation is different from anyone else's. Indeed, the situation in your household may differ from one child to another. We can't tell you what rules to make, but some rules should be made and enforced as a prerequisite for Internet access in your household. Any of these rules should be adapted to accommodate the ages and personalities of your children.

- Because most mailing programs support unique address books for each user, consider limiting outgoing e-mails to the addresses found within each child's address book. You may also want to specify that only Mom or Dad may update a child's address book. Although there is no mailer that will enforce this rule for you, most younger children will adapt to the use of address books anyway, because if they use address books they will not have to remember or type complicated addresses. Using the address book exclusively will limit the scope of your children's outgoing e-mail activity to a pool of people that you approve. When a child wants to add new names to the list, you can approve the friend, and add the name to the address book.

- Consider limiting replies to only that same trusted pool of names found in the address book. This is a harder rule to enforce, because it's so easy to respond to an e-mail message just by hitting the "reply" button. The least you can do is to make sure your child knows the person before he responds to e-mail from that person. There are a whole lot of predators out there who may pretend to be nine-year-old girls who are interested in playing with Barbie dolls, but who are actually 40-year-old men who have a sexual interest in children like your daughter.

- Insist that Mom or Dad approve any requests for materials advertised through e-mail. Most children are protected from spam-advertised products anyway, just because most of them can't be ordered without a credit card. But some products can be ordered via e-mail or through a phone number. In fact, sometimes the phone number is the part of the scam, because it appears to be toll-free and yet adds hefty charges to your monthly bill.

- All requests to join a mailing list must be approved by Mom or Dad. When one of your children requests to join a mailing list, Mom or Dad can subscribe in their own name first, and monitor the content for a couple of weeks. If it is appropriate, allow the child to subscribe. If necessary, you may subscribe and unsubscribe yourself as needed to make sure that that the list continues to meet your standards.

- All requests to post to a mailing list must be approved. Especially with younger children, don't allow them to post anything until you have approved the content of the actual message that the child wishes to send.

- There is no authority greater than Mom and Dad. Even children who follow the rules about giving out private information may be duped by hoaxes sent from "official" representatives. Children may respond to requests to supply their password if they think they have been contacted by an employee of the service provider or an official agency, especially if they feel they will lose access or get in trouble by not responding. In fact, some of the scams tell the person to respond within thirty seconds or service will be cut off. If children aren't forewarned, they may panic. Unable to get Mom or Dad's advice within the time frame that is specified by the scammer, otherwise responsible children may give out the telephone number or credit card information.

- You may wish to ask for approval before your child forwards any item of e-mail, even if the child is forwarding it to someone on his approved list of recipients.
- Consider requiring parental approval for any e-mail attachments, whether sent or received. For outgoing mail, approve each file that is going to be attached. For incoming mail, make sure you trust the source of the file being received. For incoming programs, run a virus scan on the file to make sure it is not infected. We will explain how to run a virus check later in this chapter.

Parental Controls

As explained in the previous chapter, most commercial services provide some form of parental controls that allow parents to control their children's access to some Internet features. For those who access the Internet through an ISP, there are also products designed to work with the application software you use. These products will be discussed more thoroughly in Chapter 6, because most of the controls they provide apply to web browsing.

An example of the types of controls provided for e-mail can be illustrated by looking at Version 4.0 of America Online. With that version installed, you can configure each user name with the following e-mail options:

- User cannot send or receive any e-mail.
- User can only exchange e-mail with those AOL members, Internet addresses, or domain names that have been specified.
- User can receive e-mail from all AOL users, but not from any Internet users.
- User can receive e-mail from all AOL users, plus selected Internet addresses and domain names.
- User can receive all e-mail, except for e-mail from specified AOL members, Internet addresses, and domain names.
- User can receive unrestricted e-mail.

Those options that allow inclusion/exclusion will support the use of individual mailboxes, or entire domains. Thus, specifying "BillJ@prodigy.com" would allow/block just one user, while "prodigy.com" would allow/block any Prodigy user.

Note that the next to last option could be used to protect all family members against spam or unwelcome contact from certain individuals. Just because the options are called "parental controls" doesn't mean that adults can't use them to get rid of their own spam and other nuisance messages. The only problem with using this mail restriction as a spam control is that spammers tend to change their addresses almost daily. You might add their domain to your blocking list today, only to find that they have moved to another domain by sundown.

With any of the options specified above, you may also request that e-mails be blocked that contain file attachments or embedded images.

Keeping a Low Profile

Children should be taught to keep a low profile, so that they don't attract a lot of attention to themselves through their e-mail activities. This doesn't mean they have to be paranoid and filled with fear before sending any message, but they don't need to call attention to themselves either.

As already mentioned in the last chapter, avoid creating an entry in the member directory of your commercial provider. Even those entries that are totally innocent can provide exposure to unsolicited mail from strangers, spam, and potential scams.

Family members should limit their subscription to mailing lists, and should avoid excessive posting to those lists. In the section where we discussed the operation of the mailing list managers (the programs that perform administrative functions), you might remember that some managers supported a command that would display the names and e-mail addresses of everyone subscribed to a list. This is another potential way for someone to get your e-mail address. Most of the managers support a "Set/Conceal" command that will allow you to set an option so that your address will not be displayed when this is requested. See the previous descriptions of commands, or use the "Help" command to determine if the manager software you are using supports this.

You know those little registration cards that you complete when you buy a new product? Have you ever noticed how many of those are now asking you to supply an e-mail address if you have one? Avoid providing that information unless you like spam, because the manufacturer is only interested in your e-mail address so he can put unsolicited spam in your box. Another ruse to get your e-mail address is to visit Internet sites that provide free services, but still want you to register. Avoid providing your e-mail address as part of this registration.

Delete Before Opening

Just like the real junk mail that clutters your postal mailbox, there's no law that says you cannot delete spam without even opening it. Most mailing programs allow you to delete mail right from the summary screen, without ever having to look at it.

Those who have been online for a while become quite expert at recognizing junk mail and deleting it without reading it. Some sophisticated mailers can even be configured to send certain mail straight to the trash, based on the sender or the content of the subject field.

All these savvy users have caused the spammers to become more sneaky, and it is not uncommon to see subject lines like the following:

- Here's the Information You Requested
- In Response to Your Question
- Re: What I Need to Know
- Please Forward This to Steve . . .

Even if you occasionally get fooled and open the message, just delete it and move along. Don't be fooled by such opening lines as, "It has been brought to our attention that this would be of interest to you . . . ," or, "Your name was given to us by someone who thought you would be interested . . . ." No, your name probably wasn't provided by a friend or by your service provider. These are standard openings, designed to make you feel that you are one of the privileged few.

No Reply Necessary

Teach your family members that it is never necessary for them to respond to an e-mail message, especially a message from someone they don't know. In fact, they probably shouldn't respond to those types of messages at all without getting your permission first.

Many spam messages have a polite little message at the bottom that helpfully says, "If we have received your name in error, and you would not like to receive future offers such as this, please use the Reply option and type the word Remove in the subject line." Although this appears to be a tempting option, most experts suggest that you do not try to respond to these messages. Why? Four reasons:

1. Many programs that send spam use forged headers on the message, so the person shown in the "From:" area probably did not send the message. In fact, the

information in the "From:" box is probably not even a legitimate e-mail address. Chances are good that any reply sent by you will bounce back as undeliverable. Don't waste your time by responding.

2. The odds are good that the ISP from which the spammer sent his messages has detected the activity and terminated the account. Even if the account was good when the spam was sent, any reply sent later will probably bounce back because of a closed account.

3. Some spammers consider it a good sign when they get a response, as it means they've found an active e-mail account. Thus, responding to the request to remove your name from the mailing list may even increase future spam, because your name can be added to a list of known active accounts, for which other spammers will pay even more.

4. Even on the rare occasion when you find a spammer who is honest enough to remove your name, future harvesting of new names will probably turn up your name again on a future list, and the spam from the same company will continue.

Complaining

If you have a serious problem related to an e-mail you received, there are some formal avenues through which you can file a complaint. These formal avenues are only designed for serious infractions. For example, if you post a message on a mailing list, and someone sends you a flame telling you you're an idiot, that probably doesn't justify a complaint—unless the flame was accompanied by threats.

But there are situations where a formal complaint is warranted. One example is if someone is trying to pull a scam on you by posing as an employee and asking for personal information. Another would be if you receive an e-mail that contains threatening or obscene language directed towards a member of your family. Also, most service providers do not allow spam, so report any spam that comes from within your own domain. For example, if you have a CompuServe account, and you get a spam from another CompuServe user, you should report it. Also, any offer related to child pornography should be reported. The rule of thumb to follow is that if there are any actions that break a law, they should be reported.

Your children should always report any situation online that causes them discomfort, or that they believe is wrong. You should encourage them to do this, and let them know that they should not be embarrassed, nor will they ever get into trouble for raising such concerns. As a parent, you then need to determine the seriousness of the problem. Perhaps it is just a misunderstanding that can be corrected through discussion or a change of behavior. But if your child has reported a situation that could bring harm to himself or to others, or if a law has been broken, then you need to take the actions outlined in this section.

If you belong to an online service and the person causing the problem belongs to the same service, the first thing to do is to learn whether that person has broken the service agreement with the company. Every online service has a set of rules that users are expected to read and follow. America Online calls these Terms of Service, or TOS. Other services have similar names, and there should be an online copy of these rules that you can read. If you believe that someone has violated these rules, you can report the violation to the online service, usually via an e-mail. You might want to forward the offensive material you received as part of the message.

If the offensive message was sent from another domain, there are several standard mailboxes you can use to send complaints. These complaints should be sent to the same domain from which the message was sent, except you use a different mailbox. Try one or more of the following:

Abuse

Admin

Support

Postmaster

For example, if the return address on the offensive message was from BadGuy@anyisp.com, you should send your message of complaint to Abuse@anyisp.com. If that doesn't work, then try sending in turn to each of the four mailboxes shown above. By convention, all domains should have a Postmaster mailbox assigned, and should have it inspected by a real person.

If your message bounces back and says the domain is unknown, it could be that the message you received had a phony header. If so, look down at the jumble of header information that is printed at the bottom of the message. Locate a line that starts with the tag "Return-Path," and see what domain is listed there. If a message sent to that domain bounces as well, the message was probably sent through something called a remailer that hides all evidence of the original sender, and your search is probably at an end.

If your message doesn't bounce, but you never get a reply back, there is one other thing that you can do. You can access the web site of the organization that registers domain names, and obtain information about the owners of the domain name. Try one of the following search sites with your web browser (see Chapter 6):

www.inet.net/cgi-bin/whois
www.internic.net/cgi-bin/whois

If you are searching for a valid domain, this should return the name, mailing address, phone number, and often the e-mail address of the support person for the domain. Often, several different contacts are listed for different types of issues, such as billing and technical support. Try contacting these individuals and see if they will address your complaint.

If your complaint relates to child pornography or contact with a potential child molester, consider calling the National Center for Missing and Exploited Children at 1-800-843-5678. They can answer your questions, and direct you to other agencies such as the FBI.

Mail Folders

All of the suggestions in this section thus far have related to preventing problems before they appear. We should now mention a few ideas that could be used to monitor your children's e-mail activity to make sure they are following the rules you have established. This is a sensitive subject because many parents want to protect their children's privacy, and would consider such actions dishonest.

We agree that the first principle of any rule program should be trust, and constantly spying on children will undermine any program you want them to follow. But all families are different, and all children within those families have different weaknesses and needs. The ideas in this section may be a last resort, but you may need to use that last resort in order to keep your children safe. In any case, you should know what to do in case you have to do it to safeguard the welfare of your child.

Most e-mail systems have a series of file folders that can keep copies of mail that has been read and sent. In some systems, these folders can only be accessed if you are signed on under the user name that sent and received the mail in question. If your children have not changed their passwords since you established their user names, you should be able to examine these folders by using the child's user name and password. If they have changed their passwords, you'll have to ask for the new password before you can inspect the files. (You can get around this by establishing a rule from the beginning that parents must be informed of any password changes. Your children might not like this rule, but you pay the online service bill, so they don't have much choice.)

Fortunately, many e-mail systems allow parents to inspect mail file folders without

assuming a false identity and using their child's password. For example, America
Online 4.0 has a Personal Filing Cabinet option that allows you to make copies of
incoming and outgoing mail on your hard drive. If this is configured correctly, you
don't need to be connected to access the folders, nor do you need to know the password
of the user whose mail you wish to inspect. To configure AOL 4.0 to do this, follow
these steps:

> -> My AOL -> Preferences -> Mail
> Check the two boxes with the prefix "Retain all mail . . ."
> -> My AOL -> Preferences -> Passwords
> Remove the check from the check box labeled Personal Filing Cabinet

After you make these changes, both incoming and outgoing mail will be saved in the
Personal Filing Cabinet. To access it, select the screen name you wish to inspect,
select "My AOL," and then "Personal Filing Cabinet."

A person who wants to hide his tracks can still go into the Personal Filing Cabinet area and manually delete files. Users might start doing this if they suspect you are
monitoring them, but we suspect most children will probably not take time to visit
the Personal Filing Cabinet area. In fact, most children probably won't know anything about it.

Double Mailings

The Netscape Communicator has a feature that allows you to send a second copy
of any sent e-mail to an alternate address. The user has no knowledge that this is
being done, and there is no indication on any of the sent mails. In order to set this,
perform the following options:

> -> Edit -> Preferences -> Mail & Groups (expand) -> Messages

In the section "Copies of Outgoing Messages," find the line prefixed with "Mail
Messages," and type the recipient's e-mail address where it says "Other Address."
Now any message sent from that account will send a second copy of the message to
the address you just specified.

One of Clark's coworkers has her son's e-mail system configured so that copies of
all his sent e-mail go to her work address. She will occasionally drop remarks about
things he has said in messages to friends, and he thinks his mom is a real mind reader.

Notice on the same option page that you also have the ability to save outgoing messages into a folder. This is not as good an option as sending them to another address, but it may be an alternative if you have no second address.

Scanning for Files

If you suspect family members of receiving inappropriate file attachments and then downloading them, there is a Windows find function that will search your hard drive for specific files. Use these options:

-> Start -> Find -> Files or Folders

The find dialog allows you to select a drive to be searched, and even a specific subdirectory on a drive. In order to make sure you find any files that may be hidden, you'll have to search the entire drive, and search all your hard drives. Of course, if the files are being downloaded onto floppy disks, you will be out of luck unless you have the disks. You will want to make sure the "Include Subfolders" box is checked. In the "Named" box, you place the file patterns of the files you wish to find. Multiple patterns may be specified if they are separated by a semicolon. The following example would find any files with the file extensions GIF, JPG, or ZIP. These are common file extensions for download programs, as the first two represent common graphics files, and the last represents a compressed file:

.GIF;.JPG;*.ZIP

See the appendix for a list of common file extensions. When you press the "Find Now" button, the search will begin. The results appear at the bottom of the find screen. The name of each file listed will be shown, along with its location, size, and a description of the file type. If you find a file you want to know more about, double click on it. If Windows knows how to handle a file with that extension, it will launch the program to handle that file. If it doesn't have a program registered to handle that type of file, it will notify you, and allow you to select a program from its list of known programs. If you cannot view a graphics file, download a graphics viewer from one of the free software sites listed in Chapter 7. If graphics files are the primary files you are interested in examining, we will give you a better option in Chapter 6.

The "Find" dialog also gives you some sophisticated options, such as being able to search by file size, or the date the file was created or modified. Don't rely too much on that date, however, because a downloaded file typically keeps the date it was last modified, not the date it was downloaded.

One feature of Windows may be misleading when searching for files. It may not display the file extension of files that it knows how to process. You can change this with the following action:

=> My Computer -> View -> Options -> View

Make sure the option "Hide MS-DOS File Extensions for File Types That Are Registered" is not checked, and all extensions will then be displayed as part of the file name.

Virus Scan Products

You might suspect that your computer has been infected with a virus that may have been sent as part of a file attachment. You might suspect this if your computer is behaving oddly, such as having programs fail, having to restart the machine frequently, or having a hard drive that suddenly seems to be running out of space. Even if your computer is not having any problems, it is a good idea to search for viruses occasionally, as some are written to have a dormant phase before they start causing problems for you.

There are programs designed to look for viruses on your system. As you might expect, the sooner you can find and remove them, the less damage that will occur. There are three basic kinds of programs that deal with viruses.

A scanner is a program that searches through all the files on your hard drives and looks for viruses. It usually just searches the files having extensions such as EXE and COM, as those represent executable programs. The scanners detect viruses by looking for known patterns of computer instructions that are unique to each virus. Because of that, it is important to update the scanner program regularly to check for new viruses that were written since the scanner program was produced. Most companies that make scanner programs allow you to upgrade them regularly for a fee.

An eradicator is a program that removes a virus from an infected file. It usually does this by modifying the computer instructions that do the damage so that they become harmless. It is quite common to find a scanner and eradicator function packaged into the same program.

An inoculator is a program that is always active on your computer and monitors other running programs for events that might cause damage. These programs usually start themselves when you start your computer, and then monitor critical system locations that are known places where viruses might try to infect your system. When it detects one of these potential invasions, it will usually stop the access, and ask you whether the invading program should be terminated or allowed to proceed.

If you think you need virus software, make sure you don't already have it. Many computers come with virus software already installed. Or you may have an anti-virus program that came packaged with a suite of programs, such as Microsoft Office. If none of that produces any results, check the anti-virus software sites listed in Chapter 7.

A PARENT'S QUESTIONS

Q. How do I send e-mail to a friend on another online service?
A. You need the friend's mailbox address, and then the proper domain name as shown below:

CompuServe:	user-number@compuserve.com
Prodigy:	member-name@prodigy.com
America Online:	screen-name@aol.com
Microsoft Network:	user-name@msn.com

Replace the comma in the CompuServe user number with a period, because commas are not allowed. Ignore any embedded spaces in America Online screen names.

Q. Can I change my e-mail address to something easier?
A. You're pretty much stuck with the domain name, unless you want to change to another service provider. Whether you can change your mailbox or not depends upon the service provider. Some will allow aliases, so your mail can be sent to a mailbox that is different from your user name. Services such as Prodigy and America Online will allow multiple user names, so you could just define a new user name and use it for most of your mail and online activities. If worse comes to worse, just cancel the service and then join up again in a month.

Q. How can I be assured my e-mail was delivered?
A. If there is a delivery problem, you will usually get a "bounce" message back, stating that your mail could not be delivered. Some online services offer a return receipt feature that sends you an e-mail when the message was opened by the recipient. In general, e-mail delivery is quite reliable, but you can never be one hundred percent sure that it arrived. So if you're sending something important, pick up that low-tech phone, and let them know it's on the way.

Q. Why can't service providers stop spam?
A. You can believe that service providers would like to stop spammers in their tracks, because it costs them a lot of money to process those extra letters. Although most service providers have strict rules against spam, spammers are such smooth operators that it's hard to stop them before the damage is done.

Most providers are so anxious to sign up new customers that they make it very easy to join and start using the system. This also plays into the spammers' typical method of operation. The typical spammer will open an account using a phony name, address, and credit card number. Spammers have access to software that generates valid credit card numbers, even though real accounts do not exist for those numbers, or the accounts exist in other people's names. (For a new customer, service providers usually just check for a valid credit card number. Actual charges aren't applied to the card until after the free hours have been used, by which time the spammers have moved on to other accounts.)

Once the spammers have access into a system, they install their bulk mailing programs and start sending unwanted e-mail to thousands of addresses. It is difficult for the service providers to detect these programs, because an e-mail that is sent by a spammer looks just like any other piece of e-mail. The service provider only becomes aware of the problem when recipients of the spam start complaining, or when the secondary credit card check turns up a problem.

To their credit, most service providers are quick to terminate accounts, once they are alerted to a problem. But by then the damage has been done. There are Internet sites described in Chapter 7 that will keep you informed about the status of the spam wars. There are steps being taken, both technical and legislative, to stop this mess.

Q. What can we do to get more user names?
A. Most online services allow the account holder to have multiple user names (usually five) on one account. Each user name has its own e-mail box and can have different parental control privileges. Five user names is plenty for most families, but if five user names aren't enough you can always get a second account. This would double the amount of user names your family could have, but it would also double your monthly fee.

Another option is for family members to share user names. This works well if you have two children about the same age, and who would have the same parental control settings. But it still causes a problem with e-mail, because two children would be sharing one e-mail box and would have to make sure that e-mail intended for one person didn't get read and discarded by the other.

If e-mail is the only issue, there are Internet sites that provide free e-mail access (see Chapter 7). Through the use of these facilities, two children could share the same user name, but one (or both) of them could have their mail sent to a different location that would be accessible by web browser. This is not an ideal situation, but could probably be managed by older children.

If you use an ISP for access, check with the provider about the possibility of having multiple accounts. Some of them will allow multiple e-mail aliases, perhaps for a modem fee, that will at least provide separate e-mail accounts for family members. If your ISP won't do that, look for other ISPs that might be more willing to provide the services you need, or that will provide multiple accounts for a discount.

Chapter 4—All the News That's Fit to Post

•••••

A COUPLE OF TIMES EACH YEAR, CLARK GETS TO attend various computer conventions. Prominently displayed in a public area at each convention are large cork boards for posting notes and messages. A large sign at the top of each board indicates the subject matter of the messages that should be posted there. Rather than bore you with the topics discussed at computer conventions, which would put you to sleep immediately, let's assume you're attending a convention of vegetable farmers. As soon as you registered, you immediately approached the big cork bulletin boards to see what treasures had been posted there, and were gratified to see notes on the following topics:

- Growing Bigger Carrots
- Corn Corner
- Green Bean Roundup
- The Broccoli Barn
- Spinach Secrets
- Avoiding Squash Rot

With such riveting topics as these, you decided immediately that you'd make every effort to stop at those bulletin boards several times a day, even if you had to cross the street to another hotel to do it. And today your efforts were richly rewarded, because your most recent trip to the Corn Corner topic yielded the following three messages:

"My production is down from last year, the ears are smaller, and the edges of the leaves are turning brown. What is wrong?" Tom in Kansas.

"Tom: I had the same problem, and it was because there wasn't enough iron in the soil. Try using a fertilizer that is rich in iron." Sally in Iowa.

"Tom: Iron might be the answer, but it could also be too much water and not enough sun. On cloudy days, cut down the amount of water." Bill in Nebraska.

Having visited that bulletin board, you are now ready to return to your own farm in Ohio and try the solutions listed on the bulletin board. Your diligence in returning to the topics could result in a bumper year for this year's corn crop.

So what did you learn from this? A couple of things come to mind. First, the authors of this book don't know anything about farming. (Kids: Don't try our farm tips at home!) Second, farmers' conventions look almost as boring as computer conventions. But this silly example should illustrate the concept of Internet newsgroups. Newsgroups are the electronic equivalent of the corkboards at the farmers' convention. To access a newsgroup, you use your computer to locate the newsgroups that interest you, read the messages posted there, and even add your own messages if you are so inclined.

A newsgroup is formed to let users with common interests exchange ideas. There are thousands of newsgroups, centered around such topics as TV programs, recipes, favorite authors, religion, education, genealogy, and, of course, computers and software.

Once you've found a newsgroup that looks interesting, you can read the messages that others have posted there. Just as with the farmers' bulletin boards described above, you will find questions or comments, and then usually one or more replies directed to that question or comment. You can also use your computer to post your own messages to the newsgroup.

In this chapter we will explain how to use newsgroups, including finding the ones you want, reading them, and posting your own messages to them. We will also expose the dangers associated with them, and make some suggestions that will help you avoid the problems. We will also share some ideas that you can use to make sure your kids are following the rules and are not accessing newsgroups that could pose a potential threat to them.

NEWSGROUP BASICS

Sometimes you will hear newsgroups referred to as Net News groups or Usenet groups. Actually, Usenet is the name of the network that is designed to maintain and transport the newsgroups. It is really a separate network from the Internet, although the Internet is connected to it. The various networks that comprise Usenet communicate regularly with each other to transport messages. For example, if you post a message to a newsgroup, it actually gets posted only to your local Usenet machine. But that machine communicates regularly with the rest of the network, passing along new messages, so that eventually your message will travel to all parts of the Usenet network.

Various parts of the network may choose not to carry certain newsgroups. If that is the case, the carriers just ignore any new messages posted to groups that they have decided not to carry. Also, your local online service or ISP may decide to not carry all the groups. If this is an issue for you, then question your service provider before subscribing to determine which groups are not carried.

Finding Groups

The names of newsgroups are composed of a major topic area followed by one or more subtopics. Consider the following newsgroup name:

rec.music.celtic

The major topic area is "rec," meaning recreation. Within recreation, you have the subtopic of music, and within that, you have the further subtopic of Celtic music. There may be any number of different levels of subtopics. For example, here are just a few of the other groups dealing with recreational music:

rec.music.a-cappella
rec.music.artists.debbie-gibson
rec.music.christian
rec.music.classical
rec.music.classical.contemporary
rec.music.classical.guitar
rec.music.country.western
rec.music.folk
rec.music.makers.guitar
rec.music.makers.marketplace

Remember that the first part of the newsgroup name represents the major topic. Most service providers will provide some or all of these major topic areas, plus you may even find some major topics not listed here:

alt   Alternate (a little bit of everything; it can sometimes get kinky)
biz   Business
comp Computers

k12   Education
misc   Whatever Doesn't Fit Anywhere Else
news   Newsgroup Information
rec   Recreation
sci   Science
soc   Society
talk   Discussion Groups

Most software designed for reading newsgroups allows you to find the newsgroups you want to read using one or more of the following techniques:

Collapsed Tree

The reader will display a tree of all the discussion groups that it finds, and will let you explore the branches of the tree. For example, it might show:

+   comp.* (922 groups)

This means there are 922 groups that start with the major topic "comp." To view them, click on the plus sign. Within that branch, you may find individual groups plus other branches, such as:

+   comp.ai.* (15 groups)

As before, just click the plus sign to explore that branch.

Title Search

You can search for a newsgroup by title. For example, if you search for "religion" you will find all the groups with the word "religion" somewhere in the newsgroup title.

New Groups

You can display all the new newsgroups that have been created since you last checked. The first time you do this, it will show all the groups, but there should be a function that will clear them so they will not display the old ones the next time you visit the screen.

Another option is to visit the following web site, which allows you to search for newsgroups in various ways (see Chapter 6):

www.reference.com

Subscribing to a Group

If you plan to use newsgroups regularly, you will probably want to subscribe to the groups that you want to read each day. Subscribing to a newsgroup is not like subscribing to a mailing list. Subscribing just tells the newsgroup reader the newsgroups that you would like to read on a regular basis.

When you start the newsgroup reader, it will show all the groups to which you subscribe, and also some statistics, such as the number of unread messages in each group. You can select one of the subscribed groups and start reading any unread messages for that group.

Rather than selecting a group to read, you might want to change your subscription options. If you have lost interest in a particular list, you can unsubscribe from it. If you want to subscribe to new lists, you can find them, using one of the three methods described in the previous section, and then add them to your list of subscribed groups. Some readers even allow you to read the messages in unsubscribed groups, so that you can determine if you wish to subscribe.

Depending on your service provider, sometimes the newsgroup names are shown in a more understandable fashion, such as "Folk Music," rather than "rec.music.folk." America Online gives you the option of displaying newsgroup names this way, or you can display them in the more traditional Usenet manner.

Also, sometimes your service provider will not show you the names of some of the more controversial newsgroups, and yet the software will allow you to subscribe if you know the name. So the group "alt.sex.fetish.fashion" might not appear when you list the groups, and yet you can subscribe if you know the name. This is known as the "expert add" feature when using America Online.

To give you a better idea of how all this works, we will describe the process of reading newsgroups with Netscape Communicator, one of the more popular Internet applications used by people that access newsgroups through ISPs.

When you start the news reader, it will display a "message center." Somewhere in the list of files shown, you should see an entry that lists the name of your news server. It will look something like this:

Name	Unread	Total
+ news.myisp.com		

Click on the plus (+) sign to expand this branch. After clicking, it will expand to show you the names of the newsgroups to which you subscribe, and also a count of the total messages in the group, and the number of those that you have not read:

Name	Unread	Total
new.myisp.com		
——> microsoft.public.kids	12	17
——> comp.lang.javascript	3726	3730
——> comp.software.measurement	61	61
——> comp.windows.misc	323	323

If no newsgroups appear, or if you wish to add groups to the subscribed list, choose the "Subscribe to Discussion Groups" option. It will display a new dialog, and allow you to select newsgroups in one of three ways described in the previous section. When you find newsgroups to which you wish to subscribe, click the newsgroup name, and press the subscribe button. That group will then be added to the list of groups to be displayed when you start the newsgroup reader the next time.

Reading the Group

Once you see the groups to which you are subscribed, you need to determine which one you wish to read. Once that is done, you need to select it, usually by clicking or double clicking on the group name. When you click on the group name, the news reader must actually contact the news server to request the messages within the group. Because this takes a certain amount of time, and as some groups accumulate a lot of messages, you are usually given options as to how many messages you wish to read. For example, you might define your configuration options so that a maximum of five hundred messages are to be loaded. If you select a group with more than that number of messages, you will be asked whether you wish to read all the messages, abort the read request, or read a certain number of messages that you specify. Once the messages are loaded, you should see a screen similar to Figure 4-1, which is taken from a Netscape Communicator session.

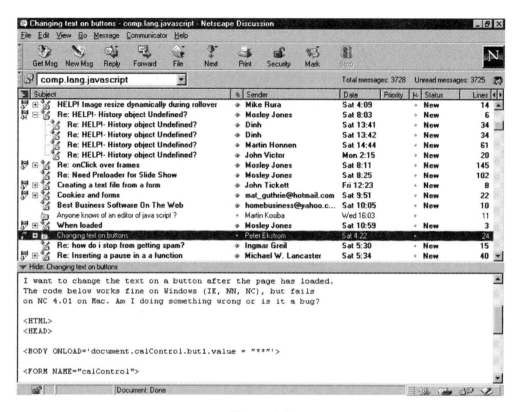

Figure 4-1

Notice how the top of the screen contains the standard Windows menu and toolbar that allow you to select the functions of the newsgroup reader. Under that, the name of the newsgroup is shown, along with message counts for the total number of messages and the number that you have not read.

The middle of the screen displays a summary of the messages in the newsgroup, shown under a title bar. The various items shown include the subject of the message, the name of the sender, the date and time it was posted, the priority, the status, and the number of lines in the message. To the left of the sender name is also a column showing a green diamond or a small gray dot. The diamond indicates the message has not been read, and it changes to a dot when the message is read. This is important, because messages you have read will not appear the next time you read the newsgroup.

You can click on a segment of the title bar at the top of each column to sort the messages in a different order. For example, clicking on the segment that says "Subject" will sort the messages in ascending (A-Z) order by subject. Clicking on it again will sort the messages in descending order (Z-A).

The bottom portion of the screen shows you the text of the current message that is being read. As you single click a message line in the upper portion of the screen, that line will be highlighted, the status will change from unread to read, and the message will be displayed on the bottom portion of the screen. If the message will not fit in that window, the scroll bars may be used to scroll through it. The size of these windows may be adjusted dynamically using the drag-and-drop technique.

To the very left of the "Subject" area, you will notice that some messages contain a plus (+) or a minus (-) sign. This is used to indicate a discussion "thread." Each thread represents a different topic of conversation. For example, one person might post a question, and then three different people might post answers to it. These answers are not posted at the end of the newsgroup, but along with the original question. The Netscape Communicator indicates threads by a plus sign. When you click on the plus sign, it turns it into a minus sign, and displays the messages that were hidden. When you click on the minus sign, it hides the messages again and displays the plus sign. Some newsgroup readers do this differently, displaying an ICON of a paper for a single message, or an ICON of a folder for a thread of messages.

Because some newsgroups accumulate hundreds of new messages per day, you need a way of disposing of new messages quickly without having to read them all. Most readers have a "Mark" function that allows you to process messages in groups. For example, you can select an entire range of messages and mark them all as read. You can also mark an entire thread as read, if that topic has no appeal. Another option marks messages as read if they are older than a certain date. Finally, you can pick and choose the messages you wish to read and then mark the entire newsgroup as read.

Most news readers also have quite powerful navigation controls that allow you to jump from one message to another. Netscape Communicator provides the following:

- Read Next Message
- Read Next Unread Message
- Read Next Unread Thread
- Read Previous Message
- Read Previous Unread Message
- Read Next Group
- Read Next Unread Group

Like e-mail readers, many newsgroup readers allow newsgroups to be read offline to limit the amount of time you have to be connected to your service provider. Once you have set this up, it will connect, download the new messages from the groups to which you subscribe, copy the messages to your hard drive, and then disconnect. You can then read through the messages at your own speed, and not have to worry about connect time.

The length of time new messages are kept in the newsgroup depends on the message activity level, and the options set by the newsgroup administrator.

If you wish to learn more about a particular newsgroup, many groups maintain a FAQ (Frequently Asked Questions) file. This may be posted to the newsgroup itself on a regular basis, or it may be posted in one of the following newsgroups:

    xxx.answers (where xxx is the major topic area of your group)
    news.answers

It is especially important to read the FAQ if you wish to post a message to a newsgroup that you haven't followed for very long. If it's a common question, the odds are that the answer is in the FAQ file, and that you will be subject to flame mail if you ask that tired old question once again.

Posting Messages

Once you have read a particular newsgroup for a while, you will probably want to ask a question, answer someone else's question, or make a comment. This will bring you to the next phase of newsgroup learning—posting your first message. There are approximately 250,000 new Usenet postings each day, so you will be in good company.

You usually get the urge to post a message when you are reading a newsgroup. At that point, there are a number of ways that you can respond to a message. Netscape Communicator supports the following options when you are reading a newsgroup:

New Message

Allows you to compose a new message to be posted to the newsgroup being read. The "To:" portion of the message is filled in with the name of the newsgroup. You need to add a subject line, the message text, and any other optional addresses to which the message should be sent.

Reply to Message

Allows you to reply to the specific message you are reading within the news-group. Make sure you are positioned on the correct message before using this option. Once you have selected this, you will be asked to choose a reply option:

❑ **1. Reply to Sender**
   Allows you to send an e-mail message to the person that posted the message. The "To:" section contains the e-mail address, the "Subject" area is filled in and prefixed with "Re:", and the text of the original message is copied to the text area.

❑ **2. Reply to Group**
   Same as above, but the "To:" area contains the name of the newsgroup, rather than the e-mail address of the sender. Your reply will be added under the sender's original message as part of the same thread.

❑ **3. Reply to Sender and Group**
   Same as above, but the "To:" address contains both the name of the news-group and the e-mail address of the original sender.

Forward

Allows you to forward the message to another user. The "Subject" area will be filled in and prefixed with "Fwd:." You will need to complete the recipient's address, and optional text that is to appear in front of the forwarded message.

When replying to a message, there should be some reference to the original mes-sage so that people who read your reply will have some indication of what you're responding to. You can either paraphrase the original message ("On January 13th, Merry Homemaker made a reference to peanut butter and licorice pies"), or you can copy portions of the original message to your text area, with an arrow placed at the left side of the text:

> When we were tired from a long day of working on the farm, Mother would often
> surprise us with one of her famous peanut butter and licorice pies.

The arrows are placed at the left side of the text so those who read your reply will be able to distinguish the original message from the comments that you are about to make. Have some mercy on the reader of your message and delete those parts of the original message that aren't relevant to the comments you are making in your reply. Because portions of messages are often quoted and requoted many times, it is not unusual to find lines with five or six arrow symbols to the left side of the text.

As with mailing lists, you should lurk for a little while before making your first post to the newsgroup. This will allow you to get a feel for how the newsgroup operates, so you don't look like a fool by immediately jumping in with a lot of postings that do not fit in the group. Don't hesitate to refer to the FAQ document first, because it may answer many of the common questions that are on your mind. As with all things you write, read the message again before you send it to check for typos and other obvious mistakes. A post that is poorly done with many obvious errors will distract from the point you are trying to make.

Signature files may also be used with newsgroups. As with e-mail signature files, try to keep them under five lines so as to not consume storage space on the machines of other users.

Like mailing lists, some newsgroups are moderated. This means the message you post to a newsgroup will really be sent to a moderator. If he likes the message, it will get forwarded to the group. If he doesn't, try again with another question later.

Imbedded Files

You should have noticed as you read through this chapter that the technology behind newsgroup software has a lot of parallels to e-mail software. Another similarity is the fact that newsgroup messages, like e-mail messages, were originally designed to handle only the 128-byte combinations that can be represented on a typical keyboard. It wasn't long before users of Usenet, however, decided that it would be really nice to deliver images and other files as part of a newsgroup post.

Enter our old friends uuencode and uudecode again—the same tools that were originally used to send files as part of e-mail messages. As you may remember, uuencode takes a file and converts it into a jumble of characters that can be represented in an e-mail message. When that message gets to the other side, the recipient runs uudecode against the message, which converts it back into the original file.

Files within newsgroup posts are so common that most software products handle them automatically, so that you don't even have to run uudecode against the message. News readers often provide a button that allows you to invoke uudecode and extract the files into a hard drive subdirectory of your choosing. More advanced news readers may extract graphics files automatically and display them as part of the message.

Because some systems limited the size of newsgroup messages, sometimes files sent via a newsgroup would be broken up into several messages. It was not unusual to find messages with subject lines such as "Betty at the Beach—Part 1 of 9."

An early convention was that newsgroups containing any kinds of imbedded files should have the word "binaries" somewhere in the name of the newsgroup. Thus, you still see newsgroups around such as "alt.binaries.pictures.teen-starlets." But this guideline seems to be generally ignored these days, and you will find imbedded files on occasion in just about any newsgroup.

Up until a few years ago, before the World Wide Web (see Chapter 6) started to become so popular, the "binaries" newsgroups were the main vehicle for exchanging pornography across the Internet. But web browsers have made it easier to preview the clean pictures you want and download them, without having to mess with newsgroup-imbedded files. This is not to say that all "binaries" groups are bad. Some of them exchange harmless photographs, or files that are not graphics files. Nevertheless, if your child wants to subscribe to a "binaries" group, you should check it out first with a cynical eye.

Newsgroup Software

If you access the Internet through a commercial online service, the news reader you will use will be built into the software. ISP users will probably use a product such as Netscape Communicator or Microsoft Internet Explorer. If you use the latter product, the news reader comes as part of Outlook Express, which comes with Internet Explorer.

Depending on your connection options, some providers might let you use your own software, or might not provide you with a news reader. If that is the case, there are several free or inexpensive programs you can download that will do a good job. Two of the most popular ones are News Xpress and Win VN, both of which can probably be downloaded from some of the sites listed in Chapter 7.

If you use your own news reader, the biggest problem you will have is getting it configured correctly. Look for a parameter with a name similar to "NNTP," and then supply the name of the Usenet news server. You may have to obtain this information from your access provider.

Newsgroup Etiquette

Here's a riddle that's been going around the Internet for a long time. You may not get a laugh out of it, but it will give you a pretty good picture of what you can expect to find in a newsgroup discussion, and it may also give you some suggestions for the kind of posting you should avoid:

Q: How many internet mailing list subscribers does it take to change a light bulb?
A: 1,331

- 1 to change the light bulb and to post to the mailing list that the light bulb has been changed;
- 14 to share similar experiences of changing light bulbs and how the light bulb could have been changed differently;
- 7 to caution about the dangers of changing light bulbs;
- 27 to point out spelling/grammar errors in posts about changing light bulbs;
- 53 to flame the spell checkers;
- 41 to correct spelling in the spelling/grammar flames;
- 156 to write to the list administrator complaining about the light bulb discussion and its inappropriateness to this mail list;
- 109 to post that this list is not about light bulbs and to please take this e-mail exchange to alt.lite.bulb;
- 203 to demand that cross posting to alt.grammar, alt.spelling, and alt.punctuation about changing light bulbs be stopped;
- 111 to defend the posting to this list saying that we all use light bulbs and therefore the posts **are** relevant to this mail list;
- 306 to debate which method of changing light bulbs is superior, where to buy the best light bulbs, what brand of light bulbs work best for this technique, and what brands are faulty;
- 27 to post URLs where one can see examples of different light bulbs;
- 14 to post that the URLs were posted incorrectly, and to post corrected URLs;
- 3 to post about links they found from the URLs that are relevant to this list which makes light bulbs relevant to this list;
- 33 to quote all posts to date, including all headers and footers, and then add "Me Too";
- 12 to post to the list that they are unsubscribing because they cannot handle the light bulb controversy;
- 19 to quote the "Me Too's" to say, "Me Three";
- 4 to suggest that posters check the light bulb FAQ;
- 1 to propose new alt.change.lite.bulb newsgroup;

- 47 to say this is just what alt.physic.cold_fusion was meant for, leave the discussion here; and
- 143 votes for alt.lite.bulb.

The above riddle wouldn't be circulated so often if there weren't so much truth in it. Sometimes, newsgroups seem like an exercise in frustration. But you can help the situation by staying out of the trivial portions of newsgroup debates.

As with any Internet application, there are certainly rules of the road that will make you a good citizen when it comes to newsgroup postings. Many of the suggestions for e-mail apply here also, but we will cover some of the specific habits to avoid if you don't want to be hated by your fellow newsgroup members. So, here are the guidelines:

- When replying to a previous message, quote or paraphrase enough of the original message so that users understand the context of your reply, but not so much that they get annoyed. There's nothing worse than someone who repeats a two-page message, only to add a new sentence or two at the bottom. Some systems prevent you from doing this if a certain percentage of the reply is not new material. Cut and paste or paraphrase as necessary so that the final message is as short as possible, and yet understandable.
- Almost as bad is someone who doesn't quote or paraphrase enough of the original message when posting a reply. Unless you do *some* cutting and pasting or referring to the original post, no one will have any idea what you are talking about once the original message has aged off the group.
- Avoid replies that don't add anything to the discussion, but only echo: "I agree" or "Me too." Unless you become a celebrity and somebody really does care about your opinions, nobody wants to hear what you have to say unless you have something new to add to the discussion. For just about any message, you can be sure that a certain number will agree, a certain number will disagree, and a certain number probably just don't care. Letting everyone know which camp has your vote doesn't enlighten anybody.
- As with mailing lists, avoid posting suspected hoaxes—and don't post anything that would break copyright laws.
- Just as you can send one e-mail to multiple people, most news readers allow you to send the same posting to multiple newsgroups—a practice known as "cross-posting." Within limits, this is not a problem, particularly if your message applies to all of those groups. But in general, avoid posting the same message to more than one or two groups.

- Remember that English may not be the primary language for some posters. This is particularly true in advice newsgroups, where people come to ask questions or solicit suggestions. Just be kind to and patient with people whose English is less than fluent, and consider that they are probably doing a better job than you would do if you had to write a coherent note in Swahili.
- Count to ten before posting a nasty reply that could provoke a flame war. Similarly, don't be overly offended if someone flames one of your messages. Clark has belonged to newsgroups where fully seventy-five percent of the message traffic consisted of increasingly hostile messages between a handful of people in the group. These wars can become so contentious that everyone finally just gives up and unsubscribes.
- Remember the readership of the newsgroup may be worldwide. Asking if anyone has a spare ticket to the local baseball game will probably irritate about ninety-nine percent of the readers of the newsgroup.
- Consider writing directly to the author of a message if your reply doesn't apply to the general conversation in the newsgroup. Recall that most news readers allow you to choose where to send your reply, so use that option if it applies in a particular situation.
- Okay, we saved the most important one for last. The number one commandment for posting in a newsgroup is: Don't post off-topic. This is another way of saying, "Stick to the subject." If the newsgroup is related to humor, don't post your grandmother's apple pie recipe. You will be surprised how many people post replies that are completely off the subject, or are personal messages to other people posting in the group. The worst of all are posts advertising something you wish to sell. There are newsgroups designed for people selling things, so put those kinds of messages in those groups.

WHERE DANGER LURKS

Stepping into the world of Internet newsgroups is like leaving the old homestead and going to New York City for the first time. Although the discussion groups on commercial online services have certain minimum standards, the Usenet newsgroups are pretty much wide open. Posting an obscene or racist message on a commercial service will probably result in a warning or the outright termination of your account. No such restrictions apply to newsgroups, which are not really "owned" by anyone. Actually, most newsgroups do have monitors that remove the worst of the messages, but their level of tolerance for diverse opinions is much greater than you might realistically hope.

There really is a lot of value in some newsgroups. If you're ever diagnosed with a rare disease, you may find out more from a newsgroup devoted to that disease than you ever will from your doctor. Other newsgroups might fill in the holes in your family tree, or keep you posted on the teen heartthrob of the minute. But anyone who subscribes to a newsgroup has to be prepared to find a little bit of chaff in with the wheat. Family members who are not mature enough to handle potentially inflammatory material should be restricted or highly supervised when accessing newsgroups.

We will now try to expose those areas with the newsgroups that could lead to problems for some families or family members.

Newsgroups Not for Kids

There are newsgroups devoted to the discussion of hundreds of topics, many of which are not appropriate for children. In fact, some newsgroups cover topics that would just as well be off-limits for adults. A quick survey of just the newsgroups in the "alt" major topic area revealed groups devoted to the discussion of the following: Aliens, astrology, atheism, beer, bigfoot, bondage, brothels, cancer, celebrities (nude), conspiracy, depression, divorce, drugs, euthanasia, forgery, gay journalism, ghost stories, herpes, Howard Stern, pagans, paranormal, prostitution, recovery, satanism, skinheads, tarot, Vietnam, and wastewater.

To be fair, this is taken from the "alt," or alternate major topic area, and many of these groups tend to appeal to those with alternate interests. While some of those newsgroups do sound appealing for adults, they are definitely off the scope for all young children, and a lot of teenagers.

Bad Messages on Good Groups

Even if you find your children the most innocent newsgroup in the world, there's nothing to stop people from posting bad messages on those groups. As with e-mail, most of these improper messages are "spam," or advertisements for products of dubious value. Just as spammer programs can send junk e-mail to thousands of users, similar programs can send the same junk to thousands of newsgroups.

In 1994 two Phoenix lawyers spammed more than 6,000 newsgroups with advertisements for an immigration service. Although this caused a major headache for a couple of days, it actually resulted in some good. Usenet administrators developed a technique called canceling that allowed them to detect such spam bombs, and cancel all of their messages almost immediately.

Canceling eliminated most of the major spammers, but sometimes a small opera-tor can post a scam on a few dozen groups and get away with it. The problem with most of these spammers is that they post their trash in groups that have no relation-ship to what they are selling, so that someone who reads a newsgroup to learn gar-dening hints is suddenly looking at an ad for a pornographic web site. The worst case of this we have ever seen was when Clark was reading a newsgroup devoted to locat-ing missing children, only to find a spam for a pornographic web site that featured sexually explicit photographs of young children. Not only do some of these guys have no ethics, but they have no class either.

Posting to the World

We made a point in the last chapter, when discussing mailing lists, that also applies to newsgroups. When you post a message to a newsgroup, you really are posting for the world to see. Your message might be read by thousands, or tens of thousands of people. Most of those people will be normal, but some of them might be a little crazy. They might flame you, or they might even go to the trouble of locating your phone number, so they can call you and express their opinions in person. All of these are good reasons for observing some of the security precautions we discussed in Chapter 2. If you follow some of those privacy suggestions, it is unlikely anyone will ever know more about you than your e-mail address, and that can always be changed.

Speaking of e-mail addresses, posting to a newsgroup is a good way to get your address on multiple spam mailing lists. Those who compile such lists use programs to search through newsgroups and "harvest" all the e-mail addresses they find. About the only way to avoid this is to have separate mailboxes for posting versus private e-mail.

AVOIDING PROBLEMS

In this section, we will give some suggestions for controlling the use of news-groups in your home. To be honest, most children are more interested in other more active Internet applications anyway, such as e-mail and the World Wide Web. So it may not be too difficult to establish rules related to newsgroups.

Parental Controls

If you access the Internet via an online service, the parental controls provided by such services usually have some provisions for controlling newsgroups. Those who are ISP users can usually get similar protection using some of the blocking software that is available for web browsers.

Using America Online, for example, the following custom settings may be applied to any user name:

❑ **Full Newsgroup Access**

User may access any newsgroup available to the news server. Without this attribute, users have access to a filtered list of common groups.

❑ **Block File Downloads**

Files imbedded in newsgroup messages may not be viewed or downloaded.

❑ **Block Groups by Word**

Newsgroups may be blocked if their titles contain certain words.

❑ **Block Groups by Name**

A list of newsgroups may be excluded by name.

❑ **Block Expert Add**

Newsgroups cannot be added, even if the user knows the full name of the newsgroup. This option disables the Expert Add feature.

❑ **Block All**

User does not have access to any newsgroups.

As with any type of parental control, parents should check it frequently to make sure the controls are still set, and that they are still effective in blocking access.

Subscription List

You may want to establish a family rule that young children may only access newsgroups to which they are subscribed, and they may not subscribe to any new groups without their parents' permission.

If children request access to new newsgroups, the parents should subscribe first and monitor the content for at least two weeks. If the content is acceptable, then the parents can help the child set the subscription list so that the new group is included in the list of groups to which the child is subscribed.

Privacy Options

Before you can use most news readers, you must establish certain options that will affect the content of your outgoing newsgroup posts. For example, many news readers ask for your name (to be printed on the message), your e-mail address, your reply address (if different from the e-mail address), the name of your company, and the name of an optional signature file to be appended to each message. Consider some of the privacy suggestions in Chapter 2 when completing this information. You should pick a name that reveals nothing about the age or gender of the sender. You may want to select e-mail addresses that will route any replies to the parents and not the children.

One technique tried by some is to configure your reader with an invalid return e-mail address, and then provide directions in your signature file for changing it. For example, let's say you are an America Online user with the user name of "JohnDoe." You could configure your e-mail reader with a return e-mail address of "John-Doe7@aol.com," and then make a comment in your signature file that says "Change JohnDoe7 to JohnDoe before replying." Why would this work? Consider that many e-mail addresses are harvested from newsgroups by software, and not by a real set of human eyeballs. Any of this harvesting software would extract the incorrect mailbox of "JohnDoe7," and any spam sent to that address would bounce. Those human beings who really want to reply to you can read the instructions and delete the "7" before sending the reply. This makes slightly more work for the humans involved, but does fool many of the address-harvesting programs.

Spam Filters

Recent software enhancements have made it possible to hide certain newsgroup posts that are considered to be spam. One such enhancement uses a technology known as NoCeM (No-See-'Em) to mark spam messages as "junk" posts. Certain news readers then give you the option to hide these messages while reading new mail. For example, when you display your subscribed groups with America Online, it tells you the number of messages in each group that are considered to be junk. If you have your options set correctly, these messages will not even appear when you display the messages in the newsgroup.

Messages may be marked as junk by newsgroup administrators, or by automatic software routines that search for spam. For example, spam messages are routinely posted to multiple newsgroups. If the same message is found in more than ten groups, the software may consider it to be spam, and may mark it as junk in all of the newsgroups where it was posted.

There are some who object to such filters, because they don't want someone else censoring what they read. If you're one of those people, you may want to experiment with the option to see if it really hides anything you consider to be valuable. In our experience, the filter has never hidden anything of value, but has cut down on a lot of the trash.

Don't expect any filter to do one hundred percent of the job. Even with filtering active, there are a certain amount of posts in every newsgroup that are not appropriate.

Mailing Postings

Some news readers allow you to send a copy of each newsgroup posting to a different e-mail address. Netscape Communicator allows you to do this for both outgoing newsgroup messages and e-mail. If you want to monitor what other family members post to newsgroups, you should configure their news reader options so that copies of postings will be e-mailed to you at a different address. If you are limited in terms of the mailboxes that can receive mail, you can establish free e-mail accounts at several web sites that are mentioned in Chapter 7.

File Folders

Many news readers also support the option of storing copies of outgoing postings in a selected file folder. This may allow you to browse through the folder and look at the messages that have been sent. This is not as good as the previous method, however, because anyone with a little bit of computer savvy can delete selected messages from the folder. This also may be more intrusive, because you may need to access the folders while using the user name and password of the person you wish to monitor.

Searching Newsgroups

There are several web sites that allow you to search most of the major newsgroups (see Chapter 6 to learn about web sites). One of the more popular ones is:

www.dejanews.com

Earlier, we discussed privacy options that usually must be set before using a news reader. These options relate to the names and e-mail addresses that get included with each posting. You can use any of this information as an option when searching for posted messages. For example, assume you have configured all your children's newsgroup options so that any replies to their posts will be sent to your e-mail address, which is TheirDad@aol.com. Using the newsgroup search facility to search for this address should show you anything they posted, as well as any other posts containing that string, such as other people's replies to their posts. If you experiment with this a little, you can probably find a technique that will easily track their posts and any related activity.

A PARENT'S QUESTIONS

Q. How long will an entry stay in a Newsgroup?
A. Because of the vast amount of messages transmitted over Usenet, most systems maintain messages for only a few days or weeks. This relates to the actions of administrators, and the amount of messages that pass through the group. Some newsgroups are beginning to keep archives on web sites, which allow you to search through all the old postings for the last few weeks or months.

Q. How do I start a new newsgroup?
A. You may not find a group for the topic you desire, and may wish to inquire about starting a new group. As easy as that sounds, it is really a very complicated process. You basically write a proposal, submit the proposal for votes, and tally the votes. If the majority of voters approve of your new group, it gets created. If you're interested in doing this, see newsgroup "news.announce.newusers" for more details.

Q. Part of this newsgroup post appears to be in a language I don't understand. What is it?
A. This is an old newsgroup trick for scrambling dirty jokes, bad language, and other material that might be offensive to some. This "secret code" is called "ROT13," and it simply involves rotating each letter forward 13 positions into the alphabet. Thus, "A" becomes "N," "B" becomes "O," "Y" becomes "L," and "Z" becomes "M." This "secret" is so commonly known that most news readers have options to translate ROT13 messages. Applying the ROT13 technique to a coded message will convert it back into the original message, so the same option can be used to both encode and decode sensitive messages.

Chapter 5—Yak, Yak, Yak

● ● ● ● ●

OUR LAST CHAPTER BEGAN WITH AN EXAMPLE OF some farmers who exchanged corn-growing tips on a message board. The computer chat room takes the message board idea one step further, and changes it from a passive medium into a very active one.

Imagine this same convention of vegetable farmers, but this time the hotel rooms each have a sign on the door that indicates the topic that is being discussed inside the room. Perhaps you find the room with the sign "Avoiding Squash Rot" and decide to enter. You find a group of farmers standing around in a huge circle, all talking at the same time. As you try to separate the conversational threads, you find that some of the farmers are indeed discussing the perils of squash rot, but one group is talking about the good features of various tractors, and another group is talking about basketball. Soon you may reach the point where you'll want to call for some amount of order, so progress can be made on the subject at hand. But most of the people in the room are entirely happy with the conversation as it is. You'll either have to weed out the comments you don't want to hear or give up in disgust and leave the room.

In a computer chat room you don't really talk, of course. You type what you want to say, and your comment is immediately sent to the rest of the group. In return, you will see a screen that contains a log of all the comments made by everyone in the room. As new comments are made they appear at the bottom, and the older comments are pushed up and scrolled off the top. Each comment is prefaced with the name of the person who made the comment, so you know who is saying what. Staying in a chat room for a while can really sharpen your powers of concentration, because there can be a dozen or more different conversations (called "threads") that are occurring simultaneously. If there are a lot of people in the room and they are all talking at the same time, you'll really have to be committed to the subject at hand if you expect to tolerate the environment for more than a minute or two.

As with a newsgroup, each chat room is assigned a topic, and those who enter should supposedly be talking about that topic. Just as newsgroups can be established to talk about anything, so can chat rooms. Individuals can also establish private chat rooms, which are only open to those who know the name of the room. The idea of a private chat may conjure up images of secret groups meeting to plot a world takeover, but the intentions of the participants are usually more benign. For a while we participated in one group that would meet at 9:00 p.m. every Thursday evening and discuss science fiction. Another group would meet once a week to discuss religion. It was fun to get together for these electronic chats, knowing that the participants were sitting in homes all across the world, but having conversations as if they were all in the same room.

What follows is an actual log from a typical chat room session. To the left is the name of the person who made the comment, and to the right is the comment that was made. We have changed the names of the users in the room, to protect their identities. It would be awfully sad if you recognized that the CEO who is leading your company into the future is actually a blithering idiot who writes in sentence fragments and who spells "all right" as one word. The comments preceded by the words "OnlineHost" are messages sent by the software running the chat room. These messages generally tell you when a person enters or leaves the room. We have also deleted comments containing profanity or vulgarity, but it should be noted that both vulgarity and profanity are common expressions in chat rooms unless ground rules have been set up ahead of time, and unless there is a moderator who can see that the rules are enforced.

OnlineHost:	*** You are in "Town Square - The Saloon 12" ***
BigBird23:	where is fire????
Tiger 1990:	BORN AND BRED THAT WAY I GUESS
Padre9:	there alright
BigBird23:	that is my color, could you kindly switch?
OnlineHost:	THEFROGMAN has left the room.
BigBird23:	nah we can share
Tiger 1990:	NO
BuilderSW:	yyyyaaaaaawwwwwwwnnnnn
BlueBetty6:	sure you are
OnlineHost:	Grinin293 has entered the room.
OnlineHost:	ABC3675 has entered the room.
Grinin293:	age/sex
BigBird23:	hey baldy, is this font ugly?
ABC3675:	20/f here
BigBird23:	yea it is
FIRE0451:	im here

Grinin293:	16/f here
OnlineHost:	BlueBoy444 has left the room.
BlueBetty6:	16/f
BigBird23:	hey fire baby
Tiger 1990:	HEY FIRE WAS UP
BigBird23:	ohhh i like this one
OnlineHost:	GreatGirl9 has left the room.
OnlineHost:	DocPope7 has entered the room.
OnlineHost:	Gravity22 has entered the room.
BigBird23:	Fire is MINE
BigBird23:	hehehehe
Tiger 1990:	SHUT UP
BigBird23:	Mark??
BigBird23:	NOOOO
BigBird23:	YOU
Tiger 1990:	I COMMAND THE TO DO MY BIDDING
BlueBetty6:	no
OnlineHost:	Gravity22 has left the room.
BigBird23:	oh get real dude
Padre9:	yeap
OnlineHost:	PRISM09069 has entered the room.
BigBird23:	okay hello
Tiger 1990:	DUDE?
OnlineHost:	SpringQHS has left the room.
OnlineHost:	CuteOne432 has entered the room.
BigBird23:	yup that whjat i said
Tiger 1990:	DUDE
CuteOne432:	hi room
BigBird23:	hahahha
Tiger 1990:	HEY DUDE
JuneBoy745:	hi
BigBird23:	fire honey??
Padre9:	brb dew k
BigBird23:	june hello
BigBird23:	okay
Tiger 1990:	HEY DUDE
JuneBoy745:	hi

BigBird23:	my word
BigBird23:	hiya
DocPope7:	what's up

As you can see, this is not exactly riveting conversation. At least, that's the opin-ion of your average adult. Unfortunately, many teenagers and even more preteens think chat rooms are fascinating. Statistics show that a good deal of online time is spent there, typically by teenagers and young adults. Pedophiles also enjoy chat rooms, but we'll get to that later.

In this chapter we will teach you how to find a chat room, how to enter it, how to leave it, and how to behave once you're inside. We will also cover the dangers of chat rooms, and make suggestions for controlling their use.

Chat Room Basics

Unlike the Internet applications discussed thus far, chat rooms are quite different when using a commercial online service versus an ISP. Because of this, in each part of this section we will describe the use of chat rooms from the perspective of both types of users. First, we will discuss using chat rooms on America Online. Second, we will discuss the chat function using a program called "ichat" that runs under a web browser such as Netscape Communicator. Although you may be using different software from these two examples, most of the concepts and features will be the same in all chat software.

Getting the Software

If you use America Online, or any other commercial service, you should have the software already in place as part of the service you are using. Refer to the manuals or online help provided with your service to make sure you have everything you need.

Users of an ISP will have to do a little more work, unless your ISP provided you with chat software as part of your membership. Chat rooms on the Internet use a technology called IRC, or Internet Relay Chat. Just as there are Usenet networks that deal in newsgroup messages, there are IRC networks that deal in chat conversation. Before you can chat, you need to obtain a chat client, which is a program specially designed to access the IRC networks and allow you to participate in chats.

Chat clients can be used that are designed to run as part of a web browser, such as Netscape Communicator. The chat client is installed as a "plug-in," or "helper application," which means that the browser invokes the chat client to handle things when you desire to enter a chat room. The plug-in that is described in this chapter is called ichat. You will learn more about web browsers and plug-ins in the next chapter.

Another option is to get a chat client that runs as its own Windows application, and is designed specifically for chatting. After you have established your connection through the ISP, you just start this program and it does its job. A good example of one of these independent chat clients is called mIRC. Free or inexpensive copies of chat clients can be obtained from many of the software sites listed in Chapter 7.

Finding a Room

America Online 4.0 users can access the chat features by selecting the "People" ICON and then the "Find a Chat" menu item. An alternate method is using the "chat" keyword, and then selecting the "Find a Chat" button.

In the chat finding area, you must first select a category that describes the types of conversation you are seeking. Typical categories will be things like "Town Square," "Friends," "Life," "Places," and "Romance."

Once you select a category, you need to decide if you want a "featured" chat room or a "member" chat room. Featured chat rooms have established descriptions, they tend to accommodate more people, and they are often monitored by America Online volunteers who try to keep things under control and report serious violations. But lest you think these featured rooms are anything like a Sunday School class, consider the rooms we found while looking in the Romance category: "Lesbian," "Gay," "Divorced Only," "The Flirt's Nook," and "Tonight's the Night."

Member chat rooms are similar, but they are started by members and usually have no official volunteer or employee to monitor them. Any member can start a chat room by selecting one of the categories named above, along with the name of the chat room he wants to create. For example, you might select the Places category and start a room called "What to See in Detroit." Anyone looking at the list of members' rooms in the Places category would see your room, and could come in for a chat. While looking at the member rooms in the Romance category one afternoon, we found the following rooms: "Female Wants to Play," "Michigan Affairs," "Unhappily Married," "Females Want Males," and "Female Home Alone."

Once you have selected a category and the type of room (featured or member), the "View" option will display the rooms of that type that are active. The list will contain the name of the room, and the number of people inside.

Without even entering the room, you can use the "Who's Chatting" option to find out about the people who are inside. Selecting this option will give you a list of the user names of the people inside. If you select one of those names, you are given the option of viewing that person's member profile or sending him an "instant message." We talked about member profiles in Chapter 2, but here's a short tutorial on instant messages.

Instant messages (IMs) are private conversations between one subscriber and another, both of whom must be signed on to the service at the same time in order to participate. When you send an IM to someone else, the software opens a window on the other person's desktop, sounds a chime, and displays what you typed. It also gives the other person an option to type something back and send it to you. You can bat IMs back and forth until you disconnect from America Online, or until you get bored and close the instant message window. This is like having a private conversation just between the two of you—which is a good thing if you know the person who's IMing you, and perhaps a not-so-good thing if you've been contacted by a stranger. More on that later.

Another option for choosing a chat room enables you to search all member chat rooms by the name of the room. You might select something like "Bored in Kansas," and it will show you any rooms with that title, the number of people in the room, and the category to which it belongs.

One final option allows you to create or enter a "private" chat room. This is like a member room, but the name of the room does not appear on any of the directories. Only those who know the exact name of the room can enter. This works well if you have a group of friends who want to get together at the same time for a private conversation. You'd better give them the name of the room in advance, however, or you may be talking only to yourself.

*****

When you chat via IRC, the names are a little different. You must first select the IRC "network" you wish to join, display the conversations taking place on that network, and then choose the "channel" (instead of a room) that you wish to enter.

In this section we will discuss finding a chat room using a web browser, and then using a plug-in module, such as ichat, to do the actual chatting. There are several web sites (see Chapters 6 and 7) that allow you to search and select IRC networks and channels. One of the best ones is the Liszt site that can be found at:

www.liszt.com

This site allows you to search for IRC channels, even though they may span across many networks. Liszt provides several ways to search for channels. You can ask to see the one hundred most popular channels, you can ask to have one selected at random, or you can search for specific words in the channel descriptions. While searching you can further tailor the search to consider only certain networks, to employ a "naughtiness" filter that will exclude certain adult channels, to sort the results in a number of different orders, and to only consider channels with a minimum number of users. The result of one such scan is shown in Figure 5-1.

The results of that scan lists twelve different matches for the word "computer." Starting at the left-hand side of the screen, the Results screen shows the channel name, the number of people in the channel, the network hosting the channel, and an optional description of what is being discussed in that channel.

Once you have this search screen, clicking on the network name will show you to active channels on that network, and clicking on the channel name will request that you be allowed to enter that channel. Now, if all goes well, you will soon be chatting.

Entering

With America Online, once you have found the room for you, use the "Go Chat" option. This will get you admitted to the room so you can start chatting. When you enter the room, you will see a message that tells you the name of the room. A notice that you have entered the room will also appear in the chat area to let others know you have arrived.

When using the Liszt web site, once you have searched and found a channel you wish to join, you should be able to click on the channel name to start the chat session. This is the point where you need to cross your fingers, because there are a lot of things that can go wrong. The first error you might see is a "Save As" dialog, similar to what Windows shows you the first time you go to save a document. This is Windows' roundabout way of telling you that you are trying to use a file that it doesn't know how to handle. Usually the file will have an extension of CHA or CHAT. You might see a different error message saying something about a "MIME-type of Application/x-chat." Either of these errors indicates that your web browser doesn't exactly know how to handle a chat channel, so you need to download a plug-in application that the browser can call to do this function in the future. Most web browsers are helpful enough to even point you to a sample site where you can download the plug-in for free. Once you have downloaded ichat, or whatever plug-in you decide to use, follow the installation instructions carefully. You may have to restart your computer or your web browser.

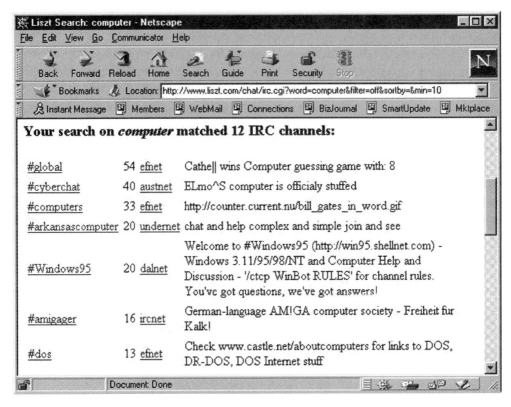

Figure 5-1

Once ichat is installed, you may still not be out of the woods. The channel you have selected may be too busy, and you will be denied access and asked to try again later. Some channels require special access codes that you probably won't have. Also, some plug-ins do not handle all of the different formats of the IRC networks. Don't get discouraged if it takes you a while to achieve success. You may have to try several channels and several networks before finding a combination that will work.

When joining a channel, ichat prompts you to enter a nickname, a user name, and a description. Other commands can be used to add more personal information, such as an e-mail address, or a mailing address. The nickname will be used to represent you in the chat session. The other items can be displayed by other people in the room if they wish to know more about you. Some of these items are optional, and even for the ones that are required, you can supply any value you wish.

When you finally connect with most channels, you are shown a series of introductory messages telling you about the channel, and about the rules that are in force there. Then you are ready to start chatting.

Making Conversation

Once the chat is started, most of your screen will contain a large text box that will contain the chat log, or the text of the conversations that have taken place in the room since you entered it. A sample of an ichat chat session is shown in Figure 5-2. When someone makes a comment, his user name will appear on the left side of the chat log, with the comment written at the right. New comments appear at the bottom of the chat log, and then scroll to the top as even newer comments appear.

Comments may also be generated by the software that runs the chat room. The comment you will most often see is when someone enters or leaves the room. In the example shown in Figure 5-2, the generated comments are prefixed with three asterisks.

If you wish to add your own comment to the discussion, there is another text box, usually underneath the chat log. Type the comment you wish to make, and then press the Enter key or press the Send button. Your comment will now appear along with the others, prefixed with your user name. In the old days, chat software used to support just standard text. Today, however, many chat clients now support colors and different fonts and text styles. This makes the conversation look prettier, even when the words themselves are devoid of interesting content.

Who's Talking?

A common feature of all chat rooms is the ability to show the other users who are in the room. This is usually done with another window on the chat screen that can be scrolled to see the names of all the participants in the chat. In the sample shown in Figure 5-2, the names of the participants are shown in the box on the right side of the screen. In the next section we will explain some of the things to do with these names.

Playing Around

Some people are content to pass the hours in a chat room just reading the conversations of others, and making an occasional comment themselves. But many people use chat rooms as a forum to meet others. They may spend some time just listening to everybody talk, or they may try to single out one or more of the room's occupants for their attention. People are different: some of them may have entirely innocent motives for singling out a person to meet, but others may have sinister purposes at hand. Chat rooms represent a huge potential threat to children, as you'll see at the end of this chapter.

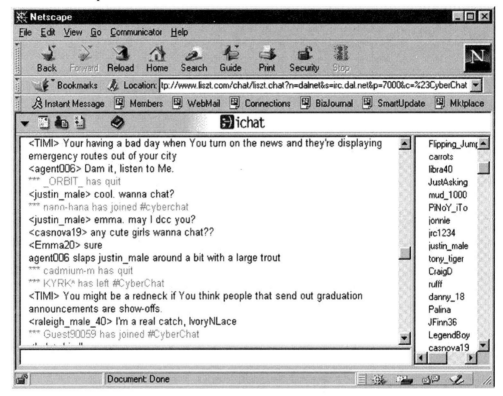

Figure 5-2

When using America Online, double clicking on a user name in the participant window will bring up a menu that gives you three options. First, you can view the member profile for that member, assuming that person has a member profile listed with the service. This might give you further information about the person who has been profiled, including that person's location, marital status, hobbies, and anything else he chose to disclose in his profile. (Keep in mind that there is no police force to make sure people tell the truth in those profiles, and that a profile which purports to be written by a thirteen-year-old girl who collects American Girls dolls can actually be written by a thirty-seven-year-old prison inmate.) If a member's profile or conversation appeals to you, the second option is to send that member an instant message, so the two of you can engage in a private conversation. The third option has the opposite effect. If someone in the chat room is annoying or obnoxious, you can check a box that says you wish to ignore any comments made by that member. This just means that any comments he makes will not appear in your chat log. This is a good feature to have when you are in a room with a know-it-all who is dominating the conversation. Ignoring a member will suppress his comments only on your chat log, and not on the logs of others (unless they have chosen to ignore him also).

Another America Online feature that we should discuss is the "buddy list." A buddy list can be used to keep track of friends that are connected to America Online at the same time you are connected. You customize your buddy list to include all the user names of the friends you wish to seek out. When you connect, the buddy list appears in the corner of your screen. If any of the people whose names are in your buddy list happen to also be connected at the same time, their names appear in the Buddy List window. If any of your friends connect or disconnect during your session, their names are added or deleted from the Buddy List window, plus a sound is played to indicate that your buddy has entered or exited the system.

When user names appear in the Buddy List window, there are a number of functions you can request. First, you can locate them. If your buddy is in a chat room, this feature will tell you the name of the room, so you can enter that room to join your friend. Another option can be used to send your friend an instant message. A final option allows you to send your friend a different message that invites him to a chat room, or to any area within America Online that you specify in the invitation.

The ichat client supports most of the same features of America Online, and then some. You can type text in different colors, to denote different emotions. You can also request that various sound effects be played, which can be heard by those participants who have the same sound files installed on their computers. (These features can be considered benefits or drawbacks, so don't overuse them just because *you* think they're cute!) You also have the option to turn all sounds off, if the noise level is waking the neighbors.

Like America Online, ichat software allows the user to send individual messages, known as "private messages," to others in the room. You can also maintain a buddy list, which lets you know if your friends have arrived in a chat room. One additional nice feature is the ability to display the names of the users who have chosen to put your name on their buddy lists. Thus, you can see who is interested in knowing where you are. You can also choose to ignore any messages sent by selected people in the current chat room.

With ichat, you can also establish moderated chat rooms, where a monitor is assigned to supervise the conversation. This could be used, for example, if a guest or celebrity were participating in the chat. With a moderated room, each participant is allowed to submit questions or comments to the monitor, who can then determine which ones to pass along to the guest. The guest can then answer the question, with the reply being sent to all the participants. This makes for a more orderly chat than when everyone is talking at the same time.

Any chat user can also request to ichat that a new room be created. The user will provide the name and whether the room is public or private. Public chats will appear on the list of current rooms, but private chats can only be entered by those knowing the name of the room. Users may also leave any chat to visit a web site, returning back to the chat when they are through browsing.

As stated previously, ichat provides a number of commands that allow you to define more personal information about yourself, such as your e-mail address or a postal address. There are also commands that allow others to display this information, based upon your user name.

The use of "avatars" is also supported by ichat. An avatar is a small picture of a person or creature, such as a wizard, a unicorn, or a frog. During the chat, the avatar is used to represent your personality, much as you might select a nickname for the chat that reflects your personality. The avatar will appear next to your user name during the chat, and will further define the personality of your chat character.

There are two options that will allow you to keep track of your friends during chat sessions, particularly if those friends like to move around from one conversation to another. The "Follow" feature allows you to specify the name of another user that you wish to follow. If the user goes into another chat room, you go with him. A similar feature is the "Go To" feature, which allows you to immediately go to the chat room where your friend is residing. You would use this when you first started to chat, if you wanted to catch up with a friend who had been there for a while.

There are options you can set to specify whether or not others should be able to follow you, or to go to your location. If the options are set to "Yes," any person can follow or join you without your permission. If the options are set to "No," then no users are allowed to follow or join. Finally, the "Ask" option will always get your permission when someone wants to follow or join you. You will be shown that person's user name, and asked if he should be allowed to join or follow you.

Some chat clients support the use of hyperlinks during a chat session. This allows users to imbed a web address (see Chapter 6) in the text they type. Those interested in visiting the site can click on the name and be taken to that web site, only to return back to the chat when they have seen enough.

Leaving

Leaving a chat room on America Online is just a matter of closing the chat window. That should take you back to the "Find a Chat" screen, and you will be able to choose another room, if you so desire.

There are more options for leaving an ichat chat room, as explained above. If you use the "Follow" or "Go To" option, you may leave the room at any time to go meet someone else in another room. That failing, the ichat window does have some toolbar options, and one of those removes you from the current room and allows you to choose another room or stop chatting.

MUDs

No discussion of chat rooms would be complete without mentioning MUDs. Depending on what you read, this stands for either Multiple-User Dimensions or Multiple-User Dungeons. A MUD uses IRC to expand the function of a chat room into an alternate fantasy world that may be explored through the use of your keyboard.

Back in the 1980s, there was a series of popular computer games called adventure games. These allowed you to explore a world and solve riddles by obtaining and using clues and objects. These games didn't have graphics, but were text only. You would communicate with simple commands, and the program would respond to those commands:

```
YOU ARE LOOKING EAST TOWARDS A MEADOW.
turn right
YOU ARE LOOKING SOUTH. THERE IS A BOTTLE.
get bottle
YOU NOW HAVE THE BOTTLE.
break bottle
YOU DON'T HAVE THE HAMMER.
inventory
YOU OWN BOTTLE, COIN, WIZARD, MAGIC LAMP.
```

Through a series of simple commands, the object was to solve the puzzles, save the world or the fair princess, and finish the game. A MUD expands this type of game to include others who are playing. Each participant will assume the roll of a fantasy character, and will interact not only with the game, but with the other players. These other players may be friendly, or may try to kill you. (Virtually, that is!)

Each MUD will have its own personality, determined by the person who created it and established the rules and laws of the MUD community. Some are designed to be played in the spirit of cooperation, with users joining their talents together to solve a common problem. Others are more "blood and guts" oriented, with emphasis on violence and dirty tricks to become the victor.

Most MUDs have remained text-only games, but some graphical MUDs are starting to appear. These show an animated world where each participant appears as a character, based on the avatar he has chosen. When a character makes a comment, the words appear next to his head in a balloon, much like a character in a newspaper comic strip.

Those who get involved with MUDs report that they can be very addictive, and more than one college student has flunked out of school because he has spent every spare moment sitting at the computer lost in a fantasy world. Parents who allow MUD access should definitely monitor its usage.

Where Danger Lurks

Due to their interactive nature, chat rooms are perhaps the most potentially dangerous of the Internet applications. Having an interactive chat session with someone can brew up trouble much faster than exchanging one or two e-mails a day. In this section we will try to identify some of the potential problems of using chat rooms.

Rough Rooms

As you might have noticed when we named some sample chat rooms earlier, some of these rooms have titles that are definitely not designed for children. When selecting categories such as Romance, you tend to find a large number of rooms with sexual themes. Even if you find interesting and wholesome room topics, there is nothing to stop someone from joining the conversation and saying things that are not appropriate for the age and interest level of the other participants. In fact, there is a segment of the online community who delights in wreaking this sort of mayhem. No matter how safe the topic, no unmonitored chat room is one hundred percent safe from intruders who wish to cause trouble.

In general, featured chats are safer than either member or private chats, particularly when using a commercial service such as America Online. But even featured chats often contain mature themes such as sexual orientation and people seeking other people for extra-marital relationships.

Because featured chats are sponsored by the commercial service, they tend to have monitors in the rooms on a regular basis. These monitors can catch the participants who most flagrantly violate the provider service rules. Of course, monitors themselves can sometimes need people to monitor them. The system is not fail-safe.

With IRC chat rooms, there is usually no monitoring, and the results may be even more inappropriate for some family members.

Private Messages

The ability to send private (instant) messages to individual chat room members is a useful feature, but can also lead to problems. Having your child participate in a group chat is one thing, but when your son or daughter starts getting private communications from other members, that is something quite different.

You should regard the senders of private messages as especially suspect when they try to persuade the receiver to give out personal information, or when they suggest that both parties enter a private chat room or initiate a meeting in person or over the phone.

Conscientious parents teach their children not to talk to strangers they meet on the street, and to avoid anyone who tries to single them out for attention. If you allow your children in chat rooms at all, you may want to consider applying the no-strangers rule to limit their private exchanges with other chat room members. Strangers online can be just as dangerous as strangers in a car, and your children should be warned on a regular basis to stay away from those strangers.

Receiving E-Mail

Once you enter a chat room on America Online, you have immediately revealed your e-mail address to the world. This is because America Online gives you no option but to list your user name as your identity in the room. Even if you never make any comments, the software will announce your name when you enter or leave the room, with a message such as "JohnDoe has just entered the room." Anyone following the chat in the room will then know that "JohnDoe@aol.com" is a valid e-mail address, and you have just exposed yourself to being placed on a spam mailing list.

We did an interesting experiment while writing this book. We had a user name that had been established for several months, which was only used occasionally. We never used it in any of the "public" areas, such as mailing lists, newsgroups, or chat rooms. In the several months we had the user name, we had never received one piece of unwanted e-mail. When Clark was researching chat rooms, he used the user name one night to visit several different chat rooms. He never made any comments, but only lurked and watched the conversation. The next day, that user name had received five pieces of spam mail, most of which were sexually oriented. It is obvious that spammers log the conversations in the chat rooms, and harvest those logs to obtain new "customers."

Chat clients such as ichat allow you to choose any identifier you want when entering a chat room. Thus, you might pick something like "NiceGuy," that has no relationship with your e-mail address. You can specify your e-mail address also, and others can display it, but at least you have the option. It is unfortunate that America Online does not allow the use of such anonymous aliases.

Displaying your user name exposes you to spam, but it also exposes you to unwanted e-mail from any of the other members in the chat room. Most people initiate private conversations with instant messages, but some may choose to use e-mail and send messages at a later time. As with spam, this danger is more applicable to systems like America Online where you cannot conceal your user name in the chat room.

Stalking

We have all heard those terrible news stories about children or adults who arranged an in-person meeting with someone they met online, only to have that meeting end in disappointment or tragedy. Although these experiences happen to a very small percentage of online citizens, they still happen often enough to keep parents awake at night. As you read the various features of chat rooms, little alarm bells should have been going off in your head. Some of the so-called "nice features" of chat rooms leave the potential for frightening consequences.

Spray yourself with disinfectant, and then let's climb into the head of A. Wacko, who is a convicted criminal. We will just use him as an example. The same techniques could be used by anyone whose motives are less than pure.

A. Wacko will first establish a user name that is harmless. He will also build a member profile that's as pure as the driven snow. His user name might be "CutiePie," and his profile might read as if it were created by a ten-year-old boy, or a twenty-five-year-old banker. He will then try various chat rooms that will tend to appeal to the type of audience he is stalking. If he is looking for children, he will enter the teen chat rooms. If he is looking for some sexual excitement, he will try the romance rooms.

A. Wacko will lurk in the room, mainly just following the conversations. As we discussed in Chapter 2, he will often be able to determine the age and sex of the participants, just by such subtle clues as participants' use (or non-use) of capital letters in their messages. If a person looks like a potential victim, A. Wacko can display the target's member profile and see what the target has to say about himself. When he finds a good candidate for his attentions, he can use an instant message to contact the target and try to initiate a private conversation. If the target responds favorably to the private messages, he might suggest that they start a private chat room. This will allow the two of them to enter their own room.

At this point A. Wacko will probably be wanting to find out more about his target. After all, there's always a chance that the target is just as phony as he is! If further investigation reveals that the target really is a potential victim, and if that potential victim is naive enough to allow A. Wacko to deepen the friendship, this is exactly what A. Wacko will do. He may ask to exchange personal information, so he can call the victim and they can visit together over the phone. Or perhaps he will insert a hyperlink for his web site, and invite the target to visit it and (supposedly) learn all about "CutiePie."

Let's assume that A. Wacko has not quite worked up the proper level of trust yet to have earned his target's confidence. He will then use the target's e-mail address to send one or more letters, describing how much he enjoyed the previous chat, and how much he would like to chat again. He might also attach a (supposed) photo of himself, and suggest that the target return the favor and send his picture back to him. If the target doesn't have a scanned picture of himself, perhaps he could just send a snapshot through the regular mail. This will not only give A. Wacko a picture of his target, but the postmark should reveal the city, and the envelope may even contain a return address.

While developing the trust with his target, A. Wacko will probably add the target's user name to his buddy list. Any time the target enters the service, A. Wacko will be notified and will be able to contact his new friend with an instant message. If his chat client supports the "Go To" function, he can jump right there and be in the same room. He can also use the "Follow" function to be near his new friend all the time he is online.

When he has established a relationship of trust, A. Wacko will attempt to get more personal information from the target, such as his name and phone number. Perhaps the target is shy about giving out this information. If so, A. Wacko will respond that the target shouldn't have any objection to calling A. Wacko collect, and just talking for a while at his expense. You can be sure that A. Wacko is equipped with caller-ID, and by the end of the conversation he will have his target's home phone number. Using that number, he can use a web site to do a reverse search to find the phone book listing for that number. Then he will have the target's phone number, mailing address, and the name of the occupants of the house.

Perhaps the target will get wise to A. Wacko and cease communicating with him. Maybe his parents will discover the situation and throw the home computer in the trash. Nothing to worry about. A. Wacko is probably grooming a whole batch of new friends, and one of them is sure to pan out.

Do not underestimate the potential danger of online stalkers. Kathy, who has been a discussion moderator for a couple of online communities, has had several periods when she's been afraid to open her front door, because she had a legitimate concern that someone may have come across the country to appear on her doorstep and cause harm. Kathy has stayed out of the chat rooms, and the online communities she moderated were as wholesome and clean as any online community. (One of them was religious in nature.) But despite these precautions, she has been stalked by three individuals whom she met through her online responsibilities.

Chilling? It most certainly is. But these are some of the techniques used to snare those who are more innocent and unsuspecting. Hopefully, using the hints in the next section will make sure this scenario is never played out for anyone you know.

AVOIDING PROBLEMS

Even though there are some real dangers associated with chat rooms, there are also some controls that will minimize the threats. We will explore these controls, and give some suggestions in this section.

Parental Controls

Most online services provide parental controls that can be used to limit some activities related to chat rooms. For those Internet users that connect with ISPs, some of the blocking software discussed in Chapter 6 also has controls for chat rooms.

America Online allows each screen name (user name) to have the following controls placed upon it related to the use of chat rooms:

❑ **Block All Rooms**

No access to any chat rooms.

❑ **Block Member-Created Chat Rooms**

No access to rooms created by other members.

❑ **Block Conference Rooms**

No access to conference rooms, which are the larger featured chat rooms.

❑ **Block Hyperlinks in Chat Rooms**

No access to hyperlinks when they are entered as part of chat text, so that they can't be followed to a web site. They are printed in the chat log as comments.

Although this is not directly related to chat rooms, parents may want to be aware that America Online also allows the option of blocking all instant messages sent to any screen name. Instant messages can be used anywhere within America Online, but are often used to start private conversations within chat rooms.

Establishing Rules

More than any other area, parents need to establish firm rules related to the use of chat rooms, and make sure that all family members understand these rules and will commit to following them.

Depending on the age of family members, parents might want to limit the rooms children may enter. If there are featured rooms, or other rooms with human monitors, stick with those. Don't allow children to enter any private chat rooms unless they get parental permission first.

Families should have strict rules about how to respond to personal attention from other chat members, such as instant messages or e-mail.

Family members should be trained to maintain a healthy dose of skepticism, and not believe everything they hear online, until proven otherwise. Not even a photograph should convince your children that the person who pretends to be ten-year-old Chuckie is not thirty-seven-year-old A. Wacko.

If family members want access to MUD rooms, parents should agree with the themes of the rooms, and should set strict time limits on the amount of daily use.

Preserving Privacy

Parents should stress again the need to promote privacy online. A child is under no obligation to reveal anything about himself if someone asks. As stated in Chapter 2, select a user name that tells little about the owner, and omit the member profile entirely, or make it general enough that it hides the age and gender and location of the owner.

When using a client like ichat, select user names and descriptions that are non-specific, and don't use the option that displays the owner's e-mail or home address to others. Regularly use the command that shows the names of the others who have added the owner's name to their buddy list. If someone the user doesn't recognize is monitoring him, he should get offline immediately.

When contributing to the conversation of the room, family members should make intelligent and thoughtful comments that reveal little about their age and gender.

If the chat client supports such options as "Go To," or "Follow," either disallow all such requests, or approve each request on an individual basis as approved by the parents.

Although the America Online buddy list feature can be annoying, there are options that actually make it work for your privacy, rather than against it. Go to the "Buddy List" keyword and select "Privacy Preferences." In the "Choose Your Privacy Preferences" section, select the option that only allows users to add you to their buddy list if they are in your buddy list. Thus, you have certain people that you want to check for online, and only those people can include you in their buddy list. Parental approval should be needed before any names are added to the buddy list.

At the bottom of the same option page, find the area "Apply Preferences to the Following Features." Check the box that says "Buddy List and Instant Messages." What you have just done is improved your privacy by only allowing instant messages and buddy lists containing your name to those individuals whose names are in your own buddy list.

America Online users can safeguard their family's chat room experience by creating a unique user name that is just used for chatting. The parental controls on this account should be configured to block all e-mail, block all instant messages, and block others from adding the user name to a buddy list. This will allow chat, but will block all attempts at communication outside of the chat itself.

Reporting Violations

Commercial online services typically have certain standards of behavior that must be followed in all areas of the service, including chat rooms. Family members should not hesitate to report chat participants whose behavior violates those standards. America Online even has a function right within the chat room that allows a violation to be reported. Even if you're not sure the person has violated their rules of service, it is better to report the offender and let the online service make the decision.

Chat rooms run over IRC networks typically have less control, and there is usually no one to whom you can report a violation. Occasionally you will find an IRC chat that is moderated, and if so, you can send any complaints to the moderator, although there is no guarantee that he will do anything about your complaint.

People who are rude and use crude and profane language should probably just be ignored. Use the "ignore" function of the chat software to hide their comments. It is difficult to say when bad behavior crosses over the line between rude and dangerous. If you think someone in a chat room is stalking, or is violating a federal law, note all the details about the incident, and contact your local law enforcement agency, or the National Center for Missing and Exploited Children at 1-800-843-5678. Note the date, time, and the name of the area (network) and chat room (channel) where the problem occurred. If possible, start the logging function so you can keep a copy of the chat room conversations. Use all possible commands to obtain information about the user name causing the problem, including such things as the member profile.

Be Suspicious and Defensive

It's a sad state of affairs to have to teach children to doubt everything they see, yet that should probably be what they do when entering a chat room. Your children should be trained to do everything possible to keep a low profile and maintain their privacy. They should be careful of the information they give out in the room, and they need to be especially suspicious of anyone contacting them directly via an e-mail or an instant message. For some reason, many children gain a sense of excitement from communicating with a stranger without their parents' knowledge. Thus, something that starts out as perhaps just a little daring can escalate into a dangerous situation. Children need to understand the potential threat of confiding in strangers, and they need to feel free to approach their parents when confronted with an uncomfortable situation.

When approached in a chat room by someone whose behavior makes them suspicious, children should be taught to just ignore the message and then use the controls that are available to limit future contact from that person. If the person persists in trying to contact your child, your child should exit the chat room, disconnect from the online service, and report the problem to an adult immediately.

A Parent's Questions

Q. Does anything good ever come from a chat room?

A. Despite their reputation as a waste of time, chat rooms have proven themselves to be a good communication vehicle in times of political crisis or natural disaster. People will often start chat rooms to ask questions of those who live within areas affected by earthquakes or floods. Many times the logs of these conversations are saved and posted on web sites so that other people can browse them and learn about the situation. Similarly, those who live in countries in the midst of revolution or other political turmoil often start chat rooms to communicate with curious family members in other parts of the world.

Chat rooms designed to help people answer questions are often also quite valuable. There are chats dedicated to discussing various computer issues, where you can usually get good advice about computer-related problems. The experts who inhabit these rooms really do seem intent on helping people, and not just hanging out to discuss the weather.

Assuming they all have computer access, families with older children spread out across the country can use chat rooms to hold regular family get-togethers. They can agree on a specific date, time, and location, and then start a private chat room just for family members. This is not as satisfying as a family reunion, but it certainly beats a letter sent once a month.

Chapter 6—Said the Spider to the Fly

•••••

HERE'S AN EXPERIMENT THAT YOU CAN TRY without getting out of your trusty reclining chair. The next time you pick up a magazine, thumb through it and look at all the advertisements. Look at the tiny print at the bottom of each one. Count the number of ads that contain statements such as:

Visit our web site at *www.bookland.com*
Visit us at *www.gymshoes.com*
Web site *www.pizzapie.com*
See us online at *www.redcross.org*
http://saverain.org
www.rosebuds.com

If you find more than ten of them, you win. Treat yourself to a free nap. But this quiz is easier than it looks, because more and more businesses are adding these tag lines to their newspaper articles, television ads, and movie previews. They represent web sites on the World Wide Web (also known as WWW, or just "the web"). This is the fastest growing segment of the Internet, and a topic to which we will devote much ink. We have already mentioned some of these web sites in previous chapters, with a promise that everything would be explained in Chapter 6. Well, that's where you are, so it's time for you to sit back and learn everything you've always wanted to know.

The funny names like those shown above are addresses you can use to get from your home to an unlimited number of locations, or "sites," all over the Internet. All you need to visit those addresses is a program called a "web browser." The function of a web browser is to visit an Internet location, retrieve the document that is stored there (called a "web page"), format the page for your computer, and then display it for you. The phrases "surfin' the web" and "surfin' the net" both refer to the process of visiting various web sites. Let's use the first example shown above. (By the way, all the names shown above were just invented for this example, so don't expect them to work.)

When you start up your browser you give it the address where you want it to go. The address we're using for this example indicates that it's a company called Bookland that is found on the World Wide Web. (The ".com" means it's a commercial site, in case you've forgotten from Chapter 1. We'll talk more about other extensions later.)

Go to: www.bookland.com

When you hit the Enter key, your browser will contact the location you specified and return the web page stored there, and will format it and display it for you to see. Depending on your modem speed and the amount of network traffic, this may take a while (which is why some people say WWW really stands for World Wide Wait).

In this example, the web page you will see will probably be information about a bookstore that sells books over the Internet. Perhaps it will just give information about the store, plus a phone number that you can call. This type of page is called an "electronic brochure," because it just gives you information and then expects you to call the company or write to them if you want to do business.

But the bookstore could also be very sophisticated. One Internet bookstore we regularly use will allow you to search for books by title, author, or subject matter. Once you have found a book, you can see a picture of the cover, read comments that other readers have made about the book, or make your own comments. The browser will also show you books with related subject matter, and will show you books that other readers bought when they purchased this particular book. Once you have selected the books you want to purchase, the company will charge them to your credit card and ship them so that they arrive within the next three days. What an easy way to shop for books, especially ones that are difficult to find!

Early web browsers would display only printed documents. This was a good way for scientists and researchers to share their papers, but it wasn't good for much else. Then enhancements were made so that pictures and drawings could be imbedded within the text and then displayed, much like you would find them in an actual book. Recent browser enhancements have allowed audio clips, video clips, and movie files to also be displayed.

One of the more valuable things that a web page can display is links to other web pages and other web sites. If your friend has an impressive site, you could include a link in your page that would say something like:

Like what you see here? Visit Bob's site.

Notice how the word "Bob's" is underlined? That means it is a link. If you click that word with your mouse, the browser will jump you into Bob's web site. This is why the Internet is called a World Wide *Web*. Many pages all over the Internet are linked together like a giant spider web.

In this chapter, we will give you many more details about how the web is constructed, and how your browser can access it and process the different types of files that are stored there. Because one of the challenges of using the web is just finding the information you want, we will also explore a valuable tool known as a "search engine."

As with previous chapters, we will also alert you to the danger spots, give hints for avoiding them, and provide tips for making sure the rules are working.

THE WORLD WIDE WEB

The World Wide Web (WWW) is really the new kid on the block when it comes to the Internet. Applications like e-mail and newsgroups seem like old-timers when compared to it. Yet it is the WWW that has really generated an interest in the Internet, transforming the Internet from a boring, text-only tool to a full-color medium complete with sounds and moving pictures. Jumping from a text-only Internet to the web is the space age equivalent of replacing an old manual typewriter with a color TV.

Information by the Ton

What if you had a magic spyglass that would allow you to peek into any home or building in the world? Wouldn't it be fun to go to Paris and visit an art museum, or to San Francisco to visit the zoo? This is basically what the World Wide Web provides. Your web browser is your spyglass, and it allows you to look through the computer files of any computer that is attached to the Internet. How many times have you heard someone tell a store employee, "Thank you very much, but I'm just browsing today"? That is what a browser does—it looks at things. You can tell your web browser to go to a specific computer on the Internet and look for a specific file. When it finds that file, it will transmit the information back to your computer and display it on your screen. The file might be a news story, or a book review, or a topographical map, or the local TV listings for your area, or a picture of your nephew. There are millions of computers that are connected to the web, and they each contain hundreds or thousands of files to be browsed. You could literally spend the rest of your life surfing the web, and not see it all. It's enough to make an information junkie break into a cold sweat.

Web Sites

A web site is an Internet address from which you can obtain information using your web browser. Most web sites use domain names, but not all domain names are web sites. Confused? You learned in Chapter 1 how domain names are assigned because they are easier to remember than IP addresses. You might send an e-mail to "Brutus@acme.com." In this example, the domain name is "acme.com," and the mail message would be sent to a mailbox named "Brutus" within that domain name.

If you forgot to put Brutus's name into the equation, and just pointed your Web browser to "acme.com," your web browser wouldn't know what to do. In effect, it would be telling the mail server, "Give me something to read." The only response the mail server could give would be, "This is not a library; this is a post office. Give me the letter you want sent!"

Some domain names are designed to read mail, some are designed for providing pages to browse, and some are designed for yet other functions. In order to use your web browser, you have to use a domain name with your browser that is designed to accept requests from browsers. Let's assume that the domain in this example, "acme.com," belongs to the Acme Anvil company. The CEO of Acme Anvil, Brutus Hardhead, wants to start a web site for providing pictures of his anvils online. Brutus cannot use the address "acme.com," because that is already used by their mail server. Since he doesn't have a creative bone in his body, Brutus obtains a new domain name called "www.acme.com." He connects that domain to something called a "web server," which is an application that is designed to talk to browsers. So now Acme has a domain name called "acme.com" that is connected to its mail server, and a domain name called "www.acme.com," which is connected to its web server.

In fact, the majority of domain names designed for web browsing have adopted this convention, so that when you see a domain name that starts with the prefix "www," you can be assured that the domain name is connected to a web server, and is just awaiting a command from your browser.

My Uncle URL

When you sit down to write a postcard, you fill in the address portion with a house number, a street, a city and state, a country, a postal code, and the name of the recipient. This is a unique address. If you've filled out the card correctly, there will only be one address in the whole world that will match what you've written. Similarly, the address you give your web browser will be the unique address of a document on the WWW.

The technical name for an address that you give your browser is a URL, or a Uniform Resource Locator. Some people pronounce this as an "Earl"; others just use the initials "U-R-L." Let's show an example of a URL you might use, and then dissect it into its various parts:

http://www.acme.com:80/products/index.html

Depending on the documentation you read, the prefix "http://" is called the protocol, scheme, access method, or technology. This basically tells the browser what to expect when it gets to this address. The code "http" tells it to expect a file that it can process using the Hyper-Text Transfer Protocol (aren't you sorry you asked). Actually, there are several different "languages" that your browser can understand, and this just tells it which one to use. Most of the time, the scheme used will be http, but we will discuss some of the other options later. The good news is that you can omit typing the entire "http://" prefix, and most browsers will just assume you want http.

The second portion, "www.acme.com," is the domain name, or host name, as described above. This is an address of a computer on the Internet that is connected to a web server.

If the domain name is followed by a colon and a number, such as the ":80" in the example above, this indicates a port number. Just as houses on a street have a house number, this is the number that the browser should use when asking for the information. If you don't code this, the browser will use a default of 80, meaning it will always go to "house" 80 if you don't give it a "house" number. Almost every site you visit will use this default, so don't even think about it unless you're given a URL with some other value.

The section of the example URL containing "/products/" is called the path name. We will discuss that more in the next section. For now, just think of it as the area on the computer where the document we want is stored.

The last item of the example URL is "index.html," and this is the name of the file we want the browser to find for us. Just like a file name stored on your hard drive, this file is composed of a name and an extension. The extension HTML means this is a document that is written in something called Hyper-Text Markup Language. We will discuss this in Chapter 7, when we teach you how to build your own web pages. For now, just think of it as the language in which most WWW pages are composed. If you don't specify a file name as part of the URL, your browser will look for a file named "index.html," or "index.htm." So the last part of the example URL really wasn't needed either, because the browser would have tried that name anyway if we hadn't so considerately provided it.

Now let's have a little quiz and see if you were paying attention during that last section. Sorry to be picky, but it is really important that you understand this. There's only one question on this quiz. If you were lazy (like most of us) and wanted to do the minimum typing possible, what would you type for the above example so that it would still work?

Okay, pencils down. The answer is: www.acme.com/products/. Actually, for the *really* lazy, you probably don't even need the last slash.

All of the rules we gave you in Chapter 1 related to domain names will apply to web site names as well. For example, most web site domains you see will end in the standard suffixes of "com" (for commercial), "edu" (for educational), etc. You will see some that use the newer standard, such as "www.library.sf.ca.us." This indicates the library system, within San Francisco, within California, within the United States. That is just an example though, so don't try it.

Rather than typing long URL names and taking the chance of making an error, remember the standard Windows technique of copy-and-paste. If you have an e-mail or newsgroup post that refers you to an interesting web site, just copy-and-paste it into the Location window of your web browser. As noted in previous chapters, web site addresses may often be embedded directly in e-mail, newsgroups, or chat room conversations as hyperlinks. They usually appear in a different color, and are under-lined. Clicking on a hyperlink will start your web browser, and pass it to the URL address it should locate. This is even easier than using copy-and-paste.

Directories and File Names

Each web site you visit may have hundreds or thousands of potential files for you to access. These files are stored on the hard drive of the computer on which the web server is running. This hard drive is organized much like the hard drive on your computer. There is a root directory that may contain files or subdirectories. Each subdirectory may in turn contain files or other subdirectories.

Remember in the example URL above, we said that the last two things you type are the path name and the file name. This is how you tell the web browser to navigate the hard drive of the computer you are browsing. If the file you want is in the root directory, you just type the file name, and you don't even need that much if the file name is one of the default file names, "index.htm," or "index.html." If the file you want is in a subdirectory, just type it before the file name with a slash on each side, such as "/tools/." You may see URL addresses such as "www.x.com/math/tables/sqroot.htm." The portion consisting of "/math/tables/" is the path name, as that tells the browser the path to follow to find the document. This basically says, "In the root directory find a subdirectory called 'math.' Within that, find a subdirectory called 'tables.' Within that, you will find the document I want called 'sqroot.htm.'"

Taking Your Browser for a Test Drive

The best way you can learn more about your browser is to fire it up and take it for a test drive. Some of the things you will learn in this section will be easier to understand if you're actually in front of a keyboard so you can experiment while you learn.

All of this is assuming that you do have a browser. Most computers come with one or more of them already installed. If you are using a commercial service such as America Online, the browser comes as part of the software you use with that service. If you subscribe to an ISP, the ISP probably furnished you with some software as part of your subscription. If neither of the above is true, you can buy a browser at your local computer store, or download one for free from a web site. We know this is putting the chicken before the egg again, but maybe you can coax or bribe a friend to help you download the software from one of the following sites:

www.netscape.com (Use the "Download" option for Netscape Communicator)
www.microsoft.com (Use the "Free Downloads" option for Internet Explorer)

The two browsers mentioned above are the two most popular, although you can buy less popular ones that work just as well. If you use America Online, the browser you are using is really Internet Explorer, even though it has been integrated into the rest of the software, so it looks just like another America Online screen. (That may change, however, now that Netscape has been acquired by America Online.)

General Navigation

When you start your web browser, it is usually configured so that it automatically takes you to a certain web site. (Don't worry, we'll show you how to change this to a location of your own choosing.) If everything works as planned, you should see a window that looks something like Figure 6-1.

Figure 6-1

The browser shown in Figure 6-1 is the Netscape Communicator, and it is visiting a web site that allows you to download free software. We will talk more about these sites in Chapter 7. The image on your browser will likely look different from this example, because you may have a different browser, and you will be looking at a different web site. But it should look similar to this.

Like most Windows programs, your browser has a menu bar that can be used to select various program functions. Most browsers will also have a tool bar under the menu bar, containing ICONs for the more common functions. Some browsers even support a personal tool bar that you can customize with your favorite options.

Near the top of the screen, you should see a small text box with a title that is something along the lines of "Address," "Location," or "Go." In this box is displayed the URL address of the current page you are viewing. If you want your browser to display a different web site, you can type over this URL with a different value, or you can delete the whole thing and type an entirely new one. Then press the Enter, or

Return, key, and your browser will attempt to display the document at the new address. To the right side of this text box, you should see an arrow that points down. If you press on this, you should see a drop-down list of the most recent URLs you have visited during this browser session. Most browsers keep track of the last ten or fifteen sites you have visited. If you see a previous site to which you wish to return, clicking on the URL should send the browser back to that site.

A small rectangular area on the bottom of the browser window is called the "status box." The browser displays messages there related to the operation you are requesting. In Figure 6-1, this contains the message "Document: Done," meaning the requested document has been accessed and displayed in the browser window. This message area changes as the document is being located, transmitted back to you, and then finally displayed.

Your browser is one of those software programs that allows you to get some use out of your right mouse button. For example, if you display a page that has a pretty picture on it, put the mouse pointer over the picture and right-click the mouse. This should pop up a menu that allows you to do a number of things, including saving a copy of the picture to your own disk drive.

In the rest of this section, we will describe some of the more common functions you can do with your browser. These functions may be requested through the menu or the tool bar:

❑ **Home**

This directs the browser to go back to the first web site that was displayed when the browser was started. This default can be changed, so your browser will always start at your favorite site, and will return to that site when you use the Home function.

❑ **Stop**

The Stop function aborts the loading of the current web page. This is a convenient feature if you can see that a partially-loaded page doesn't appeal to you or is not what you expected, or if you change your mind and decide you need to visit another site first.

❑ **Reload**

The Reload function reloads the last page that was requested. There are several uses for this feature. First, you might have aborted the load previously, but now decide you want it to proceed. Or the computer may have gotten locked up while the file was loading, and a reload could expedite the process. Another reason to use this feature is to see whether the file could have changed since you last fetched it. Requesting this feature will call up the latest version. We will discuss this in more detail when we talk about NetCams and browser caches.

❑ **Back**

The Back function takes you back to the previous page you viewed.

❑ **Forward**

The Forward function is the opposite of the Back function, and it may only be used after you have done one or more back operations.

❑ **Print**

The Print function prints a copy of the page or pages being displayed on your printer.

❑ **Save As**

The Save As function allows you to save a copy of the current page being displayed on your hard drive or a floppy drive. This is useful if you want to make a copy of the page being displayed so that it may be included in another document or application. You usually have the option to save the page as a text file or in its original HTML language. Some types of web pages cannot be saved with this option.

❑ **Copy/Paste**

As with any Windows application, you can usually copy pieces of a web page into the Windows clipboard, and then paste those portions into other documents.

❑ **Find**

The Find function searches the current page being displayed for a certain word or phrase that you provide.

❑ **New Window**

Your browser is a Windows application that supports multiple windows being open at the same time. This option opens a new browser window, so that a second web site may be accessed without disturbing the original browser window. This allows you to navigate through multiple web sites at the same time.

❑ **Search**

The Search option connects you with several popular search functions that may be used to search the WWW for documents of interest to you. We will discuss these functions (called "search engines") later in this chapter.

Hyperlinks

Hyperlinks are areas you can click that will start your web browser and magically transport you to a location on a web site. We have already discussed hyperlinks in regard to e-mail, newsgroups, and chat rooms, but they also may exist as part of the web pages you display. In fact, hyperlinks are one of the features that make the WWW so exciting. You might visit a friend's web site and find that he loves cowboy movies, and has provided a link to a site that provides movie reviews. At the movie review site, you might find a link that connects to another site that sells movie videos over the Internet. When you find that site, you might also find the company sells music CDs, and they have links to the web sites of various popular singers. Once you have followed web site links for a while, you will understand the origin of the term "web" in WWW. All of these pages are linked together like the strands of a giant spider web. Fortunately, we have never encountered a giant spider.

There are three kinds of hyperlinks that you will commonly find when you start exploring web sites:

❑ **Text**

This is a word or phrase that will be a different color from the rest of the text, and it will be underlined. To follow the link, put the mouse pointer over the word and click.

❑ **Image**

An image will be a small picture or ICON, with a colored border around it. To follow the link, put the mouse pointer over the picture and click.

❑ **Image Map**

An image map is like an image (see above), except that clicking the link does different things depending on where the mouse pointer is located when you click. For example, some web sites show a map of the United States, and will show you the current weather in any part of the country. Clicking on Vermont gives you the weather for New England, but if you click on California you'll learn what's happening on the Pacific Coast.

Text hyperlinks usually appear as blue—at least, the first time you see them. Once you have followed a link and returned to your original destination, the color of that link will change from blue to purple. This is to let you know that you have already followed that link, so you won't forget and select it again. One nice feature of this is that it will change color on any web page that contains the link. For example, both Brutus and Herschel have links to the Acme Anvil company on their web sites. You go to Brutus's site and then link to Acme Anvil. A week later you visit Herschel's site, only to find that his link to Acme Anvil is purple, meaning you once visited that link, even though you linked to it from a different web site. Magic, no? This is a handy feature when doing research, to keep you from visiting the same sources more than once.

An image hyperlink is surrounded by a colored border that reacts the same way as the color on a text hyperlink. That is, it changes color when you click on the image and visit the site. You can change the options in your browser to specify the colors of followed and unfollowed hyperlinks, as well as the number of days the browser should remember that you have visited a particular link.

Your browser does a couple of other interesting things to let you know that you are using a hyperlink. Normally, when displaying a web page, the mouse pointer is in the shape of an arrow. As you move the pointer over the page, it will change from an arrow to a hand when it is over a hyperlink. Thus, anytime you see a mouse pointer in the shape of a hand, you can click there to activate a hyperlink. Also, when the mouse pointer is positioned over a hyperlink, information will appear in the status box at the bottom of the browser window. This information will either be a description of the link, or the actual URL address that will be used if you click. This is often useful to help you determine if you want to follow the link. For example, if the web page you display has a link that says "Click here to party!", and when the mouse pointer is on the link the status box says "www.hotsex.com," you have a pretty good idea that the link won't be taking you to a kid's birthday party.

Some browsers will also show you interesting information if you right-click on a hyperlink.

Bookmarks

Just as scraps of paper can serve as a bookmark to hold a favorite place in a beloved book, all common browsers give you the ability to maintain a list of bookmarks that can help you return to a favorite destination on the Web. These bookmarks may be given different names, such as Favorites, or Favorite Places—but a bookmark under any other name will still hold your place. Every novice web surfer has had the bad experience of finding an interesting or useful web site, only to try to return later and not be able to find it. As their name implies, bookmarks are a useful way of saying, "Mark this page for me, because I like what I see, and I'm going to want to return." Browsers usually provide a combination of the following bookmark functions:

❏ **List Bookmarks**
    This lists the bookmarks you have previously created. If you see something you like, click on the bookmark and you will be taken to that location.

❏ **Add Bookmark**

This adds an entry for the current web page to your bookmark list. Use this option when you are displaying a page that you would like to visit again. The entry that is created for the bookmark is usually not the URL, but the title displayed on the web page. Some browsers give you an option to provide your own title.

❏ **Edit Bookmarks**

This allows you to create and delete bookmark folders, and to rename, delete, and move bookmarks. Folders allow you to group common bookmarks together in common categories, such as "Research," "Fun," "Sports," and "Finance."

❏ **Import and Export**

Exporting your bookmarks allows you to create a copy of them in a file. Importing is the opposite; it allows you to read an exported file and create entries in your bookmark list from them. This is useful if you wish to trade bookmarks with friends. You can each export your bookmarks onto a floppy disk, exchange disks with your friends, and then import each other's bookmarks into your own list. Rather than have the imported entries mingled with your own, the browser usually creates a new folder and places all the imported entries there.

History Folder

If you forgot to bookmark an exciting web site, all is not lost. You may still be able to find the site in what is called the "history folder." This folder keeps track of all the web sites you have visited for the past few days. If you visit the site regularly, it will stay active in the history folder. If you stop visiting it, then it will eventually age out of the folder after a few days.

Using Netscape Communicator as an example, when you open the history folder, it will show the following information for each item in the folder: Web page title, location (URL), time of first visit, time of last visit, number of visits, and the date the entry will expire if the page is not visited again. Clicking on the title bar above any column will sort the folder based on that column. Clicking it multiple times will alternate between ascending and descending sort sequence. For example, you could sort it so that the most commonly visited sites appear at the top. Double-clicking on any of the rows in the folder will cause the browser to go to that web site.

Most browsers provide the options that control how the history folder is managed. For example, Netscape Communicator allows you to set the number of days until old entries are removed from the folder. The default is nine days, but you may want to set a higher value, such as thirty. Also, there is an option that will empty the history folder and remove all the entries so you can start over again.

WHAT TRICKS CAN A BROWSER DO?

Now you know that a browser can visit any URL on the web and display what is there on your computer screen. But what kind of files can it handle? We know it does text, but what else? These are the questions we will answer in this section, as we look at the various kinds of files upon which a browser can perform its magic.

Text

Some of the first users of web technology were a group of scientists working at CERN, a physics research center in Switzerland. They wanted a tool that would allow them to write research papers and share those papers immediately with other scientists all over the world. Thus, many of the early features of HTML, the language in which web pages are written, concerned themselves with the display of text. Participants could display text using different fonts, and could use text styles, such as bold, italics, and underlining. They could also do things such as center text and provide horizontal lines.

Early browsers also supported hyperlinks, which provided a way to reference other documents that was much superior to footnotes. Instead of having a footnote refer you to another document, you could simply provide a link to that document. Those who wanted to check a scientist's source material were only a click away from it.

Tables

Because many documents contain tables of numbers, it was only natural that HTML be expanded to support tables within a document. This feature causes the browser to display a table, with user-provided data inserted into the various rows and columns. The user may specify such things as the size of the table, the titles for each row and column, the thickness of the border lines, and whether or not the table should be centered on the page. The cells within a table can not only contain numbers, but may contain items such as hyperlinks.

Whenever new features are proposed, they are proposed first in the HTML language specification. Once the enhanced HTML features are generally accepted, the software companies that write the browsers enhance them to support the new features. Thus, if you have an old browser, it may not support some of the newer features of the HTML language. This usually causes the browser to just ignore the features it doesn't understand. So what might appear as a table of numbers on a newer browser might just appear to be a jumble of numbers on an older one.

Graphics

Many documents contain figures or illustrations, so it was only natural that HTML be enhanced to allow the display of images. As noted in Chapter 0, pictures and drawings are converted into computer files with a scanner, or they are created by digital cameras and then copied to a computer. Although there are several formats for these graphical files, most browsers only support the two most common—JPEG and GIF. You can identify files in these formats because their extensions will usually be JPG or GIF.

When building a web page that includes a graphical image, the image is not embedded in the page, but is only referenced by the page. For example, the file you wish to display as part of the page might be named FIG1.GIF, and might live in a directory called "figures." When you build the web page, you simply refer to the directory name and the name of the file, something like <IMG SRC="/figures/fig1.gif">. When the browser loads the page, it also loads the graphic image and displays it at the proper location within the page. There are also other options that control the positioning of the graphic, and the flow of text around it.

One interesting variation of a GIF file is called an "animated GIF." This allows multiple images to be stored in one file, and the browser rotates through the images as it displays them. Thus, the changing image makes it appear to be animated. You will often see these kinds of images drawing attention to web sites, because they can be used for special effects such as burning fires and rotating skulls. As you might also expect, they are used quite heavily to advertise pornographic web sites.

Frames

Another common feature you will see on web pages is a "frame." Frames allow the browser window to be broken up into two or more sections, each of which can operate more or less independently. Each section can be a different size, as determined by the designer, and each section may have its own unique buttons, options, and scroll bars. Users can navigate through multiple areas in one section, while the other sections may remain constant.

A common design incorporates a small frame on one side of the screen. This frame will contain option buttons to select the various choices available. As the user chooses one option or another, the right-hand frame will change to accommodate the user's request, but the smaller frame will not change, and will continue to list options.

Forms

Support for forms allows a web page to be designed like a Windows dialog, in that the host can interact with the user and have users enter items of information. These forms can be quite complex, such as an online purchase form, or as simple as a text box and search button. Forms will support elements similar to those found on a Windows dialog, such as text boxes, check boxes, drop-down lists, radio buttons, and push buttons. Most forms will contain a button labeled "Clear," which will clear all the options on the form, and a button labeled "Submit," or "Send," which will allow the information on the form to be processed by the web page.

When you buy a new product, you typically send in a card to register the product and start your warranty period. Many manufacturers are converting to online registration, where users can contact the company's web site and complete an online form to register. It is not uncommon to find useful web sites that provide information free of charge, but ask that you register and get a password so that you can use the system. This is just another example of designing a web site using forms to obtain information from those who visit.

Audio Files

Web pages can be a virtual cornucopia for the senses. Lest you think all web pages contain content for the eyes only, there are other items designed to stimulate the ears. For example, you might visit a page sponsored by a music company that will offer small song clips from their featured artists. When you click on the name of an artist, a small sample file is downloaded, and then the browser plays it. Note that a sound card and speakers are required, and that sound files can be quite large. It is not uncommon to wait fifteen minutes for a sound file to download that then only plays for one minute. Usually when playing the file, the user is presented with a control panel that permits functions such as volume control, pause, fast forward, rewind, and search.

Some audio files are loaded automatically when a web page is fetched. For example, if you visit a Halloween site, you might hear a squeaky door when you first enter the area. This is different from files that you choose to download, but the technology for playing the file is the same.

One recent audio innovation is something called "streaming audio." Unlike regular audio files, this allows users to start playing the file as it is being downloaded, rather than having to wait for the entire file to download first. This also allows users to hear live audio, because the sound can be updated as it is being sent. Several radio stations have web sites equipped with streaming audio that allow computer users to listen to their stations live, using the speakers on their computers. Thanks to modern technology, users can sit in the comfort of home and listen to a radio station three thousand miles away. Talk about reception! Streaming audio will also play saved files, so a radio station could offer a menu of concerts, interviews, and sporting events. Users can choose the programs they wish to hear, and have the customized programs played on their home computers.

Video Files

Browsers can also play video files, allowing users to see short movies that play within a window on the web page. As with audio files, video files are usually quite large, and require long downloads for just a few seconds of footage. As a result, most video sequences are quite short, and suffer from poor resolution and choppy movement. But faster hardware and enhanced software systems are improving video quality and speed to the point that the images can be quite realistic on some of the newer machines.

Like streaming audio, streaming video allows the video to start playing while it is still being downloaded. A streaming video file may also be a live broadcast or a file saved from a previous taping.

By adding special hardware and software, some people are using this technology to hold video conferences on the Internet. This allows participants to see and hear each other, plus to have access to a "white board" for written materials. In order to do this, each participant needs a video camera and microphone attached to his computer. Like a chat room, participants can visit web sites that are hosting several conferences, and select the one they wish to join. Although Internet video conferencing is quite expensive, it is still cheaper than many commercial video conferencing systems.

NetCams

One unusual Internet application is the "NetCam." As the name implies, this is a camera in a fixed location that takes a picture every so often, converts it to a graphics file, and then saves it as an Internet file. Browsing a certain web page will load the graphics file and show users the latest image. Early NetCams were often focused on silly subjects, such as coffeepots, soda machines, and aquariums. Some amateur exhibitionists then got into the act and placed NetCams in their homes. You could then visit their web site and see them watching television, eating dinner, reading the paper, or doing whatever they happened to be doing. (This application is still popular for pay-per-view pornographic services, by the way. Users can whip out the old charge card and be "treated" to images of Missy or Buffy or some other vixen as she toodles around her house in the nude.)

Although previous NetCam applications have been somewhat silly, they do have some interesting potential. There are several weather web sites that display various NetCam views showing the weather in major cities. Some busy cities are also using them to show traffic flows along major highways during rush hours.

Viewing a NetCam site is one time when it comes in handy to use the Reload function on your browser. This causes the browser to load the latest file from the web site, which may have changed since you last looked.

Internet Telephone

How would you like to make free long-distance phone calls? That's the idea of "Internet telephone," an application that allows users to speak with someone else anywhere in the world through their Internet connections. In order to use this, both parties must be online at the same time, and must have compatible Internet telephone software. Their computers must also be equipped with a microphone and speakers.

There are many different companies that make the software for this application. Many of them provide a demonstration version that users can download for free and try out. These demonstration versions may limit each conversation to only a minute or two, to encourage consumers to buy the real version. As would be expected, many of the telephone companies are not happy about this situation, and are trying to push for legislation that would place taxes or fees on such services.

A variation of Internet telephone is used to connect to some audio chat rooms. As the name implies, these chat rooms feature actual voices, rather than typed comments.

Virtual Reality

Some web sites feature virtual worlds that are written using a language called VRML (Virtual Reality Modeling Language). The web browser reads and interprets the VRML file, and then displays the results on the computer monitor screen as a three-dimensional world. Users can then navigate through the world and manipulate objects they find there.

The first application of VRML was for games, but later applications were developed to simulate things such as flying through space, or exploring parts of the human body.

Within each virtual world, you can have links to other VRML files as well as animation files. You can also overlay graphics files onto the scene.

JavaScript

JavaScript is a programming language that is written as part of a web page. When the web page is selected for display, the JavaScript program is not displayed as part of the screen, but is extracted from the page and executed by the web browser. Although JavaScript is not used for complex programming tasks, it comes in handy for doing things such as validating the data a user entered on a web form, to make sure it is correct and complete.

For example, you might have a text area on a form and you may wish to require the user to enter something in that area. There is no way you can do this just by using the browser itself. But if you write a small JavaScript program that gets control when the form is completed, you can check the area, make sure everything was coded correctly, and issue a customized error message if it was not.

Java Applets

Java is a fairly recent programming language that is used quite frequently in the design of web pages. Although Java can produce regular programs, called "applications," it will also produce smaller programs, called "Applets," which are designed to be used specifically with web pages.

When your browser transfers a web page to your computer, it may also find that an Applet is associated with that page. If so, it will transfer the Applet program to your computer as well, and execute it there. Each Applet is given a specified piece of "real estate" on the browser screen, and is allowed to perform its function within that space. It may produce some interesting graphics, or collect information from a form and then present the results of calculations. Multiple Applets may be running at the same time, each communicating with the others and managing multiple windows on the browser screen. If you visit a web site that employs some really interesting special effects, the odds are good that you are seeing one or more Applets in action.

The thought of having a foreign program executing on your computer might be a concern to some, but the designers of Java thought of this. Java Applets are quite limited in terms of what they can do, so it is pretty unlikely that even someone with mischievous motives could do a lot of harm. For example, Applets cannot access any of the files on your disk drives, either for reading or for writing.

File Downloads

Another common use for web browsers is to find interesting files on web sites and then download them to your computer's disk drives. Chapter 7 will list a number of web sites where you can go to find and download shareware (inexpensive) or freeware (free) software programs. The web page that shows and describes each program will usually have a hyperlink beside each program name. If you want that program, you simply click on the link. Unlike a typical hyperlink that transfers you to another web page, clicking a hyperlink for a file to be downloaded will simply display a "Save As" dialog, much like the dialog displayed the first time you save any file in a windows application. When you have navigated to the proper subdirectory, and pressed the proper button, the save will proceed, and the file you are downloading will be transferred to your disk drive.

Once the download is complete, you may need to manipulate the file before it can be used. Many files to be downloaded have been compressed to save space, so that they may be downloaded faster. Compressed files on PCs usually have a file extension of ZIP. Not only are compressed files smaller, but they may contain multiple files and even multiple subdirectories within one compressed file. The process of uncompressing will extract the original files from the ZIP file, uncompress them, and store them back under their original names, in the original subdirectory structure.

The most common programs for doing this are called PKZIP (for compressing or "zipping") and PKUNZIP (for decompressing or "unzipping"). One problem with these utilities, however, is that they do not support the longer file names added in Windows 95. They will still work with Windows 95 files, but the file names will be corrupted. A better option is probably one of several Windows compression applications, such as a common one called WinZip. All of the compression programs mentioned here can be found at the software sites mentioned in Chapter 7.

One other type of common file is something called a self-extracting file. This file has a file extension of "EXE," so it appears to be an executable program. But when you try to execute the program, it proceeds to produce PKUNZIP-like messages, and uncompress a bunch of files. This type of file may also be created with one of the programs distributed as part of PKZIP. The advantage of the self-extracting program is that the person receiving it does not need to have a copy of PKUNZIP, nor understand how to use it.

Plug-ins and Helpers

Those who designed the web browsers made sure that new types of features could be installed later without having to upgrade the browser. (This is called "open architecture.") Allowing for new features is one of the things that has caused the WWW to grow so quickly, because designers can develop new applications and the software to handle them without having to contact the browser makers and have them change their software.

A browser is given orders to go to a specific URL and process the file that is there. From that first file, hyperlinks may be used to have the browser fetch other files. So the browser is a tool that navigates a stream of commands related to the processing of different files. For each of those files, the browser will use the file name extension to determine how to process the file. If the extension is HTM, the browser will recognize that this is an HTML document, and it will process the commands within it. If the extension is GIF or JPG, the browser will recognize that it is dealing with a graphics file that should be displayed on the browser screen. If the extension is not one that the browser can handle internally, it will use a table to look up the file extension and see if it knows anything about a file of that type.

If the browser cannot determine what to do with a specific file, it will just pop up the "Save As" screen, and allow you to save the file to your local disk drive. This is exactly what you want to have happen for some files, such as the program downloads that were discussed in the last section. But some files do not need to be saved. In these cases, what we really need to do is help our browser understand what it needs to do to handle a file of that type. This can be done by installing a "plug-in" that the browser will call in the future whenever it finds a file of that type.

Plug-ins are also known as "readers" or "players." Another type of similar software is called a "helper" application. The difference between a plug-in and a helper is that the plug-in usually operates as part of the main browser screen, while the helper often launches a new screen to handle the application. Both plug-ins and helpers can usually be downloaded for free from web sites. Often, the browser itself may suggest a location for downloading the needed piece of software.

YOUR MULTILINGUAL BROWSER

We said earlier that your web browser speaks a number of different languages, more properly known as "schemes." Your browser knows what scheme to use from the first few letters in the URL. Here is a brief description of the common schemes that most browsers can support:

HTTP

Hyper-Text Transfer Protocol is the most common scheme, and it is the default that will be used if you omit the scheme in the URL address. All of the browser applications discussed in the previous section run as subsets of the HTTP scheme. This includes text, graphics, hyperlinks, audio files, movie files, and NetCams. Probably ninety-five percent of the time your web browser is in use, it will be speaking HTTP.

FTP

File Transfer Protocol is a scheme commonly used to upload and download files. When you click on a web page to download a file, it actually uses FTP to accomplish the download. But you can also invoke FTP directly, and instruct your browser to go to a web site specifically designed for FTP downloads. When using a browser to run FTP, you can usually only download files, even though FTP itself will support uploading as well.

When you connect with the FTP site, your browser will typically show a tree of folders and files, much like the one you see when navigating through your hard drive with Windows Explorer. Click on the folders to open them, or click on a file to download it.

If you're going to do any serious FTP work, the best way to do it is to forget the browser and use an FTP application. There are many good free or inexpensive programs that allow FTP, such as one called WS_FTP. Some FTP sites require you to enter a user name and a password to gain access, but others allow you to use "anonymous" for the user name and your e-mail address as the password. A site that accepts such identification is known as an "anonymous" FTP site, and there are quite a few of them. Most browsers will support anonymous FTP sites, but not sites where you have to enter a real user name.

When downloading or uploading files, you often need to specify whether you want ASCII or binary transfer mode. ASCII will convert the file so that it will display properly on the computer to which it is being transferred. Binary does no conversion, but transfers the files with no changes. You usually don't have to specify this when you use a browser for FTP, because it will detect FTP and set the mode automatically.

Most commercial providers also supply some kind of interface so that you can access FTP sites. Using America Online, for example, you need to go to the keyword "FTP" and it will guide you through a series of panels to allow FTP uploading or downloading. It's not as elegant as WS_FTP, but it works.

Because of the high level of activity on some FTP sites, the more popular ones may support one or more "mirror" sites. As the name implies, each site has duplicate copies of the same files. You simply choose the site that you think will be closer to you, or that will have less traffic for the particular time of day.

Gopher

Gopher is not as popular now because of WWW search engines, but it is still used by universities and other large organizations that have been on the Internet for a long time. Connecting to a Gopher site provides a treelike menu structure that allows you to navigate through a variety of submenus, files and services. When you select an option, Gopher knows the proper protocol to use when accessing it. Each Gopher entry does not contain the actual data, but provides pointers to other Internet locations. Most of the data accessed via Gopher are displayed as text only.

Telnet

Telnet is an older protocol that allows you to connect to other computer systems as a remote user. The systems that support Telnet tend to be older, menu-driven software systems such as the electronic card catalogs you find in many public libraries. If your library supports Telnet, you can connect to the system and enter the same commands as if you were sitting at a terminal in the library.

Many systems that allow Telnet access require you to go through a "sign-on" or authentication process before using the system. If the system asks for a user name, try "guest" or "anonymous." If it asks for a password, try your e-mail address.

Because such systems are usually written for different keyboards, you might find you will need to use a different combination of keys than you usually use. For example, you might have to use the space bar at the end of each request, rather than the Enter key. Pay attention to any instructions that are given when you connect to the system. If the software asks for something called "terminal emulation," select VT-100. That is the configuration that provides the best operation with a PC keyboard. Remember also to press the Enter key after each line, because most of these systems are written to expect that.

WAIS

The Wide Area Information Server (WAIS) allows for the sophisticated searching of databases, often databases that may be scattered over a wide distance. WAIS allows you to search using normal questions, such as, "Tell me about the Empire State Building." Based on the results of your search, you can continue refining your questions until you have found the material you want, at which point the files can be transferred back to your computer.

Your web browser itself is capable of doing WAIS searches, but you have to install some specialized WAIS software and then make sure it is configured correctly. For most users, a better option is to Telnet or Gopher into web sites that support WAIS searches, and then perform limited searches from those sites.

News

Most browsers also support the same protocol used by news readers to read newsgroups. You type a URL such as "news://comp.answers," and your browser will attempt to access the "comp.answers" newsgroup. We have had mixed results in doing this because some browsers don't seem to handle the messages well, and they don't contain all the fancy features present in most news readers. But you might give it a try and see if it works for you.

Mailto

When you start browsing web pages, you will often see hyperlinks at the bottom of a page inviting you to send an e-mail message to the company or the author of the page you are viewing. If you click on this link, the browser will open a Compose Mail window, with the name of the recipient already supplied. You just need to complete the rest of the message and then send it.

This is handled by a browser protocol called "mailto." If you were to actually look at the HTML for the web page, you would find a string within the hyperlink that looks like "mailto:joe@acme.com." This tells the browser to use the "mailto" protocol, and fill in the address of "joe@acme.com" as the recipient of the message.

Most browsers also allow you to enter a similar command in the URL location area, causing the browser to display a Compose Mail screen with the address you specified in place. This could be considered a shortcut for sending an e-mail in the middle of a browsing session.

In Search of an Honest Site

One of the fun aspects of the WWW is discovering all the different information that exists in the millions of sites that comprise the web. But how does one go about finding interesting sites? Of course, there are the usual sources such as friends who pass along interesting URLs, and printed articles that describe useful sites (we'll even do a little of that ourselves in the next chapter). But what if little Billy announces on Thursday night, "Oh, I forgot to tell you I need a school paper about Galileo tomorrow." Panic time! The library is already closed. Then the lightbulb goes on, as you remember that there must be some web sites about Galileo. How do you go about finding them?

There are two kinds of electronic detectives that will help you sniff out interesting sites, both of which are described in this section.

Index Sites

Index sites are also known as "web guides" because they attempt to navigate you to useful web sites by listing the sites according to category. This is an expanded version of the bookmark feature that your browser uses.

With your browser, you may create folders to organize your bookmarks by area of interest, such as Shopping, Sports, News, and Games. Similarly, an index site shows you some general categories, such as Arts, Business, Computers, Entertainment, Health, News, Science, and Society. When you select one of those categories, you may be shown a series of subcategories. For example, if you selected Entertainment, you might see subcategories of Board Games, Movies, Music, and Television. There may be several different levels of sub-categories, as you continue to narrow down to exactly your area of interest. Finally, you will arrive at a page that contains hyperlinks to the web sites related to that topic. Next to each hyperlink there may be a description of the content of that web site. Click on the hyperlinks that look interesting to visit, and then use your browser's "Back" function to return to the listing of hyperlinks.

Let's see if we can get Billy some information for his paper using Yahoo, one of the more common index sites. From the main Yahoo index, we see a category called Science, which is where we start. Under Science, we select the subcategory Astronomy, because we seem to remember that Galileo may have had something to do with the stars. Under Astronomy, there is a subcategory called Astronomers, which looks promising. Sure enough, under Astronomers we find fourteen web sites related to Galileo Galilei. Now Billy can write his paper, content in the knowledge that Mom and Dad are geniuses.

As you can tell from the above scenario, the secret of using an index site is knowing what you are looking for, and how your subject is categorized. If you thought Galileo was a rock musician, for example, you wouldn't find very much helpful information from an index site.

Listed below are some of the more popular index sites:

www.infoseek.com
www.lycos.com
www.webcrawler.com
www.yahoo.com

Index sites themselves may be useful for finding other index sites. For example, at Yahoo you can find other index sites by selecting "Computers & Internet," then "World Wide Web@," then "Searching the Web," and then finally "Web Directories." Yahoo changes its headings on occasion, so what you see may be slightly different from that listed here.

Search Engines

As noted above, index sites work well if you can categorize your search, and you already know something about the item you're looking for. But for other occasions, a better solution is to use a "search engine." As the name implies, a search engine will go out and search for web pages that match the criteria you specify. For example, if you know Acme Anvil has a web site, you might invoke a search engine and instruct it to look for the words "Acme Anvil." That would search the WWW and return all the web pages it found containing those two words together in that order. This search might find several dozen web sites that contain those words, and hopefully one of those will be the official site for the Acme Anvil company.

Most search engines are composed of three different components. First, a program called a "Web Spider" or "Web Crawler" will search through all the pages it can find on the WWW. When a page has hyperlinks to other pages, the spider will follow those links and read those pages as well. The goal of these programs is to find and process as many different web pages as they can. The Web Spider on one popular search engine regularly searches more than 2.5 million web pages per day.

Second, the individual words on each of the web pages found by the spider are stored in a gigantic database, along with a reference to the URL for the page that contained the word.

Third, a search tool takes search orders from web users, searches the database for the words entered, and then returns the results.

Thus, when we asked the search engine to find "Acme Anvil," it really didn't search all the known WWW pages to find it, but it did use a database containing all those words from a previous exploration. Using that database, it could quickly isolate those pages containing the desired words in the desired order, and display them for us.

Much of the success of using a search engine is determined by how skillfully you compose the "search argument" (the phrase for which the search engine looks). If you make it too general, you will find thousands of matches, and will never find the one you want. If you make it too specific, you may not find any matches. Most search engines allow words such as AND, OR, and NOT to be used in search arguments, along with parentheses to group things together. Each search engine is a little different, so you should display the rules for your search engine before attempting a search. These rules can usually be displayed from the same page where you enter the search argument. Examples of common search arguments are shown below:

acme AND anvil
acme AND anvil AND (company OR corporation)
acme AND anvil AND NOT roadrunner

The first example returns all pages containing both the words "acme" and "anvil." The second example returns those same pages, but only if they also contain the word "company" or "corporation." The last example returns the same pages as the first example, unless they contain the word "roadrunner" somewhere on the page.

Figure 6-2 shows an example of the results that were returned when we asked a common search engine to find "Lincoln AND Gettysburg AND Address." This search found 1623 different web pages that contained those words. For each of those matches, the search engine calculates a match index of up to one hundred percent. The higher the index, the more likely you are going to be able to find what you want on that page. The results are displayed so that the matches with the highest index values are shown first. Each match lists the URL of the web site, the title from the web page, and a brief description of the page. As with an index site, the URLs in this list are hyperlinks, so you can just click on any link to visit the site, and then use the browser "Back" function to return to the search results list.

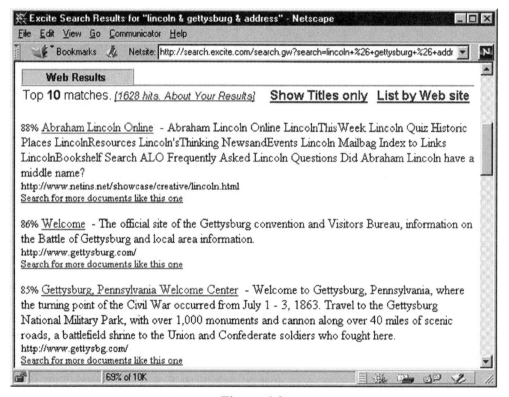

Figure 6-2

If you get discouraged using a search engine, just remember it takes a little practice to be able to find exactly what you want. Just experiment with different search arguments until you start to see the results you're looking for.

Some of the more common search engines in use can be found at the web sites listed below. Some of these support multiple searches, sending your search argument to multiple search engines, and then consolidating the results of all the searches into one list for you to see:

www.all4one.com
www.altavista.com
www.excite.com
www.hotbot.com
www.infoseek.com
www.metacrawler.com
www.northernlight.com

You will find that the line separating an index site from a search engine is becoming awfully thin. Many of the good search engines are starting to add links to interesting sites, and many of the index sites are starting to add search capabilities. Try all the different sites listed above, and you'll probably find one or two favorites that you will want to visit often as your first stop in web exploration.

WHERE DANGER LURKS

If you are a typical family, your two most popular Internet services will probably be e-mail and the World Wide Web. Because of this, you should pay special attention to the dangers that exist on the web, and you should take special precautions to protect family members from some of the more sordid material.

Unhealthy Web Sites

The most dangerous threat on the WWW comes from some of the web sites you will find there. Consider that with millions of web sites, there will be at least several hundred thousand that contain questionable material. This may be anything from pornography to racism, sexism, perversion, cults, and get-rich-quick schemes. The WWW does not discriminate. Anyone who wants a forum can get a billboard that can be seen by the whole world. If the creator of that billboard chooses to use his forum to pander to mankind's baser instincts, that's his choice.

Family members may stumble across unhealthy web sites in a number of ways. They may receive URLs from their friends, or from magazines, television, and other media sources. Search engines are another common source of unhealthy sites. Curious children seem to have it in their nature to type dirty words into a search engine and see what sites are returned. In addition, we have all read stories of a child doing a search on a supposedly innocent topic, such as breast cancer, only to find a large number of pornographic sites. These are not isolated cases, because the designers of pornographic sites often seed their pages with many sexual or suggestive words, so as to be found as many times as possible.

An unhealthy site may also be found by linking there from an innocent site. We have occasionally found personal web pages that are primarily devoted to innocent topics, such as certain movies or music. But those pages may also contain links to things that are less desirable. Perhaps little Billy searches out a link to Galileo, and he comes across a web page that is designed by an amateur astronomer. Most of the information on the page may be perfectly legitimate, but perhaps there's a section with comments like, "Here are links to a few of *my* favorite stars . . ." Billy won't know until he follows the link whether he'll be led to a site that shows Andromeda, or to a site that displays photos of some scantily-clad women.

Before you start crawling around the Internet, it's important to realize that a whole lot of people consider photos of semi-naked, beautiful women to be a harmless diversion. But remember that harmless for one person may be harmful for another, and no one else can say what is proper for your family.

We stated in previous chapters how hyperlinks can be inserted in other Internet documents, such as e-mail, newsgroups, and chat rooms. Visiting these web sites is no more difficult than clicking on a link. Much of the e-mail and newsgroup spam you will see will contain hyperlinks to sites promoting their products. This is particularly true of pornographic web sites. So all a child has to be is a little bit curious to get into some pretty sleazy stuff.

Forms

Many web sites are now taking advantage of the fact that most browsers support forms. You will often see this when you buy a new product and are given the option of registering it either by sending in the card via regular mail, or by visiting a web site and registering online. If you choose the latter option, you fill in some key items of information on a form, then press a button, and you're registered. It is usually easier than taking the time to fill in the card and find a mailbox.

Sometimes you will visit web sites that want you to register before you can use the service they provide. For example, you might visit an online encyclopedia that allows you to search and display articles. Even though the owners of the site allow you to do this for free, you still may be asked to register, and sometimes you'll have to pick a user name and/or password as part of the registration process. The owners of the site may also want items of information, such as your name, mailing address, and e-mail address.

The only real danger of using forms is that you're surrendering your privacy to the person who gets information about you. That online encyclopedia does not want you to register just for fun. The owners of the site will use that information to send you literature about why you should buy the encyclopedia in question. If you've supplied your phone number, you might also get a telephone call. And if you've provided an e-mail address, you can be sure you will start receiving spam from them.

File Downloads

Just as attached files obtained from e-mails and newsgroups can lead to problems, so can files downloaded from web sites. The primary danger is the chance of infecting your computer with a virus that has the potential of erasing your hard drive, or doing other nasty stuff. You can avoid most of these problems if you visit established software download sites, such as the ones mentioned in the next chapter. These established sites regularly scan their files for viruses.

There are also certain sites (known as "warez" sites) that carry illegal copies of commercial software. Why spend ninety-nine bucks on a word processor when you can download a copy for free from a pirate site? These sites will often feature "cracks" that are ways to fool software into thinking it is registered. For example, you might try a demonstration program that works for thirty days, but then stops working until you have paid your money, registered the product, and reactivated it with a password. The crack will enable you to alter the program so that it thinks it has been registered, without you actually paying the money. It's amazing to see how many people who would never shoplift or cheat on their taxes have no problems with making illegal copies of software. If you make unauthorized copies of software, you're breaking the law. In addition, you're driving up the prices for legal users.

Although not strictly considered downloads, graphics files from pornographic web sites are often saved to disk for later viewing with a graphics program. Such files can be quite large, and can quickly consume hard drive space that could be much better used for more tasteful files.

AVOIDING PROBLEMS

Although the World Wide Web is fraught with danger, it also comes equipped with some of the most powerful controls for limiting and auditing access. Those controls will be discussed in this section.

Parental Controls

Most of the commercial online services provide parental controls that allow certain limitations to be placed on the sites that may be visited. If you're using America Online, for example, there is a way to customize your account so a user may only visit web sites that are appropriate for children ages six to twelve. A second classification allows visits to sites that are designed for older children, ages twelve to sixteen.

As with any classification system, this does not relieve parents of their responsibilities. After all, your definition of appropriate sites may not always agree with those who decided what is appropriate for a sixteen-year-old child to see. But at least these controls will get rid of the worst web sites.

America Online also allows some controls over the types of files that may be downloaded. You can block all downloads, or you can specify that downloads are permitted only from the America Online software libraries. Using this latter option should avoid most of the problems associated with viruses or illegal software, because all of the commercial online services are pretty good about removing such software from their libraries. If you don't establish any parental controls over downloading, files may be downloaded from America Online as well as any WWW site.

Site Ratings

A discussion of site ratings is like one of those good news/bad news jokes. The good news is that there is a site rating system that allows web sites to be rated, much as movies and TV programs are rated. The bad news is that most sites have not adopted the ratings system, and at least one popular web browser does not yet support it. Nevertheless, site ratings have the potential to be a powerful tool for controlling the content of the WWW.

Microsoft's Internet Explorer browser allows you to restrict access to WWW sites based on a rating assigned to each web site. The other most common browser, the Netscape Communicator, has announced plans to also support this system, but has not done so as of this writing.

The ratings are implemented using a framework known as PICS (Platform for Internet Content Selection). It should be understood that PICS is just the vehicle that allows the rating to take place—it does not assign the rating. For example, assume someone went through each videotape and music CD in your home and affixed an adhesive label to the box or case. Then someone else evaluated each video and CD, and wrote a rating on each label. The PICS technology is the label itself. It provides a label that can be used for a rating, but does not go beyond that. The beauty of PICS is that it supports multiple rating systems for the same site. Thus, one group might rate a site as suitable for all family members, while another would rate it to exclude small children.

The default rating system that comes with Internet Explorer is called RSACi (Recreational Software Advisory Council on the Internet). It allows each web site to be rated based on four different attributes. These attributes, and the possible settings for each, are shown below:

❑ **Violence**
    Level 4: Rape or wanton, gratuitous violence
    Level 3: Aggressive violence or death to humans
    Level 2: Destruction of realistic objects
    Level 1: Injury to human beings
    Level 0: None of the above or sports-related

❑ **Nudity**
    Level 4: Frontal nudity (provocative display)
    Level 3: Frontal nudity
    Level 2: Partial nudity
    Level 1: Revealing attire
    Level 0: None of the above

❑ **Sex**
    Level 4: Explicit sexual acts or sex crimes
    Level 3: Non-explicit sexual acts
    Level 2: Clothed sexual touching
    Level 1: Passionate kissing
    Level 0: None of the above or innocent kissing; romance

❑ **Language**
    Level 4: Crude, vulgar language or extreme hate speech
    Level 3: Strong language or hate speech
    Level 2: Moderate expletives or profanity
    Level 1: Mild expletives
    Level 0: None of the above

In order to determine the rating of a web site, the owner will visit the RSACi web site and complete a brief survey, based on the content of the site. Based on this survey, a rating will be assigned to the site based on each of the four content areas mentioned above. After that, when someone uses the Internet Explorer to access that site, the ratings will be obtained and compared against the rating limits set in the browser. If any of the four ratings exceed the maximum specified for the user, the site may not be displayed, depending on the other options set.

If you are using Internet Explorer and you want to activate the ratings feature, perform the following steps. First, locate the security panel:

-> View -> Options -> Security

In the "Content Advisor" section, push the "Settings" button. If you have not already specified a supervisor password, you will be asked to enter one twice. Make sure you remember this password, because it will be needed whenever you want to change any of these options in the future.

Select the "Ratings" tab. In the "Category" section, you can click on the four different ratings categories (Language, Nudity, Sex, and Violence). For each of those, use the slider bar to select the rating you desire, as listed above or described on the panel.

Now click the "General" tab, on the same dialog, and refer to the "User Options" section. This contains two important options that you will need to set. The first checkbox has the caption, "Users can see sites which have no rating." If you check this box, then unrated web pages will be displayed, just as if no rating system were in effect. Consider that the vast majority of sites on the WWW are not rated, so checking this option has the potential of letting a lot of bad material get by. On the other hand, not checking it will stop family members from visiting many useful and non-offensive sites that just have not been rated. We are not sure what to recommend for this option, because neither option is very good. Much depends on the age of your children, and the amount of time you expect to be around while they are browsing. Try the most restrictive setting first (box unchecked). If that doesn't work, then check the box, and see how much offensive material gets through.

The second checkbox has the caption, "Supervisor can type a password to allow users to view restricted content." This means that when an unapproved page is accessed (either because it is not rated, or if the rating exceeds what you allow), a dialog box will ask for the supervisor password. If the password is entered correctly, the requested page will be shown. This is a useful option, because it allows you as the parent to override the ratings system for sites that you know are acceptable.

The "Change Password" button in the "Supervisor Password" section on that same page can be used to set a new supervisor password. Be sure to change that password on a fairly regular basis, especially if you are typing in the password a lot to override access.

The "Advanced" tab allows you to pick an alternate rating system, other than RSACi. Although RSACi is the only ratings system delivered as part of Internet Explorer, there are other ratings systems that can be installed as part of other products.

When the above options are set, pressing the "OK" button will return you back to the "Security" tab. Now all that remains to be done is to press the "Enable Ratings" button in the "Content Advisor" section, and your rating system is in force.

As we said previously, a web rating system has the potential for implementing a truly flexible protection system, but the current system is flawed because of the lack of browser support, and the limited number of sites that participate in the ratings process. Perhaps these conditions will change in the future, and will provide a system that offers more protection for family members.

There are also some civil libertarians who disagree with the PICS system. They argue that any ratings system is a double-edged sword that could also be used by oppressive governments to deny access to controversial materials. These arguments are not without merit, and they may serve to discourage further adoption of any rating system.

Blocking Software

If you use an ISP and access the Internet directly via a browser, there is little control that can be imposed on access to web sites. Your two options are to implement site ratings, as mentioned above, or to install blocking software. This software works with your browser to limit access to unhealthy sites.

Most blocking software works by examining the URLs that the web browser attempts to access. These could be URLs entered directly by the user, or those contained as hyperlinks on other pages. The blocking software checks the desired URL against a database of "bad" web sites. This database may exist as part of the blocking software, or it may exist on a web site and be accessed by the software. The URL itself might also be scanned for offensive words, so that sites such as "www.nude-girls.com" would not be allowed.

Because thousands of new web sites appear every day, it is important that blocking software be updated regularly with a new list of unhealthy sites. This is not a problem if the database is accessed dynamically on a web site, but it may be a problem if you are expected to visit a site regularly and download updates. If your software employs the latter system, make sure you perform the updates in a timely manner.

Some blocking software uses the PICS site rating system, although they provide a replacement for RSACi that is more comprehensive, and rates more sites.

Listed below are some of the common features of blocking software that you should consider when evaluating them:

.

- Parents can add their own sites and either allow or disallow access.
- Parents can regulate hours of access and the amount of access time.
- Passwords allow override of individual sites or all blocking controls.
- Parents can limit the file types that can be uploaded or downloaded.
- Parents can also block newsgroups, FTP sites, e-mail and chat rooms.
- A history log can be maintained listing all the sites visited.
- The product can run in "quiet" mode, and just log all acccsscs.
- Some products check outgoing text for bad words or personal information.
- Some products work with both commercial sites and ISPs.

Listed below are names of some of the more common software products that permit blocking of web sites and other Internet materials. Also listed for each product is the web site where you can obtain more information. To see other products not on this list, visit the Yahoo site (www.yahoo.com), and use the search function to search for "Blocking Software":

Cyber Patrol	www.cyberpatrol.com
CYBERsitter	www.solidoak.com
Net Nanny	www.netnanny.com
SafeSurf	www.safesurf.com
SurfWatch	www.surfwatch.com

As we've tried to stress throughout this book, having some kind of software policeman in place does not relieve you of your responsibilities as a parent. Blocking software and site ratings both suffer from the same flaw—by using them, you are relying on someone else to establish what is acceptable for your children. Although you will probably agree with many of their decisions, such as blocking sites with hardcore pornographic material, there are other decisions that will not be as clear-cut.

Should teenagers be allowed to view sites related to some of the more extreme musical groups? What about sites that advocate abortion, homosexuality, tattoos, or body piercing? How about access to famous literary works that some would consider to be erotic? There are many of these gray areas that are bound to cause differences of opinion between different sets of parents. You need to monitor the job your blocking software is doing. If it is not stopping access to sites you believe are offensive, you may need to change the options to block additional sites that you have specified.

Even if you're satisfied that the blocking software is working as you want it to work, you need to test it regularly to make sure it is still doing its job. There was an article in the newspaper recently telling how one young man had a part-time job disabling the blocking software that parents had installed on family computers. There are even pirate web sites that provide instructions or "crack" programs to disable the various blocking programs. To make sure the software is working, try to access a known "bad" site, and make sure it stops you.

Browser URL History

Regardless of the types of controls you have on your browser, it doesn't hurt occasionally to take a look and see where it's been. As you learned earlier in this section, there are a couple of places where most browsers maintain a recent history of the web sites they have visited. This is useful if you forgot to bookmark a useful site, but it is also handy to check occasionally to see what your family members have been browsing.

Most browsers, including the browser built into America Online, will have a down arrow to the right of the box where you type in a URL address. Pressing this down arrow will display a drop-down list showing approximately the last fifteen sites that were visited. Note that you have to be using the proper user name, however, to be able to see the site list for that user.

Most browsers also keep a more comprehensive history file, containing a list of all the sites visited for the past few days. If you are using the Internet Explorer or America Online (which uses Internet Explorer), use one of the following command sequences:

Internet Explorer: -> View -> Options -> Navigation
America Online: -> My AOL -> Preferences -> WWW -> Navigation

In the "History" section, you can specify the number of days that a site should be kept in the history file. If you have not revisited the site within this number of days, it will be removed from the history folder. From this menu, you may also choose to view the history folder, or delete all the entries from it.

Using the Netscape Communicator, set options for the history file by starting with the following command sequence:

-> Edit -> Preferences -> Navigator

In the "History" section, you can specify the number of days that a site should be kept in the history file, or you can delete all the entries from it. Viewing the history file requires a different command sequence:

-> Communicator -> History

Once you open a history file, several statistics will be shown that are related to the web sites visited in the recent past. Depending on the browser, you will see variations of the following items:

- Title from the web page
- Internet address (URL)
- Date/time last visited
- Date/time first visited
- Expiration date
- Number of times visited

Most browsers allow you to sort the file based on any of the above items, and to sort in either forward or reverse sequence. Double clicking on a row will also cause the browser to attempt to revisit that site.

Obviously, the history file does not provide a foolproof audit trail. Each browser supports the option of clearing the history file at any time. If the history file has always been cleared when you start the browser, that in itself might be a good indication that something unsavory may be occurring. Also, individual entries may be deleted from the history file, so a very cautious snoop will be able to cover his tracks. But for those younger children who are less sophisticated in the ways of deceit, the browser history file may prove to be a valuable tool.

Bookmarks

Most browser users will establish a set of bookmarks (or "Favorites" for Internet Explorer users) for the sites they like to visit regularly. This makes it easy to visit these common sites without having to remember their URLs.

But bookmarks can also help provide you some clues to the sites that are being visited by family members. Review all bookmarks on a periodic basis, and check out any name or title that looks suspicious. This certainly will not catch all improper sites, because sites can be visited on a regular basis without the convenience of using bookmarks. But it will show you if sites that are not on your approved list have been added to the list of bookmark locations.

For younger children, the use of bookmarks will help enforce your rules about the sites they can visit. Build their bookmarks so that only approved sites are present, then have a rule that a site may only be visited with a bookmark. When your child has a new site he wishes to visit, the parents can test it out and create a bookmark if it meets the standards they have set.

Browser Cache Directory

A common browser feature designed to improve performance will also allow you to monitor previous browser activity. When you visit a web site for the first time, your browser must request that the file you have specified be transmitted from the web site on which it resides. Depending on the size of the file, this may take a long time. Also, many web pages you display will contain images. As already explained, these images do not exist within the web page itself, but are stored on the web site as graphics files. These files must also be transmitted to your computer. This transfer of data is particularly wasteful if you regularly visit a group of common sites. Why transmit each page and each image every time you visit the site? To solve this problem and improve browser speed, most browsers implement an option called a cache. This is a subdirectory on your hard drive where web files are kept for a temporary period.

When you visit a web site for the first time, the files and images transmitted are displayed by your browser, but they are also stored in the cache directory, usually with a meaningless name determined by the browser. If you visit the same site the next day, the browser will look in the cache for those files. Because they are present, they will be displayed by the browser, without having to have the browser request that they be transmitted again. The browser has a way of detecting when a file has changed on the web server, so it will ignore the cache copy and transmit again from the web site if the file is different. Using the browser's "Reload" function will always request a fresh copy from the web site, which is why you should use reload with functions such as NetCams that are updating the files on the web server.

In any case, looking in the browser's cache directory will allow you to get an idea of the kinds of documents and graphics files that have been displayed recently.

You may access the cache feature by using one of the following command sequences, depending on whether you are using Internet Explorer or America Online:

Internet Explorer: -> View -> Options -> Advanced
America Online: -> My AOL -> Preferences -> WWW -> Advanced

In the "Temporary Internet Files" section, the name of the current hard disk subdirectory used for caching will be shown. Using the Settings button will allow you to specify a different subdirectory or delete the files from the current cache. The View Files button will display a summary of the files that are in the cache. For each file, the following items of information will be shown:

- Name of file
- Internet address (URL)
- Size of file
- Date file expires (is removed from cache)
- Date last modified
- Date last accessed
- Date last checked

As with the history folder, you can click on the title bar above any of these items to sort the file in forward or backward sequence. You may also double click on any item to request that the browser try to display that item.

Users of the Netscape Communicator use a slightly different command sequence to access the cache options:

-> Edit -> Preferences -> Advanced -> Cache

On the Cache Options screen, you can specify the maximum size of the cache, specify that it be moved to a different subdirectory, or specify that all files in the cache be deleted. The screen also displays the name of the current subdirectory that is being used for caching. Notice that there is no direct way to display the contents of the cache under Netscape Communicator. But now that you know the subdirectory, you can use the Windows Explorer or some other utility program to browse the files in that directory.

The same limitations apply to the cache directory that apply to the history file. Someone wanting to cover his tracks could easily empty the cache after each session, or delete selected files from it. But the browser cache director remains a pretty good tool for all but the most sneaky web users.

Customizing Your Browser

Do you get annoyed by repeatedly having to view the same home page that is displayed when you start your browser? Whatever that home page is, it's probably an advertisement for somebody. Most browsers allow you to change this default, and you can select a different URL that is more useful, or that is better suited for other members of the family. Your default home page can be any URL address, or may even be the name of a file that lives on your computer's hard drive.

In the next chapter, we will show you how to build your own web pages. You might consider designing a home page tailored specifically for your family, and have that page displayed when the web browser starts. This will not only protect family members from inappropriate material, but will also guide them more quickly to the sites they will visit most frequently. Younger children will also be impressed by the magic of seeing their own family picture and their names when they start the browser.

For the Netscape Communicator, use the following sequence to change the default home page:

-> Edit -> Preferences -> Navigator

In the "Home Page" section, type the starting URL you wish to use in the "Location" text box. If you want to use a home page that resides on your hard drive, press the Browse button and navigate to the proper file, then select it.

If you're using the Internet Explorer or America Online, start with one of the following command sequences:

Internet Explorer: -> View -> Options -> Navigation

America Online: -> My AOL -> Preferences -> WWW -> Navigation

In the "Address" text box in the "Customize" section, type the URL of your home page. Unlike the Netscape Communicator, there is no browse function, but you can still specify that your home page resides on your hard drive. Simply type in the file address in the "Address" box, instead of a URL. This address consists of the drive number, a colon, the subdirectory, and the file name. For example:

C:/WEBPAGES/SMITH.HTM

Note that, unlike DOS, you use forward slashes for the path name, and not backward slashes.

Once you have connected to America Online 4.0, you can display your home page by clicking on the ICON of the house that is on the left-hand side of the toolbar.

Privacy Concerns

The same rules of privacy associated with other Internet activities should apply when family members encounter web sites that contain forms. Just because you visit a web site containing impressive-looking pages and forms doesn't mean you are obligated to complete those forms. Family members should be reminded that they should not provide personal information requested in an e-mail from someone unknown to them. Similarly, they should feel no obligation to provide the same information using a form on an unknown web site. After all, just about anyone can build a web site and publish it on the WWW. Children should not assume the designer of the form is any more legitimate just because he has a web site. Especially for younger children, Mom and Dad should probably approve any request to provide the information requested on a form.

Web sites run by well-known organizations and companies, as well as sites used for new product registrations, are probably safer in terms of completing forms. But even with these sites, you should ask yourself what they are going to do with the information. If you provide your mailing address, there is a good chance you will be added to a mailing list. If you provide your e-mail address, there is an equally good chance you will start receiving e-mails about future sales or special offers, or perhaps even have your address sold to other spam lists. Unless you are specifically requesting that something be sent to you, it's best to provide the minimum amount of information required on the form. Some forms also give you the option of requesting that you receive no further mailings or that your personal information not be sold or given to anyone else. Make sure to exercise these options, when present, although there is no guarantee the company will respect your wishes.

Scanning for Files

In Chapter 3, we suggested that you occasionally scan your hard drive for files that may have been attached to e-mails, and then downloaded. This same advice should apply for files that have been downloaded from web sites. Use the Windows Find function described in Chapter 3 to look for unusual files, particularly archive files (file extension of ZIP) or graphics files (file extensions of BMP, JPG, and GIF).

If you find a subdirectory containing a large number of graphics files, you may want to use a graphics viewer program to examine them. This type of program is also useful for examining the cache subdirectory used by Netscape Communicator, especially because Communicator has no built-in function to display these. Displaying a

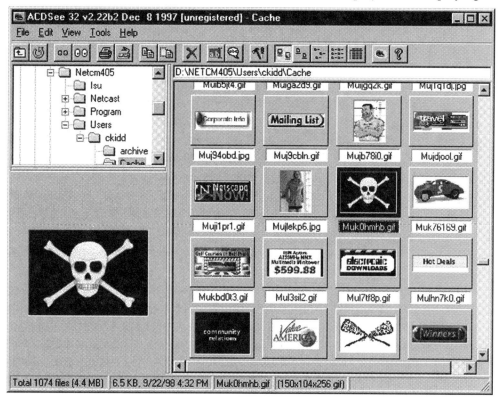

Figure 6-3

browser cache directory with a graphics viewer will show any embedded graphics contained on pages that were viewed by the browser. Because many of the buttons, boxes, and drawings on web pages are actually small graphics, this will give you a pretty good idea of the kinds of places your browser has been visiting recently.

If you don't have a graphics viewer program, there are several inexpensive versions that may be downloaded from the software download sites mentioned in the next chapter. Figure 6-3 shows a screen from one of these programs, called ACDSee, that makes it easy to scan through your hard drive and view graphics files. The upper-left-hand portion of the screen is used to select a hard drive and a subdirectory. If the selected sub-directory contains any graphics files, they will be displayed on the right-hand side of the screen in a scrollable area. The images displayed here are called "thumbnails," because they are shown at thumbnail size—just large enough for you to make them out. If you click on one of these images, a larger version of it will be displayed in the lower-left-hand portion of the screen. You may adjust the size of any of the three areas on the screen for better viewing.

A PARENT'S QUESTIONS

Q. How can I speed up a browser that runs like molasses?
A. The popularity of the World Wide Web has resulted in increasingly slow page loading, especially during busy times of the day, or at busy web sites. First, make sure you are running a modem that is fairly new and that supports a reasonable speed. If this is not the case, you can improve browser performance by investing a little money in a new modem. If that doesn't help, perhaps the delay is caused by your online service or ISP. See if other friends on other providers are having similar slow results accessing the same sites at the same times. If some sites are slow and others are not, it is probably just an overload on the particular site that is slowing your response time. Perhaps there are a lot of people accessing it, or it is being run by a web server running on a small computer.

A good deal of page-loading delay is caused by the graphics that are embedded in most web pages these days. A typical page might require the transfer of a 12 KB HTML document, followed by four 60 KB image files. It is not hard to see what is causing the delay. Most browsers have an option that allows you to turn off the loading of graphics. When this option is set, pages will load, but the embedded graphics within them will not. There is usually a browser button, such as "Show Graphics," that will reload the page again, and include the graphics this time. Although ignoring graphics shows pages that are not as pretty, it may be a reasonable trade-off for the improved speed of the page loading.

Q. Is there any way I can use my own web browser through an online service?
A. Check with your online service to see if it will support access to the Internet with other applications. For example, America Online will allow you to use Netscape Communicator for your browser, rather than using the built-in Internet Explorer. In order to do this, you must first connect through America Online, and then start Netscape Communicator. Your America Online connection must remain actively connected for as long as you are browsing. There are some features that don't work when using this technique (such as newsgroup access through Communicator), but most of the browsing features work just fine. You may also need to make some configuration changes to make sure Parental Controls are enforced when using Communicator. Contact your online service for more information.

Q. Why do I get an "Error 404" when trying to connect to a web site?
A. The 404 error is kind of a general-purpose browser error that is used whenever the operation you requested could not be completed. Some web sites have software in place to trap 404 errors and display them as messages that are a little more meaningful. If you typed in the URL, make sure you typed it correctly, and that the capitalization is correct. If you got the error trying to follow a hyperlink, you have probably found what is called a "dead link." This just means that the document that used to be at that URL address is no longer there. The domain name could have been removed, or the directory on the web server was changed, or the file specified was renamed, moved, or deleted. You will find this happens more often than it should when you are following hyperlinks.

In some cases, a 404 error may be received because of a temporary environmental error. Perhaps the web server was too busy with other requests, and couldn't get to you. Or perhaps the web site has been taken down temporarily to fix a problem or to make backup copies of the data. For these types of errors, try accessing the site again on a different day or at a different time of day.

Chapter 7—OK, What's the Good News?

● ● ● ● ●

NOW THAT YOU'RE INTO THE HOME STRETCH OF THIS BOOK, we hope you have a balanced view of the Internet. There are certainly dangers there, to be sure. But some of that danger is caused by ignorance about what is out there, and a feeling of powerlessness at not being able to control it. We hope we have been able to eliminate this type of fear by turning you into a knowledgeable Internet user, and giving you the tools you'll need to keep your family out of the pitfalls and traps.

But there are great treasures to be found out in this vast electronic jungle known as the Internet. While alerting you to the dangers, we hope we have also been able to generate some curiosity, and give you a small glimpse of the way this technology can be used to enrich your life, and the lives of each family member.

In this chapter, we want to accentuate the positive by covering topics that give you a showcase of the beneficial aspects of the Internet. And there are many benefits, as evidenced by the Internet's phenomenal growth.

A recent government survey measured the speed at which different technologies were accepted by the public. This is what they found:

- Radio took thirty-eight years to reach an audience of 50 million.
- Television took thirteen years to reach an audience of 50 million.
- The Internet took four years to reach an audience of 50 million. [1]

As the statistics can easily show you, the Internet is here to stay. That being the case, let's forget about the potential dangers for a little while, and concentrate instead on having some family fun.

First, we will show you how to go about building your own web site. As you read through the last chapter and surveyed all the different types of web sites, you may have found yourself thinking, "You know, it would be really fun to have a web site for our family. We could tell a little about each family member, maybe show some photos of the family or of last year's vacation. We could even provide links to other web sites that our family really enjoys. Yes, that would be kind of nice. It sure beats writing a Christmas letter."

As you'll find in this chapter, building a web site isn't all that complicated. Once you reach the end of this book, you'll have some idea of how to get started. Don't expect to be a web wizard when you're through, though. Entire books can be (and have been) written about this subject, and we can't expect to go beyond the basics with just one chapter. But we will help you get your feet just a little bit wet. If you find you like the water, you can jump in and buy one of those other books, and soon have a second career designing flashy web sites.

Second, we will point you to some web sites that are really fun, and that may feature useful information for your family. As with web design, there are entire books dedicated to just listing and summarizing good web sites. So again, we will just get your toes wet. Once you find out there aren't any sharks in many of the Internet waters, you just may like the water enough to do some advanced swimming on your own.

CREATING A PERSONAL WEB SITE

Although a good number of web sites are run by million-dollar companies and organizations, many are run by ordinary people such as you. The content of these sites is as varied as the people who create them. Some people display photographs or drawings they have produced, or let you read stories or poems they have written. Some devote space to their hobbies and interests, such as information about their favorite movie, television show, or entertainment personality. People who suffer from a particular disease or problem may build a site to inform others and share information about treatments they have found to be effective.

The World Wide Web allows everyone to have his fifteen minutes of fame. You can have yours by creating a little corner of the Internet where you can publicize your family. Whether you want to show your comic, serious, silly, or creative side is up to you.

Getting the Space

The first step to building a web site is to get some space to locate the pages and images. This is called web space, because it is located out on the World Wide Web. Your first question might be, "Why can't I just use some space on my hard drive?" Actually, as you learned in the last chapter, you can place web files on your hard drive and your browser can access them fine. In fact, as you will learn later, this is a good way to test the pages that you build. But your pages have to live out in web space so that other users can find them. Your computer is certainly not connected to the Internet twenty-four hours a day, and even if it was, your computer does not have its own domain name so that other people can find it. If you want others to see your work, it has to live out in web space.

Most online services provide a small amount of web space for each user. For example, America Online allows each user name to have up to 2 MB of web space. Because you can have up to five user names on one account, this means a maximum of 10 MB of web space per America Online account. Although you may not think this is a lot of space, you can actually do quite a bit with it.

If your service provider does not provide web space, there are several companies mentioned later in this chapter that provide free web space. The catch is that these sites display advertising as part of your web site, so anyone browsing your site will see the family picture, plus an advertisement for aftershave or corn remover or some such product.

Once you have your space, how do other people go there? Usually they use a domain name assigned by your service provider, plus a unique pathname assigned to each user. For example, if your America Online user name is "EarWig," you could access your web space by using the following URL:

http://members.aol.com/EarWig/

America Online users can access their web space by using the domain name "members.aol.com," followed by a pathname that matches the user name.

Think of the web space itself as being like a smaller version of a hard drive. The web space can contain files or it can contain subdirectories. Files should have extensions that describe their content, such as HTM or HTML for text pages, and JPG or GIF for image files. As you learned in the last chapter, if you point a browser to a directory and don't give it a file name, it will look for a default file named "index.htm" or "index.html." You should always make sure to have a file by this name as a courtesy to users that come to visit.

Companies that provide web space also usually provide you with the tools needed to maintain that space. This allows you to do such things as upload, download, rename, and delete files, and to create and destroy subdirectories. America Online users manage their web space by using FTP (go to the "FTP" keyword).

Some may wonder about the option of establishing your own domain name. Perhaps you want to start your own company, and you want it to have a web site. Obviously, a domain name like "www.mycompany.com" is easier for people to find than "members.aol.com/mycompany/." To establish your own domain, you will need to be willing to spend a little money. First, you will need to contact a local service provider and see how much it charges to host a site. There may be a flat monthly charge, plus a charge for the web space that you use. You will then need to select an unused domain name and register it. The service provider should help you do this also. The cost for a registered domain name is about one hundred dollars for the first two years, and then fifty dollars per year after that. The service provider may charge you a service fee on top of that, but it shouldn't be excessive. Compare prices among the service providers, as the rates they charge for web site hosting tend to vary a bit.

For small businesses and serious users, you can buy a permanent Internet connection for your home and connect a PC to it that runs a web server program. Then you can register a domain name and have it routed to your PC, so that it literally becomes a permanent part of the Internet. Thus, the hard drive space on the host PC really does become web space, and any user connecting to your domain name will be able to access the files on your PC. Expect to leave your system powered up all the time, because there's no sense in hosting a web site unless it's available to customers twenty-four hours a day.

Building the Pages

Now that you have the web space, you will need to create your web pages. Although you may want to immediately jump in and start writing, the best thing is to do some planning first. It is much easier to revise a design when it is still on paper than after the pages are all composed. Give some general thought about what you want on each page, and how you want the pages to flow together. Experienced web surfers will tell you that for every good web site there are at least ten bad ones. They even publish books that are just collections of very bad web sites. You don't want your work to appear in such books, so do some planning first.

Text web pages are written in a language known as HTML, or Hyper-Text Markup Language. This is not a difficult language to understand, and many people have learned much of the language just by looking at sample pages. Look at the sample home page shown in Figure 7-1. This is a pretty basic page, but it does have a number of features. It has blocks of text that use special styles, such as bold and centering. It also has an embedded graphic. It has a link to another web page, in case you are interested in seeing more pictures like the one shown. It has hyperlinks to two different web sites, one that is a search engine, and one that is an index site. Finally, it has two different "mailto" links, so that you can send e-mail to either of the two owners of the home page.

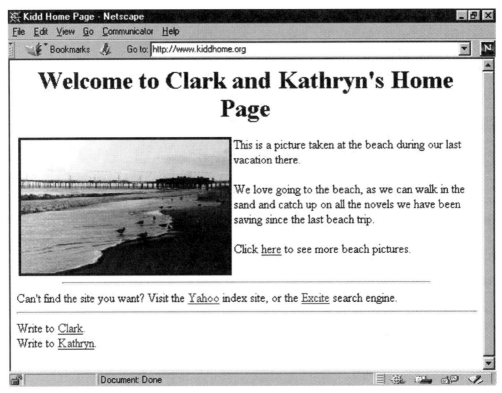

Figure 7-1

Now let's look at the HTML file that was displayed by the browser to produce the results shown in Figure 7-1:

```
</HEAD>
<BODY>
<CENTER><H1>Welcome to Clark and Kathryn's Home Page</H1></CENTER>
<IMG SRC="beach.jpg" BORDER=3 ALIGN=left>
This is a picture taken at the beach during our last vacation there.<BR><BR>
We love going to the beach, as we can walk in the sand and catch up on
all the novels we have been saving since the last beach trip.<BR><BR>
Click <A HREF="beach.htm">here</A> to see more beach pictures.
<BR clear=left>
<HR WIDTH=80%>
Can't find the site you want?
```

```
Visit the <A HREF="http://www.yahoo.com">Yahoo</A> index site, or the
<A HREF="http://www.excite.com">Excite</A> search engine.
<HR>
Write to <A HREF="mailto:Clark@acme.com">Clark</A>.<BR>
Write to <A HREF="mailto:Kathryn@acme.com">Kathryn</A>.<BR><BR>
</BODY>
</HTML>
```

You will notice HTML uses tags, that are surrounded by brackets. Some tags are paired, such as <CENTER> and </CENTER>, and some appear individually, such as <BR>. They may be typed in either upper- or lowercase. It is beyond the scope of this book to explain all the different tag values. If you're really interested, buy an HTML book or find a guide on the WWW. In many cases, the sophistication of current web authoring tools make it less important to be an expert on the various HTML tags.

If you insist on doing it the "hard way" and coding your own HTML files, you can create them using the Notepad or Wordpad programs that come with Windows, or with most word processors. The secret is that your work must be saved as text files. Most word processors save documents in a compressed format that your browser will not understand. Make sure when you save the document, you override the file type so that it will be saved as a "Text Only" or "MS-DOS Text" file.

Most providers of web space also provide some type of tools for building basic web pages. These tools spare you from having to know the details of HTML, even though the final results of your efforts will be an HTML file. The tools provide basic functions, such as font colors, text styles, and image insertion. Most provide a library of images that can be selected and inserted into your web page. The problem with these "fill-in-the-blank" tools is that all the pages they produce tend to look alike, and you are usually limited to just a subset of the features that HTML supports. They might get you started, but your pages will never win any awards.

Another option for building web pages might be as close as your favorite word processor, assuming you are running a recent version of the software. So many people are creating web pages these days that the latest versions of most popular word processing programs support HTML format. You can compose your page the way you normally would, using formatting techniques such as bold, italics, and centering. Then when you save the document, the program will insert the proper HTML tags to reflect those styles. When composing an HTML document, you will probably see some new options, such as the ability to insert hyperlinks or images.

Not to be outdone, the popular web browsers have also added support for the composing of web pages. Internet Explorer comes with a product called FrontPage Express, which is a smaller version of the FrontPage web authoring tool. The Netscape Communicator also comes with a feature called Composer. To give you an idea of what you can do with these tools, we have listed below the features that come with the Netscape Composer:

- Supports multiple type fonts in various sizes
- Supports different text colors
- Supports various text styles (Bold/Italic/Underline)
- Supports both Bulleted and Numbered lists
- Contains a spell checker
- Supports text indentation
- Supports text alignment (Left/Right/Center)
- Provides standard Windows text manipulation (Cut/Paste/Copy)
- Supports image insertion and manipulation
- Supports tables
- Allows placement of horizontal lines
- Supports internal and external hypertext links

That last feature probably needs a little more explanation. An internal hypertext link takes you to another location within the same document. This is often used like a table of contents. When you first display the page, you see the various topics, and may click on one to go directly there. Or, you can just scroll down the page and view the topics in sequence.

An external hypertext link refers to an Internet resource different from the current document. This could be another web page, or a Gopher, or an FTP site, or perhaps even a "mailto" tag for sending e-mail to someone.

A final option for composing web pages is to use web editor software designed specifically for creating web documents. Although these programs are not always easy to use, they usually provide the most flexibility, and the strongest support for all the features of HTML. Many HTML books come with CDs that provide demonstration versions of the most popular web editors. Invest in one of these books, give all the editors a try, and select the one you like best. Another option is to visit the software download sites mentioned later in this chapter and see what is available. One program that is quite easy to use is called HotDog. You can download a trial version that expires after thirty days from the web site *www.sausage.com.*

When composing your pages, avoid the temptation to make them too complex. When we're learning something new, we all have a temptation to try every little bell and whistle, and include all of them in the final result. Thus you have a page containing dozens of fonts, colors, and styles, plus a busy background and lots of inserted images. This is fine for learning, but throw away the final result, and don't pollute your web space with yet another page that causes eye indigestion!

A picture may be worth a thousand words, but an example is often worth two thousand. Sometimes the best way to learn something is to just observe the creations of others. Most web browsers give you the option to save a web page, or view the HTML source. For example, in Netscape Communicator, you use the command sequence:

-> View -> Page Source

This displays the current page you are viewing, but shows it without interpretation, so you see all the HTML tags, just the way the browser sees it. So if you come across an interesting page while browsing, use this option to look "under the covers" and see how the author performed his magic. Another option is to save the page itself, and then use your own web editor to change the page, and use it for the basis of your own work. If you do this, please just borrow a feature or two, and don't plagiarize the whole page.

Testing It Out

As noted in the last chapter, web browsers have the ability to fetch documents from your hard drive, as well as from the Internet. When designing a web site, most authors create their files in a hard drive subdirectory, only uploading them to web space after the pages are in their final format and have been fully tested. Most web editors allow you to jump back and forth between the editor and your favorite browser. This allows you to compose a page, check it with the browser, make revisions as needed, and continue the process until you are satisfied with the results.

Let's show you an example of how you would test out some of your newly-created web pages using the Netscape Communicator. First you must select the first file you want to display with the following command sequence:

-> File -> Open Page-> Choose File

This allows you to navigate through your drives and subdirectories and select the file you want. You may also choose whether to open the page in the Navigator or the Composer. The former will simply display the page as the browser would show it, while the latter will let you start the editor and make changes to it. When you first start your browser, you may get an error because you have no Internet connection. Unless you are running an older version of Windows, you can just ignore this error and proceed to open your test file. You can avoid this error by setting your browser options so that no home page is displayed when you start the browser.

Once you start your test, you should be able to load images and navigate through your pages just as if you were using a real web site. Keep in mind that if you try to link to an external resource (such as another web site), it will not work unless you have established an Internet connection before you started testing.

After your pages are fully tested, you need to upload them to your web space and then test them again. The reason for this is to make sure that all the hyperlinks still work. A link could be broken if you forgot to upload all the files, or if you changed a file's name when uploading it. Also, if you specified a link incorrectly, it might still point to a location on your hard drive. For example, the link "c:/webpages/vacation.htm" will work fine when the pages are on the hard drive, but will fail when they are uploaded. A better solution is to use a nonspecific name such as "vacation.htm" that will work either when the page is being tested or when it is uploaded. If you don't specify a pathname as part of a link, it will use the pathname from which the last page was fetched. This is exactly what we want, because it yields the same result regardless of whether the pages live in web space or on a hard drive.

Another thing to keep in mind while testing is that different pages may function differently when using different browsers. In theory, all browsers should process HTML the same; in practice, they don't. We have designed pages that look great using Netscape Communicator, but that look pretty sloppy when viewed with Internet Explorer. If you are planning to start a web business, or do other things that will attract a lot of people to your site, make sure you view it with all the common browsers to make sure they all leave a good impression with the viewer.

Updating the Pages

It is one thing to build a web site, but it is quite another to build a site that people will want to come back to frequently. The key to repeat visits is to always update your content. That is a fancy way of saying the information on your pages has to change frequently. Perhaps this is unimportant to you, because you are only building a web site for friends and family members. But even that audience would appreciate not seeing the same thing every time they drop by. The derogatory term "electronic brochure" is used to describe a commercial site that never changes its content. These are usually sites where the company hires someone to design the pages (so that they can have a presence on the WWW), but then the pages never do anything more than tell something about the company and give a phone number. Indeed, such sites provide little more than a brochure would, and you can be certain they will never be visited more than once.

For ease of updating, keep the master copies of the web files on your hard drive. This should not be a problem, because they should still be there from when you were developing and testing them. When you want to make changes, update and test the local copies, and then update the changed pages to your web space. The alternative is to download pages from web space, update them, upload them back into web space, and then test them. This option adds extra steps and discourages careful testing.

If your site has hyperlinks to other sites, you should test them on occasion and make sure they still work. Having a flock of dead links is another sign that a web site has been neglected for so long that it has grown cobwebs.

SAMPLE SITES TO VISIT

Below we have listed a number of web sites that we consider useful, educational, or just plain fun. These are our own personal favorites, plus ones recommended by friends, plus sites we came across while researching this book. Keep in mind that there are millions of web sites, so we cannot even cover one percent of them in a list such as this one. This list will only serve to get you started until you find your own favorites, which you should be able to do easily by following links from these sites or using index sites and search engines.

We have also included web sites that were mentioned earlier in the book, so that you will have a complete list here of any web site mentioned anywhere in the book.

You will find a few web sites mentioned more than once, if we believed the web site provided more than one type of service. We concluded it was better for us to duplicate a few listings rather than for you to be unable to find what you want.

The sites are listed alphabetically by category, and we tried to select category names that would describe the service being provided by the sites. Take special note of three categories for which you will find multiple entries:

• "Buying . . ." identifies sites where you may purchase merchandise online.

- "Finding . . ." identifies sites that will help you locate things.
- "Free . . ." will lead you to merchandise or services with little or no cost.

Before you jump right in and start browsing these sites, please take note of several cautions and disclaimers:

1. Not all of the sites listed below may be suitable for all family members. There are a good many for young children and teenagers, but others are more useful and interesting for adults.

2. The content of a site may have changed since this book went to press. What was once acceptable content for all family members may have changed.

3. You may find some dead links, as various sites may have changed their URLs or gone out of business. This is just a fact of life on the WWW.

4. As computer people are fond of saying, "Your Mileage May Vary." Just because we find these sites interesting and useful, does not mean you will.

5. Many of these sites want you to pay money to subscribe to the services they provide, but they also provide a few free services so that you will visit. For example, a site for investors may allow you to obtain stock quotes for free, but may restrict other services to only subscribed members. Just take advantage of the free services, and subscribe if the site seems of value to you. The bottom line is that you need to review any of these sites before recommending them to other family members. We cannot make judgments about what material is suitable for your individual family situation—only you can do that.

Now without further delay, let's jump in and start surfing!

Anti-Virus Software

If your computer didn't come with anti-virus software, here are a few sites that provide information about their products. Some of these used to provide a trial version that you could download and run on your machine. Sadly, it appears that most have discontinued this policy.

www.av.ibm.com
www.drsolomon.com
www.nai.com
www.quarterdeck.com

Automotive

Want to find out how much the old junk heap is worth before you trade it in, or do you just have an interest in cars in general? In either case, visit these sites to satisfy your thirst for all things automotive.

carpoint.msn.com
www.cartalk.com
www.edmunds.com
www.kbb.com

Blocking Software

In Chapter 6 we discussed blocking software that could be used to limit the operation of your web browser, and protect tender eyes from some pretty raunchy material. Listed below are sites that will tell you about some of the more common blocking programs.

www.cyberpatrol.com
www.netnanny.com
www.safesurf.com
www.solidoak.com
www.surfwatch.com

Buying Books

To some people, the idea of buying books without being in a bookstore is sacrilege. Although buying books online cannot compete with browsing through piles of musty books, there are some advantage of online book shopping. Some of the software running these sites are really quite advanced. They can recommend books, show you similar books to the ones you are buying, and allow you to submit comments about books and read the comments from others. Give it a try.

alldirect.com
futfan.com (Science Fiction and Fantasy)
www.amazon.com (Our personal favorite)

www.barnesandnoble.com
www.books.com
www.borders.com
www.clbooks.com (Computer Books)

Buying Computer Hardware

Need to upgrade your computer, or buy a new printer or hard drive? There are many online companies that sell individual hardware components, as well as entire systems. Many of these provide better prices than what you will find locally, plus they provide technical support by phone. Our past four computer systems have been purchased online, and we have been happy with the quality and the service.

www.accessmicro.com
www.buycomp.com
www.compaqworks.com   (Refurbished Compaq Computers)
www.dell.com
www.gw2k.com
www.insight.com
www.outpost.com
www.pcconnection.com
www.techstore.com
www.warehouse.com
www.winbook.com

Buying Computer Software

You can also purchase software online, and can get some great deals if you look carefully. As there is a fine line between hardware and software, some of these sites may deal in hardware as well.

www.beyond.com
www.buydirect.com
www.buysoftware.com
www.cdw.com
www.chumbo.com
www.egghead.com

Buying Flowers

Need to send some flowers for that special occasion? Using an online florist is easy and convenient. It's simply a matter of viewing the online catalog, selecting an arrangement, and providing the delivery address and the billing information. You can even compose a customized message that will be delivered with the flowers.

flowerrose.com
www.1800flowers.com
www.1stinflowers.com
www.flowersusa.com
www.ftd.com
www.iflorist.com
www.liveflowers.com

Buying General Merchandise

Although many online shopping sites handle specialty items, such as books and flowers, there are also sites that carry general merchandise. Here you will find online versions of established department stores, as well as other shopping services.

bid.com (Online Auctions)
cybershop.com
www.americandreammall.com   (American Dream Mall)
auctions.yahoo.com   (Online Auctions)
www.auctionuniverse.com (Online Auctions)
www.bloomingdales.com
www.brooksbrothers.com
www.bugleboy.com
www.ebay.com (Online Auctions)
www.eddiebauer.com
www.firstauction.com (Online Auctions)
www.gap.com
www.gemm.com
www.have2have.com
www.holtoutlet.com (Toys)
www.imall.com

www.jcpenney.com
www.llbean.com
www.macys.com
www.qvc.com
www.sharperimage.com
www.shopping.com
www.spree.com
www.valueamerica.com
www.virtualemporium.com

Buying Music and Videos

Music and video stores were among the first to open online versions of their stores, and there are quite a few of them. You can buy music and videos, and some stores even run a video rental service through the mail. The prices are competitive, they pay the postage both ways, and they carry a wide assortment of obscure movies.

www.camelotmusic.com
www.cdnow.com
www.cduniverse.com
www.emusic.com
www.goodnoise.com
www.lasersedge.com
www.mgmhomevideo.com
www.musicblvd.com
www.reel.com
www.towerrecords.com
www.tunes.com
www.videoserve.com

Educational

There are many educational sites on the World Wide Web, designed to teach both children and adults. The sites for kids can generate interest in new things, and help with school assignments. The sites for adults can help you learn all kinds of new skills.

gsn.org (Global Schoolhouse)
www.ala.org/parentspage/greatsites/amazing.html
www.ancestry.com (Family History)
www.bellsouth.net/dp/educ/
www.crayola.com
www.exploratorium.edu
www.kids-space.org
www.learn2.com (Learn many new skills)
www.mamamedia.com
www.m-w.com (Dictionary)
www.nova.edu/Inter-Links
www.parentsplace.com
www.pbs.org
www.productreviewnet.com
www.sil.si.edu
www.solariagames.com
www.student.net
www.tvweather.com (Weather links)
www.uexpress.com (Comics and newspaper columns)
www.unitedmedia.com (More comics)

Employment

Looking to find a job or improve your current job? There are online sites that allow you to search the "help wanted" ads from many large newspapers. There are also sites that will teach you important job-finding skills, such as learning how to interview well or provide a job history.

www.aboutwork.com
www.ajb.dni.us
www.careerbuilder.com
www.careerpath.com
www.dbm.com/jobguide
www.dice.com (Computer jobs)
www.jobsmart.org
www.monster.com

Financial

Many sites exist to help investors manage their money. You can check stock prices, and read articles and advice about financial matters. Not even listed here are sites that allow you to buy and sell stocks online.

invest-faq.com
quote.yahoo.com
www.bloomberg.com
www.brill.com
www.cnnfn.com
www.companiesonline.com
www.corptech.com
www.financecenter.com
www.fool.com
www.homepath.com
www.hoovers.com
www.investor.msn.com
www.investorama.com
www.money.com
www.morningstar.com
www.personalwealth.com
www.quicken.com
www.quote.com
www.stocksmart.com
www.streeteye.com
www.techstocks.com
www.thestreet.com

Finding Domain Information

In Chapter 3 we listed some sites that would allow you to find information about the owners of a particular domain name. That list is repeated below for your convenience.

www.inet.net/cgi-bin/whois
www.internic.net/cgi-bin/whois

Finding Internet Service Providers

In Chapter 1 we listed some sites that would allow you to find an Internet Service Provider (ISP) in your area. That list is repeated below for your convenience.

thelist.internet.com

boardwatch.internet.com

www.ispfinder.com

www.thelist.com

www.yahoo.com

When you visit the Yahoo site, follow the links "Computers & Internet," "Internet," "Commercial Services@" and "Access Providers." Yahoo changes their headings on occasion, so what you see may be slightly different from that listed here.

Finding Newsgroups, Chat Rooms, and Mailing Lists

The most difficult part about using a newsgroup or a mailing list is finding one that is right for you. There are several sites that allow you to search for these. Some of them also maintain archived versions of popular newsgroups and mailing lists, so you can browse them online, rather than subscribing. The DejaNews site allows you to search newsgroup postings for specific contents. The Liszt site also allows you to search for IRC chat rooms, and then connect easily to them.

www.dejanews.com

www.egroups.com

www.escribe.com

www.liszt.com

www.neosoft.com/internet/paml

www.reference.com

Finding People or Businesses

Would you like to find that long-lost buddy from high school? Would you like to see the yellow pages for a distant city that you plan to visit? There are several sites that allow you to display and search phone book listings for any state. Using some of these sites is a bit unsettling, as you realize how much information about you is available to anyone with a browser.

www.555-1212.com
www.bigbook.com
www.bigfoot.com
www.four11.com
www.fpf.com
www.infospace.com
www.lookupusa.com
www.searchamerica.com
www.semaphorecorp.com
www.switchboard.com
www.the-seeker.com
www.whowhere.com

Finding Web Sites

Listed below are the search engines and index sites we described in Chapter 6. These help you find interesting web sites, either by category or by searching for a given topic or phrase. It is often difficult to distinguish a search engine from an index site, because many are starting to provide both features. Parents should check out the America Online site (www.aol.com). You don't have to be an America Online customer to access it. The site provides good hyperlinks for children, and it also provides a search engine that is supposed to find only safe sites.

www.all4one.com
www.altavista.com
www.aol.com
www.askjeeves.com
www.dogpile.com
www.excite.com
www.highway61.com
www.hotbot.com
www.infoseek.com
www.looksmart.com
www.lycos.com
www.mckinley.com
www.metacrawler.com
www.nerdworld.com

www.northernlight.com
www.pathfinder.com
www.search.com
www.sites.com
www.webcrawler.com
www.yahoo.com

Fraud

If you hate spam as much as we do, you will want to check the first site on this list to catch the latest developments in the war against spammers. The other sites may be used to investigate other kinds of fraud, either online or in the real world. If you're thinking of doing some online shopping, some of these sites will also rate online merchants, and give you tips for avoiding problems.

spam.abuse.net
www.bbb.org
www.cauce.org
www.consumerworld.org
www.fbi.gov
www.ftc.gov
www.fraud.org
www.junkbusters.com
www.publiceye.com
www.sputum.com

Free E-mail

There are several sites that provide you with the ability to get and receive free e-mail. Why would you want this? Perhaps your provider only gives you one or two mailboxes, and you would like each family member to have his own. Or perhaps you travel a lot and would like to pick up your e-mail from any computer that has a web browser. Once you register with these sites and get a password, you can access them from any web browser to read and send your mail. The software supports common mailer functions, such as address books, file attachments, spellcheckers, hypertext links, mail folders, and signature files. The reason the service is free is because of advertising that appears at the web site and attached to the bottom of each e-mail you send. Most sites have a limit as to how many messages can be saved.

The Juno service is a little different, because it does not require a web browser. You can get a copy of their software by calling them or visiting their web site. You use the software to access them through a local number, or a web browser if you so choose. This truly is free e-mail, as it requires no additional Internet connection. Anyone with a computer, a modem, and a phone line can get free e-mail without spending a cent.

    www.angelfire.com
    www.geocities.com
    www.hotmail.com
    www.juno.com
    www.mail.yahoo.com
    www.mailexcite.com
    www.rocketmail.com
    www.whowhere.com

Free or Cheap Software

Listed below are sites that specialize in the distribution of software that is either free (freeware) or reasonably priced (shareware). Sometimes a person will write a program for his own use, and will then give it away to others. Other times, you are encouraged to try a program for free, and then pay if you decide to continue using it. Some programs enforce this trial period through an expiration date, while others just use the honor system. As noted, a couple of these sites deal in specific programs, while others carry many different programs that can be downloaded.

    www.download.com
    www.hotfiles.com
    www.jumbo.com
    www.microsoft.com   (Internet Explorer web browser)
    www.netscape.com   (Netscape Communicator web browser)
    www.sausage.com   (HotDog web editor)
    www.shareware.com
    www.tucows.com
    www.winzip.com   (WinZip compression program)
    www.zdnet.com

Free Web Space

The sites below are those that were mentioned earlier as providing free web space for the construction of web sites. Most of these will give you 5 to 15 MB of space, in exchange for advertising that appears when someone accesses your site. Most of these provide built-in web editors, or you can upload pages you have created with other tools elsewhere.

Many of these make you choose a "neighborhood" or "pod" where you wish to have your pages live. These can have themes, such as science fiction, sports, home improvement, military, science, television, and kids. You are assigned a password that you must supply whenever you wish to update your web space.

www.angelfire.com
www.geocities.com
www.tripod.com
www.whowhere.com

Fun for Adults

These sites aren't for adults only, but they're geared to the tastes of adults. Be warned—we have a weird sense of what's fun. If you'd enjoy seeing the Gettysburg Address translated into redneck, these sites may appeal to you.

www.judgejudy.com	(Legal advice with a sense of humor)
www.novalearn.com/wol	(Writer On Line)
www.psyclops.com/translator	(The Universal Translator)
www.queendom.com/test_frm.html	(All the tests you'll ever want to take)
susiesplace.simplenet.com/fonts.html	(Free Typefonts)
www.thesmokinggun.com	(Inside Scoops)
www.wwnonline.com	(Wild supermarket tabloids)

Fun for Kids

Although the kids may have told you they needed a computer for school, the real reason they wanted it was for fun. You may have learned the same thing in your own computer experience. But you can get even with your children by leading them to sites that allow them to learn while having fun. Not all of these sites fall into that category, but a good many of them do.

kidswriting.miningco.com
www.4kids.com
www.4kidz.com
www.cyberkids.com
www.cyberteens.com
www.disney.com
www.kidpub.org
www.kidscom.com
www.previews.net   (Many sound files)
www.realkids.com
www.safelinks.com
www.sikids.com   (Sports Illustrated for kids)
www.stonesoup.com
www.thekids.com
www.woi.com/woi/kids.html
www.yahooligans.com

Health and Medicine

The advent of managed care has made us all more responsible for the health care that we receive. Although health care web sites are no substitute for good medical care, they can help you understand certain conditions, and help you decide if a problem should be treated at home or referred to a physician. Some doctors feel Internet medicine is dangerous, but others are convinced that using the Internet makes for more informed patients. You will have to be the judge for your family.

www.eatright.org
www.healthfinder.gov
www.mayo.ivi.com
www.medmatrix.org
www.nim.nih.gov
www.obgyn.net

www.wellweb.com
www.yahoo.com/health

Internet-Related Sites

The sites in this list are all found in other parts of the book. They are used for common Internet functions such as registering web pages and locating information about the owners of domain names. The comment to the right of each URL will describe the function it provides.

www.boutell.com/faq	(Learn more about HTML)
www.lycos.com	(Register web sites to search engines)
www.submit-it.com	(Register web sites to search engines)
www.yahoo.com	(Register web sites to search engines)

Mapping Software

Are you planning to drive to see your long-lost aunt, and you're not sure how to get there? There are several sites that will help you find her house and will then draw a map of her neighborhood. If you're going on a trip, these sites can produce driving maps and directions for getting from your starting point to your destination. You can buy software that does the same thing, but these sites are free, and they are updated regularly.

www.mapquest.com
www.mapsonus.com
www.yahoo.com
www.zip2.com

Movies

If you love the movies, there are several sites you will enjoy. Some provide general movie information, or allow you to search a movie database. Most of the sites are run by motion picture companies, and they obviously provide promotional material about their own products. Not listed here are sites that are created just for specific movies. You often see these in the fine print at the bottom of movie previews or television commercials.

imdb.com	(Movie database)
mgmua.com	(MGM/United Artists)
www.film.com	(General movie information)
www.fox.com	(20th Century Fox)
www.paramount.com	(Paramount Pictures)
www.sony.com	(Sony Entertainment and Products)
www.universalstudios.com	(Universal Studios)
www.warnerbros.com	(Warner Brothers)

Newspapers and Magazines

Many newspapers and magazines have online versions of their publications. This makes it easy to keep up with the events in a different part of the country or the world. Many of these sites provide hyperlinks to online newspapers, usually classified by state and city.

crayon.net
update.wsj.com
www.enews.com
www.news.com
www.newspapers.com
www.usatoday.com
www.worldwidenews.com
www.wsj.com

Shipping

All of the major shipping companies provide sites that are useful for shipping your packages and then tracking them. The U.S. Postal Service site can help you calculate and compare different postage rates. Both of the other sites allow you to track the shipment of a package if you have the tracking number. It is really a lot of fun to check on a package as it makes its journey across the country.

www.fedex.com
www.ups.com
www.usps.gov

Television

Although it seems somewhat of a conflict of interest, most of the television stations and networks have web sites. These include the national networks, plus a good many of the cable stations. Visit these sites to view upcoming attractions, or to read articles about current programs.

TCM.turner.com	(Turner Classic Movies)
vh1.com	(The VH1 Music Channel)
www.abc.com	(ABC TV Network)
www.aetv.com	(Arts & Entertainment)
www.amctv.com	(American Movie Classics)
www.betnetworks.com	(Black Entertainment Networks)
www.bravotv.com	(Bravo!)
www.cartoonnetwork.com	(Cartoon Network)
www.cbs.com	(CBS TV Network)
www.cinemax.com	(Cinemax Premium Service)
www.clicktv.com	(General Information Site)
www.cnbc.com	(C-NBC)
www.cnn.com	(Cable News Network)
www.cnnfn.com	(CNN Financial News)
www.comcentral.com	(Comedy Central)
www.country.com/tnn/tnn-f.html	(The Nashville Network)
www.c-span.org	(C-Span)
www.discovery.com	(Discovery Channel)
www.disneychannel.com	(The Disney Channel)
www.familychannel.com	(The Fox Family Channel)
www.foxnetwork.com	(Fox TV Network)
www.foxnews.com	(The Fox News Channel)
www.fxnetworks.com	(FX)
www.hbo.com	(Home Box Office Premium Service)
www.historychannel.com	(History Channel)
www.lifetimetv.com	(Lifetime TV)
www.msnbc.com	(Microsoft / NBC News Channel)
www.mtv.com	(MTV—Music Television)

www.nbc.com	(NBC TV Network)
www.nick.com	(Nickelodeon)
www.odysseychannel.com	(The Odyssey Channel)
www.ovationtv.com	(The Ovation Arts Network)
www.pax.net	(PAX TV)
www.pbs.org	(Public Broadcasting System)
www.scifi.com	(The Sci-Fi Channel)
www.showtimeonline.com	(Showtime Premium Service)
www.showtimeonline.com/TMC	(The Movie Channel Premium Service)
www.thewb.com	(Warner Brothers Network)
www.tnt-tv.com	(Turner Network Television)
www.ultimatetv.com	(General Information Site)
www.upn.com	(United Paramount Network)
www.usanetwork.com	(The USA Network)
www.weather.com	(The Weather Channel)

Travel

You can use the WWW to plan your travel and even make your reservations. If you would rather use your friendly travel agent instead of strangers, you can still use these sites to learn about the area before starting your travel planning. There are bargains to be found here, but you have to be patient and thorough. Don't just grab the first offer you see; do a little research.

expedia.msn.com
www.180096hotel.com
www.amtrack.com
www.atevo.com
www.bestfares.com
www.biztravel.com
www.city.net
www.flifo.com
www.hotelbook.com
www.itn.net
www.leisureplan.com
www.preview-travel.com
www.thetrip.com
www.travelocity.com
www.travelweb.com

United States Government

The U.S. government has jumped into the WWW in a big way, and shown below is just a listing of the more common sites you might want to access. Not all of these sites are run by the government, but they are government-related. The voter information sites will allow you to identify the elected officials from your state, and will even help you compose e-mail to them.

thomas.loc.gov	(Status of legislation)
www.fbi.gov	(FBI)
www.ftc.gov	(FTC)
www.house.gov	(House of Representatives)
www.irs.ustreas.gov	(IRS)
www.loc.gov	(Library of Congress)
www.mrsmith.com	(Voter information)
www.sec.org	(SEC)
www.senate.gov	(Senate)
www.un.org	(United Nations)
www.vote-smart.org	(Voter information)
www.whitehouse.gov	(White House)

A PARENT'S QUESTIONS

Q. Why can't the common search engines find our family web site?
A. Even though it may seem like it, search engines don't search all of the web. Whether or not your web space gets searched depends on the provider of your web space. It may not be a bad thing that your site cannot be found. Perhaps you would like to restrict it to only those who know the URL, and thus keep it away from the eyes of search engines. But there are other cases, particularly when you are trying to advertise an online business, where you want as much exposure as possible. There are several sites that allow you to register your site with most of the common search engines:

www.lycos.com
www.submit-it.com
www.yahoo.com

You usually just provide your starting URL address, and the registration software will scan all the related pages and make them known to the search engines.

Q. Where can I learn more about HTML and related languages?
A. If you don't want to buy a book, use a search engine to see what's online. You can also refer to the web site *www.boutell.com/faq.*

Q. Should I download a 16-bit or a 32-bit application?
A. If you visit some of the software download sites mentioned in this chapter, you may be asked which version of a particular software package you wish to install. Only users running Windows 3.1 should run 16-bit applications. Users of later Windows versions should try using the 32-bit version first, and should only try the 16-bit version if the other version doesn't work. If your operating system supports them, 32-bit applications are usually faster and less prone to programming errors.

Q. Can my web browser display a file with a BMP extension?
A. BMP is the acronym for "bit-mapped graphic." Because this is a Windows feature, most browsers do not support them. Besides, BMP graphics take up far more space than other formats, and they'll eat your precious web space in no time. Currently, only the GIF and JPG graphic formats are supported by most browsers. Convert your file to one of those formats with a commercial graphics program such as Photoshop or CorelDRAW. If you don't have such a program, consider a shareware program such as Lview Pro, which is available through many of the software download sites listed previously.

Q. If I buy online, will my credit card number get stolen?
A. Despite concerns about fraud, the number of online shops and shoppers continues to grow. In 1997 there were an estimated 10.3 million online Christmas shoppers. That number was expected to grow to 16 million during the 1998 holiday season.[2] People like online shopping because it is convenient, you can find better discounts, and there are more stores coming online all the time. The major fear, however, is credit card fraud.

There are Internet experts who can trace communication lines and sneak peeks at packets as they go through the system. But considering the millions of transactions that go through the system each day, do you think these guys are just sitting there looking through random messages and trying to find credit card numbers? It is much more likely your credit card number will be stolen from a discarded charge slip or credit card statement. Most online shopping sites also employ an option called a "secure connection" that encrypts (scrambles) your order before it gets sent, and then decrypts (unscrambles) it on the other side. Your main chance of getting cheated is if you use an online shopping service that is dishonest. If you use a service that is trusted, and has been around for a while, your chance of getting cheated should be no greater than with any other charged purchase. Get recommendations from friends, or from published reviews in newspapers and magazines.

Many online businesses are starting to form groups that are designed to calm customer fears and build consumer confidence. Businesses that join these groups agree to follow certain guidelines that protect the buyer. In return, they earn the right to display a membership seal on their promotional materials. If these groups continue to grow, they should provide consumers with an added measure of confidence that they are dealing with a company that can be trusted.

Q. My son wanted to visit the White House but got pornography instead. What happened?

A. Your unfortunate son was the victim of an impostor web site. Some folks register domain names that are close to other domain names, hoping to attract those people that type the names incorrectly. For example, the URL of the White House is *www.whitehouse.gov*, while the URL of the site your son typed was *www.whitehouse.com*. A simple typing mistake can make a whole lot of difference in terms of what your browser shows.

In addition to being used by pornographers, impostor sites are purchased by companies trying to steal business from their competitors, or by activist groups who want to make political statements against groups they oppose. For example, one animal rights group has purchased domain names that people might try if they were looking for the circus. Instead of getting circus information, visitors to those sites get a message telling them that the circus is cruel to animals. The moral of the story is that you should know where you want to go, rather than trying to guess the URL.

Notes

1. *Wired*; August 1998; p. 78-79.
2. *Inter@ctive Week;* September 7, 1998.

Epilogue—Responsibility in the Information Age
•••••

As we come to the end of this book, we hope that you have been able to follow the ideas presented here, and that you are now confident enough to wade out into the electronic jungle and do some more exploring on your own. Although we have tried to use lots of examples and stories, there's no getting around the fact that the Internet is a technical subject that takes some concentrated effort to understand.

When Clark was a college student, he questioned his father on the value of a college education. He was afraid that the things he was learning would either be forgotten or obsolete by the time he got his first job. His father wisely replied that people attend college not to learn, but to learn how to learn. Given that your typical bookstore has hundreds of books on various Internet topics, you can be sure that we have barely scratched the surface with this book. But we hope you have "learned how to learn" about such subjects, and you can continue your education with more confidence and direction.

As the authors, we hope this book has equipped you to become a responsible electronic citizen within the walls of your own home. But does your responsibility stop there? Do you also need to be involved in your community, in your state, and at the national level?

If you would like to take an active role in keeping the Internet safe for your children, there are avenues that can be taken. In these last few pages, we will explore some of the things you can do to make yourself an effective spokesman for families, without coming off as obnoxious or pushy. We will also focus on the ways your efforts can have the most effect and do the most good.

Like it or not, every technology seems to attract people who want to make a buck by pandering to the most primitive of human desires. As you've seen in the pages of this book, the Internet is replete with opportunities for mankind to wallow in the mud. There's online sex. Pornographic film clips and videos. Internet porno sites. Chain letters. Hot stocks. Business opportunities. If there is a dollar to be made on basic human lust and greed, there will be someone trying to put a hand on your wallet. Although sleazy web sites represent a small percentage of the information you can find on the Internet, the purveyors of garbage know exactly how to throw themselves at you while you're trying to mind your own business.

Your first instinct might be to fight this problem with legislation. If that's what you want to do, write your congressional representative an e-mail, and tell him you want this stopped. There is only one flaw with attacking the problem with legislation alone—it won't work. Here are three reasons why:

1. The Constitution of the United States guarantees freedom of speech, and that includes the Internet. Although the content of some Internet information is truly vile, do you really want to give the government the power to shut people down? Doesn't that open the door to abuses that are even more of a threat to freedom than a few dirty words or pictures? Whether you agree with this reasoning or not, the current temperament of the Supreme Court is such that any attack on Internet freedom is bound to be overthrown on constitutional grounds. This is not to say that legislation is never effective, but that it has to work with the Constitution, and not against it.

2. The current members of Congress are not children of the digital age, and they do not understand it. This was never more apparent than with the Communications Decency Act of 1996, which was later overturned in court. Not only was the CDA unconstitutional, but it also contained provisions that were totally unworkable and unenforceable. Rather than pass something that had a reasonable chance of working, the CDA was more of a symbolic bill that allowed Congressmen to crow about how they really were trying to look out for families, while passing an ostrich of a bill that couldn't possibly fly.

3. Because the Internet is truly an international medium, it is difficult to pass laws that would control it, except in the unlikely event that all nations adopted the proposed laws. The U.S. government has already encountered this problem, as the online casinos they have tried to outlaw have only moved offshore to international waters.

Parents who want to legislate Internet behavior should encourage their leaders to really understand the technology, and then to pass laws that work with the Constitution, rather than against it. For example, there is no way to pass a law that would outlaw pornography. But you could encourage laws that would prohibit advertising such material to those who have not requested it. It is a travesty of morals when children receive unsolicited spam inviting them to view pornography. Users should not be exposed to such garbage unless they specifically indicate they want to receive such mailings. As an alternative, users should have the option of placing themselves on a registry of people not interested in such material.

The flood of all types of spam could be slowed with similar laws that require spammers to honor the requests of users who don't want to receive such material. Similar laws were quite effective a few years ago when junk fax ads were rampant, and they would work equally well with spam.

Many adult sites have started limiting access to registered users only. As part of the registration process, users must provide a credit card number and pay a small monthly fee. This makes it more difficult for minors to gain access, because most credit card companies will not issue cards to those under eighteen years of age. This is another technique that could be encouraged through law. If all such sites were required to provide this registration, this would still provide a constitutional solution that would deny access to those who shouldn't be there.

One other way to fight for Internet changes is to complain to your online service or service provider. Services such as America Online have spent a lot of time and money investigating ways to make the online experience more enjoyable. These services have implemented e-mail and newsgroup filters, as well as other parental controls. Your provider relies on you to pay a regular access fee, so you can be sure that the service wants to keep you happy—and will listen to your complaints. The smaller the service you use, the better your chance of being heard. Don't just rant and rave, but provide specific complaints and give specific suggestions of what you'd like to see done to improve the protection that is offered to subscribers. Many of the current features provided were probably added in response to user complaints.

Some of the most promising solutions to a safer Internet are to be found in some of the technology solutions developed by the industry itself. Examples of such technologies include the NoCeM newsgroup filters and the PICS web page rating facility. You can use your influence to encourage providers and software vendors to adopt such solutions. Netscape has continued to promise support for the PICS system, but as of this writing that support is still not in place.

Even if both major browsers supported PICS, there is currently no incentive for web page authors to rate their sites. But if both browser manufacturers announced the eventual implementation of mandatory ratings (so that unrated pages couldn't even be displayed), you can be sure that web sites would start adding ratings almost overnight.

When you do find or receive offensive material, consider complaining to the source of that material. Although directly replying to spammers is usually counterproductive, you can complain to the postmaster at the domain name. Similarly, most web sites allow e-mail to be sent to a webmaster that maintains the pages. This is particularly effective with commercial sites, who want to keep their customers happy and should be receptive to your suggestions.

Finally, parents should also get involved with Internet issues at a local level. Not only are these just as important as the other items mentioned above, but this will be an arena where your opinions will carry more weight. Your children probably have access to computers at school. Ask questions about what access is available, and how closely the children are monitored when they are using the computers. Many local libraries also provide computers with Internet access. Do they have controls on what can be accessed? How closely are children supervised when using the machines? Can patrons request that blocking be turned off? If so, what is the procedure, and what protections are in place for other patrons who may be nearby?

In summary, there are several ways that concerned parents can be involved outside the walls of their own home:

1. Contact your legislators, and encourage them to learn about the Internet and pass laws that will protect children without taking away the rights of others.

2. Work with your commercial service or service provider to make sure they take steps toward providing tools to better protect your family.

3. Complain to the postmaster or webmaster when you find material on the Internet that you find to be offensive and harmful to children.

4. Encourage software vendors and service providers to adopt software solutions that will provide increased protection for Internet users.

5. Work with schools, libraries, and other local groups to make sure protections are available for the citizens using those services.

The Internet has great potential for increasing our knowledge, simplifying our lives, and magnifying our possibilities. Yes, there are dangers and things that should be corrected. But all new technologies have their share of growing pains. As the Internet matures, hopefully it will get beyond some of its current baseness, and truly become a light on the hill that can change all of us for the better.

Appendix—Common File Extensions

• • • • •

MOST OF THE FILES SAVED ON A COMPUTER RUNNING THE DOS operating system have two-part names, with the first part and the second part being separated by a period, or dot. Examples would include RECIPE.DOC, and TAXES.XLS. Usually, the first part of the name is the title of the file, and the second part of the name describes the type of file. In the two examples above, DOC is a file created by a word processor, and XLS is a file created by the popular Microsoft Excel spreadsheet program.

This second part of the name is called the extension, and it follows the period in the file name. Although newer Windows versions will allow longer extension names, most file extension names are still three characters in length.

File extension names are important when using the Windows operating system, because that is how Windows keeps track of what a file contains, and how Windows should process it. For example, if you start the Windows Explorer program and browse through your hard drive, you may find the example from above called TAXES.XLS. If you are curious about what the file contains, you can double-click on the name, and Windows will try and display it for you. All you have to do is click on the filename TAXES.XLS, and let Windows do the rest.

How does Windows know what the file contains and how it should be displayed? The file extension is the key. Windows maintains a registry of common file extensions, together with the program that should be invoked to display a file of that type. So when you click on TAXES.XLS, Windows recognizes that file is an Excel file, so it will start the Excel program and tell it to open the TAXES.XLS file. This is one of the happy benefits of the Windows operating system, designed so you won't have to remember what program created which file. Enjoy this feature and remember it fondly next time Windows crashes and trashes the work you've spent hours putting together.

File extensions are also important to web browsers, which use the extension to know how to process the file. But why is any of this of interest to you? Offhand, here are three good reasons:

1. Windows has a nifty Find function that allows you to search an entire floppy or

hard drive looking for files with a particular file name. For example, assume you couldn't remember exactly where you put our friendly TAXES.XLS file, but you did remember that it was an Excel file (and thus had an XLS extension), and that it started with a "T." You could start up the Find function and then search your hard drive for files with a name of T*.XLS. The asterisk is a wild card, meaning Windows should ignore any letters it finds in those positions. In a short period of time, the Find command should display all the files matching the name pattern you gave it. You should find TAXES.XLS in the list. Once you do, you can double-click on the name and Windows will start Excel and have it open the file.

2. Using the same procedure outlined above, you can search your hard drive for specific kinds of files that may have been saved during Internet sessions. For example, most photographs that are displayed on web pages use either a file extension of JPG or GIF. You can search for both these file types at the same time by separating the file names with a semicolon—*.JPG;*.GIF. Find should soon give you the names of all the files it finds saved in these two graphics formats. If you find a file called NUDE-BABE.GIF, you may want to do some investigation and see just what little Billy has been saving during his online adventures. If you have a graphics viewer installed on your system, you can probably just double-click on the file name and the picture will be magically displayed.

3. If you see a new extension you don't recognize, this appendix is a good reference for looking it up and finding out what it contains. Of course, there is a chance it won't be listed here either. If that is the case, just double-click on the file and see what Windows tries to do with it. The worst that can happen is that you will get an error message stating that Windows doesn't know what to do with it.

Shown below is an alphabetical list of file extensions, and a short description of what files with that extension usually contain (there is no guarantee that they do). Sometimes more specific information about the program that uses the files is contained in parentheses after the description. After the file list, you will find a more detailed description of each file type.

AIF	Audio File
AIFC	Audio File
AIFF	Audio File
ARJ	Compressed Archive File
AU	Audio File
AVI	Video File
BAS	Programming File (Basic)

BAT	Command File
BMP	Graphics File
C	Programming File (C)
COM	Program File
CPP	Programming File (C++)
CSV	Spreadsheet File (Excel)
DAT	Document (Word Perfect)
DCX	Graphics File
DIF	Spreadsheet File (Excel)
DLL	Program File
DOC	Document (Word)
DOT	Document (Word)
EXE	Program File
FDF	Document (Adobe Acrobat)
FON	Font File
GIF	Graphics File
H	Help File
HLP	Help File
HTM	WWW Browser File
HTML	WWW Browser File
ICO	ICON
INI	Configuration File
IQY	Spreadsheet File (Excel)
JAVA	Programming File (Java)
JFIF	Graphics File
JPE	Graphics File
JPEG	Graphics File
JPG	Graphics File
JS	Programming File (JavaScript)
LDB	Access File
LZH	Compressed Archive File
MAD	Access File
MAF	Access File
MAK	Programming File
MAM	Access File
MAQ	Access File
MAR	Access File

MAT	Access File
MDA	Access File
MDB	Access File
MDE	Access File
MDN	Access File
MDW	Access File
MDZ	Access File
MID	Audio File
MMM	Video File
MOV	Video File
MPG	Video File
PAK	Compressed Archive File
PCX	Graphics File
PDF	Document (Adobe Acrobat)
PFM	Font File
PIC	Graphics File
PIC	Video File
PJP	Graphics File
PJPEG	Graphics File
POT	Powerpoint File
PPA	Powerpoint File
PPS	Powerpoint File
PPT	Powerpoint File
PS	Document (PostScript Printer File)
PWZ	Powerpoint File
QT	Video File
RA	Audio File (RealAudio)
RAM	Audio File (RealAudio)
RM	Audio File (RealAudio)
RMI	Video File
RTF	Document
RTS	Audio File (RealAudio)
SHTML	WWW Browser File
SLK	Spreadsheet File (Excel)
SND	Audio File
TGA	Graphics File
TIF	Graphics File

TIFF	Graphics File
TTF	Font File
TXT	Document (MS-DOS Text)
WAV	Audio File
WBK	Document (Word)
WIZ	Document (Word)
WLL	Document (Word)
WP	Document (Word Perfect)
WPD	Document (Word Perfect)
WPG	Document (Word Perfect)
WPT	Document (Word Perfect)
WRI	Document
WRL	VRML File
XBM	WWW Browser File
XIF	Graphics File
XLA	Spreadsheet File (Excel)
XLB	Spreadsheet File (Excel)
XLC	Spreadsheet File (Excel)
XLK	Spreadsheet File (Excel)
XLL	Spreadsheet File (Excel)
XLM	Spreadsheet File (Excel)
XLS	Spreadsheet File (Excel)
XLV	Spreadsheet File (Excel)
XLW	Spreadsheet File (Excel)
ZIP	Compressed Archive File
ZOO	Compressed Archive File

*****

Access File

These are files created by Microsoft Access, a database program used for keeping track of items such as customers and inventory.

Audio File

These files represent sound recordings. They are often used on web sites and can be played using browser plug-in or helper applications. There are also separate programs that can be used to record and play sound files.

Command File

A command file contains a sequence of MS-DOS commands that are executed when the file is run. You can edit and view command files with the Windows Notepad program.

Compressed Archive File

An archive file is created with a program such as PKZIP or WinZip. Each file contains one or more regular files that have been compressed to save space. These files are often used when downloading software to reduce transmission time. The files must be processed with the proper decompression program before they can be used.

Configuration File

Configuration files are used by Windows programs to keep track of the options you have set. You should not usually modify such a file, although you can view it with the Windows Notepad program.

Document

Documents are created by any of the various word processing or desktop publishing programs. Some files can only be opened by the program that created them, but others that save documents in text format can by opened by the Windows Notepad program.

Font File

Each font file represents a typefont that can be installed in Windows. Although Windows comes with a certain number of fonts, you can obtain your own font files and then use Windows to install them. Windows applications will typically have access to all the installed fonts, so they can be used in word processing and other programs.

Graphics File

Graphics files represent digital versions of drawings and photographs that can be displayed on your computer monitor. You can create graphics files with scanners, digital cameras, and other drawing programs. Graphics files are often embedded within web pages and displayed by your web browser. Such files are also commonly downloaded from web sites. If anyone has stored pornographic still photos on your computer, they will have been saved in one of these formats.

Help File

Help information for Windows programs often exists in separate files with these extensions. There is a Windows help program called Winhelp that may be able to read these files.

ICON

Those little pictures that Windows uses to represent applications and files can be stored as separate files. There are shareware software programs that may be used to display and manage groups of ICON files.

Powerpoint File

Microsoft Powerpoint is a business application that is used for preparing handout materials and overhead transparencies for talks and presentations.

Program File

Files in this group represent programs that can be run on your computer, plus the helper routines that those programs sometimes call. Be careful when downloading files of these types, because they are the most likely to contain viruses.

Programming File

Files in this group are those that are used for producing your own programs. These programs can be written in several different programming languages, such as Basic, C, C++, and Java. These programs are processed by a program called a compiler that turns the written program into a program file that may then be run on the computer.

Spreadsheet File

Spreadsheet programs allow users to build calculation worksheets, and then save those sheets as files. Most spreadsheet software is used in conjunction with budgeting or financial reporting. Examples of common spreadsheet programs include Microsoft Excel and Lotus 1-2-3.

Video File

These files represent video clips that can be played on the computer like short movies. Some of them also include sound. These files are often used on web sites and can be played using browser plug-in or helper applications. There are also separate programs that can be used to record and play video files.

VRML File

VRML software allows you to design three-dimensional worlds that can be saved as files and then later explored with other software. Web browsers will also allow navigation through VRML worlds if you have installed the proper plug-in or helper application.

WWW Browser File

These files are designed to be read and processed by web browsers. Typically, such files are written in a language such as HTML that directs the browser to arrange and display text or load graphics images. You can view these files with your web browser, even if they live on a hard or floppy drive.

Index

•••••